MEDITERRANEAN VEGETARIAN COOKING

ALSO BY PAOLA GAVIN

French Vegetarian Cooking
Italian Vegetarian Cooking

MEDITERRANEAN VEGETARIAN COOKING

Paola Gavin

M. EVANS
Lanham • New York • Boulder • Toronto • Plymouth, UK

Published by M. Evans
An imprint of The Rowman & Littlefield Publishing Group, Inc.
4501 Forbes Boulevard, Suite 200, Lanham, Maryland 20706
http://www.rlpgtrade.com

10 Thornbury Road, Plymouth PL6 7PP, United Kingdom

Distributed by National Book Network

British Library Cataloguing in Publication Information Available

Library of Congress Cataloging-in-Publication Data
Gavin, Paola.
Mediterranean vegetarian cooking / Paola Gavin.
    p. cm.
Includes index.
ISBN 13: 978-1-59077-091-7 (pbk: alk. paper)
1. Vegetarian cookery. 2. Cookery, Mediterranean. I. Title.
TX837.G345   2005
641.5′636′091822—dc22   2005018310

Typeset and designed by Chrissy Kwasnik

♾™ The paper used in this publication meets the minimum requirements of
American National Standard for Information Sciences—Permanence of Paper for
Printed Library Materials, ANSI/NISO Z39.48-1992.

Printed in the United States of America

To Francesca,
Seana, and
Bianca

CONTENTS

INTRODUCTION

This book is about simple, easy to prepare Mediterranean vegetarian food. I like fast, fresh food, made with quality ingredients—food that tastes of what it is and is, above all, healthy.

Mediterranean vegetarian food is probably the healthiest and most delicious in the world. It is traditional, peasant food passed on from parent to child for generations. It is based on pulses and grains, an abundance of fresh fruit and vegetables, nuts and seeds, and a small amount of dairy produce. Extra virgin olive oil is the main cooking medium and wine—except in Muslim countries—is usually served with meals. Meat has always been a luxury around the Mediterranean and only eaten on Sundays or for special occasions.

Each of the fifteen or so countries around the Mediterranean has its own unique culture and cuisine, but they all share the same climate, geography, vegetation, and lifestyle. In other words the same food is prepared from one end of the Mediterranean to the other. Of course, each country has its own specialties and ways of preparing food, but everywhere you will see the same ingredients: broad beans, peas; and artichokes in spring; eggplant, zucchini; and peppers; at the height of summer; mushrooms, pumpkin; and corn in the fall. In every open air food market in the Mediterranean you will find huge bunches of herbs and greens; spinach, Swiss chard, rocket, purslane, lamb's lettuce, parsley, coriander, dill, mint, basil, marjoram, and oregano, or a mixture of wild herbs, called *horta* in Greece, *preboggion* in Liguria, and *zelje divlje* in Croatia. Flavorings also vary—parsley, dill, and fresh mint are widely used in Greece and Turkey, while basil and oregano are preferred in France and Italy. Moroccans like to flavor their tajines with an exotic mix of spices (saffron, tumeric, ginger, cinnamon, sweet and hot pepper), while Algerians and Tunisians prefer *harissa* (a fiery hot sauce made with garlic and chili). Croatians often flavor their desserts with *prošek*, while marsala is used in Italy and sherry in Spain. Everywhere a wide selection of fresh fruit is served at the end of a meal—apples, pears, cherries, nectarines, peaches, apricots, plums, strawberries, grapes, and all kinds of melons and citrus fruit.

In recent years, much has been written about the benefits of the Mediterranean diet and how it lessens the risk of heart disease, cancer, and other chronic diseases—the same can be said for the vegetarian diet. Put the two together and you have a recipe for good health.

The recipes I have chosen for this book are my own personal favorites that I have collected over the years while living and traveling around the Mediterranean. Most are very simple and easy to prepare. No great culinary skill is necessary. Mediterranean cooking is based on home-style, peasant cooking. I hope the recipes evoke for you, as they do for me, the spirit of the Mediterranean.

THE COUNTRIES AND THEIR CUISINES

Our destination, the isle of Rab, lay before us, the mountains
bare as Krk, its shores green as spring . . . but the scent of
myrtle and rosemary and thyme was as strong and soothing
a delight as sunshine.
—Rebecca West, *Black Lamb and Grey*
Falcons: A Journey Through Yugoslavia

Land of Albania let me bend mine eyes
on thee, thou rugged nurse of savage men!
—Lord Byron, "Childe Harold's Pilgrimage"

Istria lies in the northeast corner of the Adriatic where the Apennine and Balkan peninsulas meet. Most of Istria is part of present-day Croatia, except for the far north which belongs to Slovenia. Istria's strategic position at the "gateway to the Adriatic" has made it a battleground for invading peoples for much of its history. Around 900 B.C. Istria was inhabited by an Illyrian tribe, the Histri, who gave Istria its name. Istria flourished under the Romans as an important trade center, exporting Balkan olive oil, wine, and walnuts to other parts of Europe. In the centuries that followed the fall of the Roman Empire, Istria was overrun by the Visigoths, Huns, Slavs, Franks, Germans, and Austrians. From the fifteenth century, it was divided between Venice and Austria. It was the Venetians who first introduced foodstuffs from the New World—haricot beans, pumpkins, and squash. (Corn was not introduced until the seventeenth century, via Egypt, Romania, and Hungary.) Venetian rule lasted nearly four hundred years until Napoleon conquered Venice in 1797. After Napoleon's defeat at Waterloo in 1815, Istria became part of the Austro-Hungarian empire until the end of World War I. After the war, Istria was given to Italy, where it was incorporated into the province of Venezia Giulia. It was not until the end of World War II that Istria was finally united with the Kingdom of the South Slavs, or Yugoslavia. Even today, most Istrians speak Italian and retain strong cultural links to Italy.

Istrian cooking is a mix of Italian and central European cuisines. All kinds of pasta dishes are made, especially *krafi* and *zlikofi* (ravioli) and *fuzi* (homemade noodles). *Fuži* are often served with truffles that are found in the region around Koper (Capodistria) in the northwest. Istrians are also fond of thick vegetable soups similar to Italian *minestroni*, which usually include potatoes, cabbage, herbs, dried beans or chickpeas, and pasta or barley. *Zgroub* or *zgroubi* (a thin cornmeal or buckwheat porridge) is often served for breakfast. One of the glories of the Istrian kitchen is *struccolo* or *štrukli* (a kind of strudel), which may be baked, boiled, or steamed. *Struccoli* are made with various stretched, rolled, or yeasted doughs. Fillings include potatoes, rice, spinach, or *pujine* (a fresh cheese similar to Italian ricotta). Sweet versions are made with apples, pears, cherries, plums, or apricots. Other desserts of note include *buzolai* (ring-shaped biscuits dusted with powdered sugar), *gibaniča* (a rich layered pastry filled with apples, walnuts, raisins, poppy seeds, and cinnamon), *palačinke* (jam-filled pancakes), and all kinds of *fritule* (sweet fritters) that usually include raisins, pine nuts, candied citron, and grated chocolate.

Dalmatia consists of a narrow coastal strip that stretches along the Croatian coast from Pag Island to the borders of Montenegro. This coastal strip (seventy miles wide in the north and only ten miles wide in the south) is backed by the Dinaric Alps—a bare wall of limestone mountains that run parallel to the coast for hundreds of miles. Throughout Dalmatia's history, this mountain wall has made access to the hinterland very difficult, which is why the Dalmatian people have always been more influenced by the sea and Italy than their Slavic neighbors in the interior. Dalmatia's rugged coastline with its numerous bays and inlets, and hundreds of offshore islands, is probably the most dramatic in the Mediterranean. Like Istria, its coastal towns—with their arcades, piazzas, and *campanilis*—reflect four hundred years of Venetian rule.

Dalmatia is named after the Dalmatae, one of the Illyrian tribes that occupied the land in the first millennium B.C. The Illyrians were followed by the Celts, who swept down from the Danube and settled in the western part of the Balkan peninsula as far south as present-day Albania. These early communities were mainly cereal eaters. They grew barley and millet and several strains of wheat, and ate a variety of fresh fruit and vegetables including onions, garlic, cabbage, black radish, and lentils. After the fall of the Roman Empire, Dalmatia was ruled by the Byzantines, the Hrvati or Croats, and the Hungarians. In the fifteenth century, the Venetians ruled the whole of the Dalmatian coast except for the independent city-state of Ragusa (present-day Dubrovnik), while most of the Balkan lands on the other side of the Dinaric Alps were swallowed up by the Ottoman Empire. After Napoleon's defeat in 1815, Dalmatia, like Istria, came under Austro-Hungarian rule until the end of World War I. In 1918, Dalmatia was incorporated into the newly founded Kingdom of Serbs, Croats, and Slovenes, which later became known as Yugoslavia.

Dalmatian cooking is classic Mediterranean fare based on olive oil, garlic, and herbs, especially flat-leaf parsley. The Italian influence is very strong with a liking for pasta in all its forms, as well as *njoki* (gnocchi) and *palenta* (polenta). *Riži-biži* (rice and peas) is the Dalmatian version of this well-known Venetian dish. Bread is a staple and eaten at every meal. Bread is made with wheat flour, rye, cornmeal, or potatoes, and often flavored with rosemary, sage, or cinnamon.

The dry Mediterranean climate is very suitable for growing olives, eggplant, sweet peppers, and zucchini. The cooking is simple and rustic. Most vegetables, especially green beans, carrots, spinach, cauliflower, and potatoes are boiled and dressed with olive oil, salt, and black pepper. *Blitva pirjana* is a popular dish of Swiss chard and potatoes, dressed with olive oil, garlic, and parsley. Zucchini, peppers, and eggplants are often stuffed with a mixture of bread crumbs, olives, capers, garlic, and parsley. A wide variety of fruit is grown including figs, apricots, nectarines, peaches, plums, melons, and table grapes. Dalmatia is famous for its *marasca* cherries which are made into jams, syrups, and, of course, cherry brandy, which rivals *sljivovica* (plum brandy), the national drink.

Various cheeses are produced: *Formaio de Novaia* (a hard ewe's milk cheese similar to pecorino), *Formaio de Ludro* (a pungent goat cheese that is sometimes served with olives as an appetizer), *pujine* (a fresh cheese similar to ricotta), and *formaiele* (a small goat cheese that resembles Italian *Caprini).*

Meals usually end with fresh fruit, cheese, or a light dessert such as *rožada* (caramelized baked custard that is usually flavored with marasca liqueur). Traditional cakes and pastries include *savijaca od orhua* (a kind of walnut strudel), *pogače* (a light yeasted cake scented with rosewater and lemon rind), and *fritule dalmatinske* (sweet fritters flavored with *sljivovica* that are made on Christmas Eve). *Medenjaci* (honey biscuits) and *paprenjaci* (pepper biscuits) are usually served with *Prošek* (a sweet wine similar to port that is made from grapes that are left to dry out on the vine to increase their sweetness).

Albania, or Shqiperia (Land of the Eagles) as it is called by the Albanians, lies along the western coast of the Balkan Peninsula between Montenegro and Greece. It is a land of great beauty with rugged mountains, thick forests, deep lakes, and a spectacular coastline—called the Riviera of the flowers—that stretches for nearly 80 miles along the Ionian littoral between Vlora and Saranda.

The Albanians are direct descendants of the *Albanoi*, an Illyrian tribe that inhabited the land in the first millennium B.C. The Albanian language, which is unlike any other, is the only surviving language to derive from ancient Illyrian. The Albanian people are very proud of their unique heritage and traditions, which they have managed to retain despite two thousand years of occupation by the Greeks, Romans, Byzantines, Bulgarians, Normans, Serbs, Venetians, and Ottoman Turks.

Albanian cooking has been greatly influenced by five hundred years of Turkish rule. *Mezet* (appetizers) and vegetable dishes such as *havjar me patëllxhan* (eggplant caviar), *dollma me fletë hardhi je ne oria* (vine leaves stuffed with rice, pine nuts, and currants), *qofte patatesh* (potato croquettes), and *byreçka* (triangular filo pastries filled with white cheese, pumpkin, or leeks) have obvious Turkish origins. Albanians also have a liking for hot peppers, which were introduced by the Turks in the sixteenth century, probably via Egypt.

Bread, rice, and pasta (*makaronash*) are staples. *Kabuni* (rice with sultanas, butter, sugar, and cinnamon) is the national dish. *Misërnike* (cornbread) and cornmeal porridge (*kaçamak* or *memelige*) also play an important role in the Albanian diet. Along the coast, the Italian influence is still apparent. *Mëmëlige me djathë* (a layered pie made with slices of polenta, cheese, and tomato sauce) is reminiscent of polenta pies made in northern Italy.

Excellent *kos* (yoghurt) is made usually from sheep's milk, as well as several cheeses including *kaçkavall* (a full-fat hard cheese made from cow's milk), *Djathë* (a white cheese similar to feta), and *gjize* (a kind of cottage cheese).

The Albanians have also adopted the Turkish love of sweet pastries filled with nuts and coated in syrup such as *bakllava* and *kadaif*. Other Albanian desserts of note include *petulla* (yeasted fritters dusted with powdered sugar), *zupa* (a kind of trifle that derives from the Italian *zuppa inglese*), *shandatlie* (walnut biscuits coated in syrup), and *pure me kungull në furrë* (a light pumpkin pudding with ground walnuts, sultanas, and cinnamon). Albanians are also very fond of *akullore* (ice cream).

> *Here nature and man are in closer harmony than*
> *anywhere else in France. Buildings . . . have become part*
> *of the landscape, baked into it by the synthesizing heat*
> *of the Provençal sun . . . You cannot live there without*
> *becoming aware of the vigorous pulse of the south.*
> —Waverley Root, *The Food of France*

The South of France is one of the most beautiful regions of the Mediterranean. The breathtaking coastline of the Côte d'Azur, the fortified hilltop villages of Provence, the wild massifs of the Alpilles, and the mountains of the Luberon have inspired artists and writers for centuries. Languedoc-Roussillon is the lesser known western half of the south of France that lies between the Rhone and the Spanish border. Its southern lowlands are often referred to as the Midi—a region that has no specific boundaries—that can apply to anywhere between Perpignan and Marseilles.

The people of southern France are descendants of Ligurian and Iberian tribes that inhabited the land in the first millennium B.C. In the seventh century B.C., the Phocaean Greeks settled along its shores and introduced the olive and the vine. They also founded the cities of Agde, Nîmes, Anitibes, Nice, and Marsillia (Marseilles), the oldest city in France. When the Romans took over from the Greeks, they called the land *Provincia Romana Narbonensis*, with Narbo (Narbonne) as its capital. Roman rule lasted more than five hundred years. The Romans drained the marshes of the Rhône delta and improved agriculture in the hinterland. They also left an impressive legacy of their architecture including the Pont du Gard aqueduct and the amphitheatre in Nîmes, which is better preserved than the Coliseum in Rome.

After the Fall of the Roman Empire, much of the land was overrun by Visigoths, Franks, and the Moors, or Saracens as they are usually called in France and Italy. The Saracens had little effect on the cooking of the Languedoc except for encouraging a wider use of spices and a liking for sweet, layered pastries. Between the tenth and thirteenth centuries, most of southern France was divided into fiefdoms ruled by counts, viscounts, and minor lords—the most powerful of which were the Counts of Toulouse, the Counts of Barcelona, and the Counts of Provence. This was the time of the Troubadours and the Cathars or Albigensians, a heretical sect that believed in reincarnation and who were strict vegetarians. The Counts of Toulouse were tolerant of the Cathars, but the King of France, King Phillipe Auguste, seized the opportunity to crush the Cathars in order to gain control of their land. At this time, France was not much bigger than the Languedon. Phillipe joined forces with Pope Innocent III and launched a crusade against the Cathars that lasted over thirty years. It ended with their savage slaughter and the Languedoc submitting to French rule. In the early fourteenth century, the Pope acquired the Comtat Venaissin and set up the seat of the papacy in Avignon, where it remained for almost a century. *Aubergines des Papes,* or *papeton,* a kind of soufflé or mousse made with sautéed eggplant that was originally made in the shape of a crown, was created by a papal chef of this period. The County of Provence remained independent for a further two hundred years of wars, famine, and pestilence before it was finally bequeathed to France in 1486.

Roussillon lies in the southeastern corner of the French Mediterranean coast next to Spain. Roussillon did not become part of France until 1559; it previously belonged to the Catalan Kingdom of Aragon. Even today Catalan is widely spoken. Both Catalan and Provençal are dialects of the language of *oc* (meaning "yes") that was once spoken all over southern France, as opposed to the language of *oil* that was spoken in the north.

The County of Nice, which had been under Italian rule for five hundred years, was ceded to France in 1860, after Napoleon II helped Vittorio Emmanuele II create the future kingdom of Italy. The Italian influence is still very strong, especially on its cuisine. All kinds of pasta are made—*les nouilla* (noodles), *lasagna,* and *cannelon,* as well as gnocchi and polenta. Raviolis are often stuffed with Swiss chard and cheese.

Provençal cooking is Mediterranean cooking at its best. Although it evolved out of *la cuisine des pauvres,* it is based on the finest ingredients: superb olive oil, garlic, tomatoes, and the herbs of Provence: thyme, rosemary, sage, savory, fennel, parsley, marjoram, oregano, and basil. Meals usually begin with fresh fruit such as figs or the famous melon of Cavaillon, steamed artichokes served with *aïoli,* the garlicky mayonnaise that is often called the "butter of Provence," or perhaps a light salad of tomatoes or roast peppers, bathed in olive oil and garnished with capers or small black olives from Nice.

One of Provence's most famous soups is *la soupe au pistou* (a thick vegetable soup similar to the Italian minestrone that is flavored with a garlic and basil sauce reminiscent of the Ligurian pesto). Another soup much loved by the Provençals is *aigo-boulido* (garlic soup flavored with sage).

Vegetables are held in high esteem. *Les farcis*—a colorful array of stuffed vegetables (eggplants, zucchini, pepper, tomatoes, and onions) are served throughout the summer months. The same vegetables appear in the well-known Provençal stew—*ratatouille*. All kinds of vegetable *tians* (gratins) are made with spinach, artichokes, pumpkin, eggplant, zucchini, and rice.

Provence produces superb fruit: especially figs, watermelons, apricots, cherries, strawberries, table grapes, pears from the Bouche-du-Rhône, and peaches from the Var, so it is not surprising that fresh fruit is usually served for dessert. A variety of pastries, cakes, and fritters are made: *les bugnes arlésiennes* (sweet fritters flavored with rum), *la tourte de blettes* (a sweet tart made with Swiss chard, pine nuts, and currants), *les pignoulats* (pine nut biscuits), and *la pompe à l'huile* (a yeast cake flavored with saffron and orange flower water that is served at the end of the *Gros Souper* on Christmas Eve).

A few cheeses are produced: *les banons* (small cheeses made from cow's or goat's milk that are sometimes wrapped in chestnut leaves), *les brousses* (fresh cheese made from ewe's milk that may be sweetened or salted), *le broussin* (a *fromage fort* that is so pungent that the locals claim that it will make a man of you), and *les picodons* (small goat cheeses that are marinated in vinegar before they are wrapped in walnut leaves and stored in earthenware pots).

The cuisine of the Haut Languedoc (Upper Languedoc) is not Mediterranean cooking, although the Arabs did introduce white beans called *nounjetas* or *favots*. However, the cooking of Bas Languedoc (Lower Languedoc) is classic Mediterranean fare based on olive oil, garlic, onions, and tomatoes. Fine vegetables are grown, especially eggplant, which are prepared in numerous ways. All kinds of mushrooms are gathered in the hills: *cèpes*, *morilles*, *oronges*, *lactaires*, *trompettes de la mort*, and *bolets*. Truffles are found in the *garrigues* (the aromatic shrub that covers much of the hillsides in the Cévennes). Chestnuts are collected from the hills and made into creamy soups, stews, and stuffings.

Desserts include various fruit tarts—apple, pear, cherry, grape, and *myrtille* (bilberry), and a variety of sweet dishes made with honey or nuts such as *la crème d'Homère* (a kind of caramelized custard made with eggs, honey, and white wine), *omelette aux pignons sucrées* (a sweet pine nut omelet), and *les Jesuites* (puff pastries filled with an almond cream). *Oreillettes* (deep-fried pastries flavored with rum) are made in Montélimar for Carnéval (Shrove Tuesday).

The cooking of the Roussillon is French Catalan cooking with a liking for tomatoes, sweet and hot peppers, saffron, and bitter oranges. *All-i-oli* (a garlicky mayonnaise) is similar to the *aïoli* of Provence. Meals often start with *el pa y al* (slices of bread rubbed with garlic and liberally sprinkled with olive oil). Catalans are fond of egg dishes, especially flat omelets made with eggplant, mushrooms, tomatoes, and asparagus. *Oeufs à la catalane* are fried eggs served on a bed of sautéed tomatoes and eggplant strongly flavored with garlic and parsley. Eggplant, zucchini, and peppers are stuffed in numerous ways or made into delicious gratins. *Poivrons farcis à la catalane* are sweet peppers stuffed with rice, green olives, capers, currants, pine nuts, saffron, and herbs.

Rousillon has the sunniest climate in France with a growing season that is virtually all year round. In spring, it provides the rest of the country with early beans, parsley, and new potatoes, tomatoes, and cucumber in summer, and lettuce, escarole, and *mâche* (lamb's lettuce) in winter. Excellent fruit is produced, especially plums, cherries, apricots, peaches, and melons, as well as such exotic fruit as jujubes and medlars. Corbières is famous for its fine almonds.

Desserts and pastries, too, are more Catalan than French. *Bunyetes* (deep-fried pastries) and *rousquilles* (almond biscuits) are reminiscent of the *bunyols* and *rosquillas* that are found across the border in Spain. *Le soufflé Roussillonais* is a peach soufflé flavored with *eau-de-vie*. Black nougat is a specialty of Perpignan. The only cheese made in the Roussillon is *lait caillé* (fresh curds) and *fromage frais*.

Corsica is the most mountainous island in the Mediterranean. The rugged gorges, deep ravines, dense forests of pine and chestnut trees and fantastic beaches have earned it the name of L'Île de Beauté. Much of the island is covered with *macchia* (shrubland that is fragrant with myrtle, broom, lavender, sorrel, borage, pennyroyal, sage, thyme, marjoram, and many other aromatic plants that are only found in Corsica).

Like Sardinia, Sicily, Malta, and the Balearic Islands, Corsica has been inhabited since the Stone Age. The first wave of settlers was the Ligurians in the seventh millennium b.c. They were followed by the Torreans, Greeks, Etruscans, Carthaginians, Romans, Vandals, Saracens, Pisans, Genoese, and the French. Even the British ruled Corsica for two brief years at the end of the eighteenth century. All these invasions and occupations have given Corsicans a strong sense of identity and family honor. There is a Corsican saying: "So corsu, ne se fienu," which means "I'm Corsican, and I'm proud of it."

Corsican food is simple country fare. Soups are substantial. *La suppa corsa* (a vegetable soup that is similar to the Italian *minestra* and usually includes onions, tomatoes, potatoes, broad beans, and cabbage). *Minestra incu i ceci di Jovi Santu* (a chickpea and pasta soup) is usually served on Good Friday. Chestnut flour is widely used in cooking. Chestnuts were first introduced by the Genoese in the fourteenth century. When the Genoese began to levy high taxes on wheat, the rebellious Corsicans refused to grow it and used chestnut flour instead. Today, chestnut flour is used to make *brilluli* (a kind of porridge), *nicci* (pancakes), and *pisticchine* (a chestnut galette). It also appears in various desserts such as *flan à la farine de chataigne* (a kind of cream caramel thickened with chestnut flour) and *la torta castagnina* (a rustic walnut cake).

Several cheeses are made in Corsica: *Bleu de Corse* (ewe's milk cheese that resembles Roquefort, various goat cheeses, and *brocciu* (a fresh goat cheese made with ewe's milk that is similar to Italian ricotta and *les brousses* of Provence). Brocciu is also made *demi-sec and sec*. Fresh *brocciu* appears in many Corsican dishes: as stuffings for omelets, ravioli, and cannelloni, and in sweet and savory fritters. It is also used in numerous desserts such as *fiadone* (a cheesecake flavored with lemon rind and *eau-de-vie*), *l'imbrucciati* (cheese-filled puff pastries), and *strenna* (a *brocciu* cheese tart that is made in Vico on New Year's Day). *Brocciu sec* or dried *brocciu* is used, like Italian Parmesan, for flavoring soups and pasta. Other pastries of note are *i canestri* (ring-shaped pastries that are traditionally made for Easter), *merzapani* (almond macaroons), and *fugazzi* (a sweet bread flavored with *pastis* and white wine that is made in Bonifacio on Good Friday.)

Light acquires a transcendental quality, it is not the
light of the Mediterranean alone, it is something more,
something unfathomable, something holy. Here the
light penetrates directly to the soul. Opens the doors
and windows of the heart, makes one naked, exposed,
isolated in a metaphysical bliss which makes everything
clear without being known.
                    —Henry Miller, *The Colossus of Maroussi*

You should see the landscape of Greece.
It would break your heart.
                    —Lawrence Durrell, *Spirit of Place: Letters*
                                    and Essays in Travel

Greece is a land where East meets West, where the past is seamlessly interwoven with the present, where myth and legend are fused with history. It is a land of extraordinary beauty, with dazzling light, dusty red earth, clear blue sea, whitewashed villages, wooded hills, and rugged mountains. Greece has over 1,400 islands, but only 169 are inhabited.

The state of Greece, as we know it today, is not very old. Half of Epirus, Macedonia, Thrace, Crete, and most of the Aegean Islands were only united with Greece after the Balkan Wars in 1913. Before then, Greece was ruled by the Ottoman Turks, Franks, Venetians, Catalans, Genoese, Byzantines, and the Romans.

Greece as a country has not existed for two thousand years, yet the spirit of Greece (its language and its strong sense of identity) have survived throughout its long history of invasions and occupations. Around 7000 B.C. early farming communities developed in Macedonia and the fertile plain of Thessaly, where they grew barley and wheat, and kept sheep and goats. In the Bronze Age (c. 3000–1400 B.C.), the Minoan civilization in Crete was the most advanced in Europe. The Minoans were a great maritime power, trading olive oil, wine, and honey around the Mediterranean. On the mainland, the Mycenaean civilization thrived until 1100 B.C. when the Dorians swept down from the north and plunged Greece into a Dark Age that lasted more than three centuries. Over the following three hundred years, city-states or *polis* evolved—the most powerful of which was Athens. This was the beginning of

Greece's Golden Age, when she produced more men of genius—in philosophy, politics, geometry, and the arts—than any other time in history.

The diet of classical Greece was based on cereals, olive oil, legumes, and wine. The main staple was *maza*—a grain-paste or cake similar to the Roman *puls* but made with whole-grain barley flour. Wheat flour was used to make bread. (According to Athenaeus, more than seventy-two varieties of leavened and unleavened bread were made.) Legumes and seeds were highly prized for their nutritional value. Chickpeas, lentils, fava beans, and vetch were boiled and made into *etnos* (a kind of porridge). Ancient Greeks were fond of onions and garlic and ate a variety of dark-green leafy vegetables such as lettuce, watercress, purslane, orache, and turnip tops. They also ate plenty of cheese, almonds, and walnuts and a variety of fresh and dried fruit, especially figs, grapes, apples, pears, melons, quinces, and pomegranates. Meals were washed down with wine—often thinned with water—or *kykeon* (barley water flavored with mint). The poorest peasants drank diluted vinegar instead of wine.

Meat and fish were luxuries in ancient Greece. Meat was mainly associated with sacrificial practices as an offering to the Gods and only small quantities were eaten after the ceremonial rites had taken place. *Garos* (the fermented fish sauce called *garum* by the Romans) was originally made in Corinth.

Greece was under Byzantine rule for over a thousand years, from classical times to the Fall of Constantinople in 1453. The Byzantines encouraged a wider use of vegetables and spices and a liking for sweet pastries. This was mainly a result of Christianity and the Greek Orthodox Church being adopted as the official religion, which increased the number of holy days in the calendar year when the eating of meat was prohibited—Pentecost, the forty days of abstinence for Lent, and the forty days following November 15 for Christmas. Meat was also never eaten on Wednesdays and Fridays. This is why there are so many traditional pies and stuffed vegetables in Greece that are made without meat. Special pastries were made to celebrate each holy day (as they were in most Mediterranean countries) such as *tahinopita* (a sweet tahini cake) for Lent, *tsourekia* (braided buns flavored with aniseed) for Easter, *Christopsomo* (Christmas bread decorated with walnuts and sesame seeds), and vasilopita (a sweet yeasted bread that is made on New Year's Day). *Vasilopita* is named after St. Basil of Caesarea—one of the three Hierarchs of the Greek Orthodox Church.

The Ottoman Turks, who ruled Greece for nearly four hundred years, were another important influence on Greek cooking. Many dishes in Greece today have names that derive from Turkish: *domates* (stuffed vine leaves) from the Turkish *dolma*, *bourekia* (fried filo pastries usually filled with cheese or vegetables) from *börek*, *pilafi* from *pilav*, and so on. The Greeks claim that many Turkish dishes have Greek origins. For example, it is often said that *yiahni*, the Turkish word for food sautéed with onions, may derive from the Greek word *ahnizo*, meaning *to sauté*. *Moussaka*, one of Greece's most famous dishes, is often thought to be a creation of Ottoman cooks who were sent to France and Italy to study cooking, and returned with béchamel sauce, which they added to a Byzantine dish of eggplant and lamb. Today there are many vegetarian versions of *moussaka*.

Modern Greek cooking has much in common with Italian and Turkish cuisines. The Greeks claim their culinary traditions go back to the days of Ancient Greece, and that both the Italians and the Turks have been influenced by the Greek cuisine. It is certainly true that Greek chefs were much sought after in the ancient world. The Romans often employed chefs from the Greek cities of Sicily and Southern Italy (then part of Magna Graecia) to prepare their banquets. It is also true that in the Renaissance the Italians were greatly influenced by the art and culture of Ancient Greece. Also, many of the Greek Islands—the Cyclades, the Sporades, Euboea, Crete, Rhodes, the Ionian, and the Aegean Islands—had, at one time or another, been ruled by the Venetians. Some dishes on the islands, such as *pastitsio* (a baked macaroni pie), still have Italian names.

The Greeks are avid cheese eaters. Most Greek villages produce their own cheese for local consumption. The most well-known Greek cheeses are: feta (a semi-soft, crumbly cheese made from goat or ewe's milk), *Kasseri* (a mild creamy-colored cheese that is usually eaten on its own or with bread), and *Kefalotyri* (a hard sheep's milk cheese that is mainly used in cooking or for grating over pasta). *Mizithra* is a soft, unsalted cheese that is often served sweetened with honey or sugar. It is also used in various sweet or savory pastries.

*The charm was, as always in Italy, in the tone and
the air and the happy hazard of things, which made
any positive pretension or claimed importance a
comparative trifling experience.*
—Henry James, *Italian Hours*

Italy is a country of superlatives. It has some of the most beautiful cities, towns, and villages in the world, some of the most spectacular coastlines in the Mediterranean, and more fine art and architecture than anywhere else in Europe. It has also produced some of the world's most famous artists, poets, and musicians: Dante Alighieri, Petrarch, Giotto, Piero della Francesca, Donatello, da Vinci, Michelangelo, Raphael, Bellini, Vivaldi, and Verdi, to name a few.

One of the charms of Italy is its diversity. Each of its nineteen regions has its own atmosphere, dialect, culture, and cuisine. In fact almost every town has its own style of cooking: *alla napoletana, alla milanese, alla genovese, alla fiorentina,* etc. This is not surprising because Italy has only been united as one country since 1861—before then it was broken up into a patchwork of kingdoms, republics, duchies, and papal and city-states.

Italy has a long and complex history. In the second millennium B.C., most of northern Italy was inhabited by the Ligurians, while the rest of the country was occupied by various migratory Italic tribes: Sabines, Aequi, Piceri, Ombri, Latins, and Messapians. By 800 B.C., much of the south was colonized by the Greeks, who called the land Magna Graecia (Greater Greece), while the Etruscans ruled the land between the Tiber and the Po. Legend has it that Romulus founded Rome in 752 B.C. By 175 B.C., the Roman Republic had overrun the Etruscans and the Greeks and spread across the entire Italian peninsula. After the Punic Wars, the Romans seized the Carthaginian territories of Sardinia, Corsica, and Spain, and by A.D. 106, the Roman Empire had taken control of the whole of the Mediterranean and most of Europe south of the Rhine.

Roman cooking was greatly inspired by the cooking of Ancient Greece, Asia Minor, and Etruria. A staple of the Roman diet was *puls* or *pulmentum*—a kind of porridge usually made with barley, millet, or spelt—that the Romans adopted from the Etruscans. *Pulmentum* was the forerunner of *polenta*—now made with cornmeal—that is still eaten in much of northern Italy today. As the poor of Rome had little cooking equipment and often suffered fuel shortages, they ate a good quantity of uncooked food such as olives, raw beans, figs, and a kind of cottage cheese made with ewe's milk, with *pulmentum* or, as milling processes improved, with coarse bread. They also ate a variety of herbs and greens, especially nettles, chard, and mallow.

The food of the rich was, of course, another matter. Roman banquets were renowned for their lavishness. Foodstuffs were imported from all over the Empire: pomegranates from Persia, apricots from Armenia, and pickles from Spain. Other sought-after delicacies included elephant trunks, flamingo's tongues, peacock's brains, camel's feet, well-fattened hedgehogs, dormice, and snails. The Romans were also keen agriculturists and produced a wide variety of vegetables (turnips, carrots, leeks, sorrel, broccoli, onions, cucumbers, radishes, cress, leeks, endive, numerous varieties of peas, horseradish, rocket, the finest asparagus in the ancient world, and cabbage), which they regarded as a panacea.

The Romans liked to disguise the taste of their food with strongly flavored sauces such as *liquamen,* or *garum* as it was sometimes called. The exact ingredients are disputed but it was very salty and usually contained the entrails of red mullet, horse mackerel, or anchovies. They were also very fond of spices, and sweet and sour sauces made with pine nuts, sultanas, grapes, mint, vinegar, wine, and musk—which roughly resemble the *agro dolce* sauces that are still in use in Italy today. Cheesecake was invented by the Romans, as well as the omelet—which derives from *ova mellita* (honeyed eggs).

The collapse of the Roman Empire was followed by wave after wave of invasions, by Visigoths, Vandals, Ostrogoths, Lombards, and the Franks. In the ninth century, Sicily was overrun by the Saracens. The Saracens introduced new irrigation systems and set up the first rice plantation in Europe near Lentini in southwest Sicily. They also brought the eggplant, spinach, buckwheat (still called *saraceno* in Italian), dates, pistachios, sugar cane, oranges, and the lemon, which quickly replaced *verjus* (the juice of unripe grapes) in sauces and dressings. The Saracens also taught the Sicilians the art of making ice cream and sherbets, and introduced various sweet pastries and cakes including *cassata* (the well-known Sicilian sponge cake filled with sweetened ricotta and candied fruit). The name *cassata* derives from the Arabic *qas'ah,* the deep-sided dish in which it was originally baked.

When the Crusaders set off in the Middle Ages to rescue the Holy Land from the grip of Islam, they were often transported in Venetian ships. Venetian merchants returned with cargoes of silks, dyes, perfumes, and spices from the East: cinnamon, cloves, saffron, ginger, cardamom, and especially pepper, which was so highly prized it was worth its weight in gold. Fortunes were made. Genoa and Pisa also prospered on the Spice Trade, but the power and wealth of Venice were unrivalled. By the middle of the fifteenth century, the Republic of Venice had taken control of Istria and most of the Dalmatian coast, as well as a string of Greek islands including Corfu and Crete. After the Fall of Constantinople in 1453, the Spice Trade was threatened and Venice was forced to trade with Muslims in the Near East. Prices soared, which was the main incentive for the Portuguese to find new trade routes to the East by circumventing Africa.

At the same time the Renaissance—the rebirth of the art and ideas of Ancient Greece—brought a renewed interest in the culinary arts. The first printed cookbook, *De Honestate Voluptate ac Valetudine (Concerning Honest Pleasure and Well-Being)* written by Bartolomeo Scappi (also known as Platina), was published in Cremona around 1475. In it, Platina recommended starting meals with fresh fruit. He also preferred to season food with lemon or orange juice, or wine, rather than the Roman excessive use of spices. Many of his recipes are very simple and healthy, such as broad bean or squash soup poured over slices of bread.

At the height of the Renaissance, Florence had the most sophisticated cuisine in Europe. In 1533, when Catherine de Medici married the Dauphin who became Henry II of France, she took her Florentine cooks to the French court. They taught the French the art of making fine pastries and cakes such as *frangipane*, macaroons, and cream puffs. They also introduced the French to a variety of vegetables including artichokes, broccoli, Savoy cabbages, and tiny peas, which the French quickly adopted as their own.

Gradually new foodstuffs appeared from the New World. The first sack of corn was brought to Venice in the sixteenth century via Turkey. The Venetians, thinking the new grain was Turkish, called it *granturco*, which corn is still called in Italy today. Haricot beans soon took preference over broad beans, especially in Tuscany where they became so popular that Tuscans became known as *mangiafagioli* (bean eaters). Both the potato and the tomato were initially thought to be poisonous and were not widely used in cooking until the eighteenth century.

Italian cooking today is regional cooking. Each of Italy's nineteen regions has its own style of cooking. The elegant cuisines of Emilia and the Veneto are very different from the rustic cooking of Apulia and Sardinia. Foreign influences, too, are still apparent—French in Lombardy, Piedmont and the Val D'Aosta, Austrian in Trentino and the Alto Adige, Central European in Venezia Giulia, Spanish in Naples and the south, and Arab in Sicily.

There is also a dichotomy between the cooking of the north and that of the south. In the north, there is a liking for soft, flat ribbons of pasta rich in eggs, while hard, tubular, factory-made pasta predominates in the south. Traditionally, olive oil was the main cooking medium of southern Italy, while pork fat was used in the center, and butter in the north, where the land was more suited to cattle rearing than the growing of olives. Today less pork fat is eaten and the use of olive oil has become more widespread. Tomato sauces strongly flavored with garlic, basil, oregano, chili, olives, and capers, which are fundamental to the cooking of the south, are seldom used in the north. In some regions of northern Italy, especially Lombardy and the Veneto, rice and polenta are eaten more than pasta.

Vegetables, too, play an important role in the cooking of every region of Italy. Vegetables are stuffed, made into fritters, all kinds of *frittate* (omelets), delicious gratins, and pies. Each region has its own repertoire of vegetable specialties such as *la torta pasqualina* of Liguria (an elaborate pie filled with beet greens), *Prescinsens* (the local soft white cheese, cream, and whole eggs), *tortino di carciofi* (a kind of baked omelet from Tuscany), and *timballo di melanzane* (a layered pie made with fried eggplant, Scamorza cheese, beaten egg, and grated pecorino from Abruzzo). Italy produces some of the finest cheeses in the world: Gorgonzola, Bel Paese, and Dolcelatte from Lombardy, Fontina and Robiole from Piedmont, pecorino from Sardinia, Rome, and the south, and provolone from Campania and Apulia. The king of Italian cheeses is, of course, Parmegiano Reggiano, which is made in specified areas of Parma, Reggio Nell'Emilia, Modena, Bologna, and Mantova.

Many Italian desserts are world famous: *zabaione* (a frothy mixture of eggs, sugar, and Marsala) from Piedmont, *panforte* (a rich flat cake made with chopped nuts, honey, sugar, dried and candied fruit, cocoa, and spices), and *tiramisù* (a chilled pudding usually made with layers of sponge cake soaked in coffee and liqueur, a mascarpone and egg cream and grated chocolate, which is a fairly recent invention from Treviso). There are so many regional cakes and pastries in Italy that it would be impossible to mention them all. Some of the most notable include: *castagnaccio* (a flat cake from Tuscany made with chestnut flour, sultanas, walnuts, pine nuts, and fennel seeds), *pastiero* (a Neapolitan pastry filled with a mixture of ricotta, candied fruit, eggs, spices, and grains of wheat that have been softened in milk), and *gubana* (a rich pastry roll from Friuli that is filled with a mixture of chopped nuts, sultanas soaked in rum, dried figs, prunes, candied orange rind, and chocolate).

Concerning the spices of Arabia let no more be said.
The whole country is scented with them, and exhales
an odor marvelously sweet."
—Herodotus, *The Histories*

It is said that there is a language of flowers.
In the Middle East there is a language of food.
—Claudia Roden, *A Book of Middle Eastern Food*

The Middle East has been called the Cradle of Civilization. The fertile Crescent of Mesopotamia and the Valley of the Nile are thought to be the sites of the world's first cultures. Jericho, which was built around 7000 B.C. is one of the oldest cities in the world. The Middle East lies on the crossroads of three continents—Europe, Asia, and Africa. It is also the birthplace of three religions—Judaism, Christianity, and Islam.

The cooking of Islam extends beyond present-day boundaries. It has a shared heritage that, at its height, was the most influential in the Mediterranean world. Little is known of the diet of its ancient inhabitants (Assyrians, Babylonians, Aramaeans, Phoenicians, etc.), although there is no doubt that these prosperous kingdoms had highly developed cultures and culinary traditions. From the Bible, we know that the Israelites ate a variety of beans, chickpeas, lentils, dates, figs, raisins, grapes, nuts, olives, capers, wild leaves, and bitter herbs—which are still eaten for Passover today.

In 539 B.C. the Persians conquered much of the region, followed by the Macedonian Greeks, Romans, and the Byzantines. After the death of Mohammed in 632 A.D. the newly converted Arab Muslims defeated the Persians and the Byzantines and took control of Antioch, Damascus, Jerusalem, and Alexandria. The Arabs, who were used to a frugal diet based on cereals, dates, milk, and small amounts of mutton, quickly assimilated the Persian love of good eating. From the Persians, they learned the subtle use of spices, to add dried fruit and nuts to savory dishes, and new, more sophisticated methods of preserving foods with salt and vinegar, or lemon juice and honey, as well as the crystallization of fruit. The seat of the Caliphate was set up first in Damascus and then in Baghdad. Food-stuffs from all over the Middle East, as well as exotic spices from India and China, found their way into the markets of Baghdad and the tables of the Abbasid Caliphs. Over the following one hundred years, the Arabs swept across the whole of North Africa into Spain, Sicily, and Southwest France, introducing new foods and cooking techniques to more than half of the Mediterranean world.

The next great culinary influence in the Middle East was the Ottoman Empire. Although both Ottoman and Arab cuisines had much in common, there were some differences. The Ottomans had adopted many recipes from the Balkan lands under their control, such as stuffed vegetables and vegetable *moussakas*. The Ottomans also introduced the Arabs to yoghurt, burghul, and *börek* (savory pastries), as well as sweet pastries such as *ba'lawah* (baklava) and *k'nafeh* (shredded wheat pastry).

After World War I, the Ottoman Empire was broken up and Syria and Lebanon became independent states under French mandate until the end of World War II when they, as well as Iraq, Saudi Arabia, and Egypt, finally regained their independence.

Syria and Lebanon lie along the east coast of the Mediterranean between Turkey and Israel. They were once part of one country called *Bilad al-Sham* (the Land of Greater Syria) and have shared a long history of invasions and occupations by Hittites, Canaanites (who later became known as the Phoenicians), Egyptians, Assyrians, Babylonians, Persians, Greeks, Romans, and Ottoman Turks.

The cuisines of both countries are virtually identical, although the names of some dishes are different. However, Lebanese cooking is more diverse, with a wider selection of vegetarian recipes. Before the Civil War, Beirut claimed to have the best restaurants in the Middle East.

The variety of Lebanese *mezze* and salads is enormous. In recent years, many have become world famous such as *hommus bil-tahineh* (a chickpea and sesame-seed paste flavored with garlic and lemon juice), *baba ghanouge* (an eggplant and tahini dip), *tabbouleh* (a tomato, parsley, and *burghul* salad), and *falafel* (a dried broad bean and chickpea rissole). *Mezze* are always served with khoubiz (Arabic flat bread). There is a liking for *mahashi* (stuffed vegetables), especially eggplant, zucchini, peppers, Swiss chard, and vine leaves stuffed with a mixture of rice, tomatoes, herbs, cinnamon, and *summa* (sumac), which adds a distinctive, tangy, lemony flavor. Various savory pastries are made including *sambousak* and *fatayer* which are usually filled with spinach, curd cheese, or potatoes.

Kibbeh is the national dish. *Kibbeh el-heeleh* (vegetarian kibbeh) is made with a mixture of mashed potatoes or pumpkin, *burghul*, nuts, onion, and spices. *Kibbeh* can be baked, fried, or simmered in a yoghurt, tahini, or *kishk* sauce. *Kishk* is a kind of flour made with fermented and dried yoghurt and *burghul*.

Various cheeses are made from goat's or ewe's milk: *Jibneh khadreah* (a fresh goat cheese made in the Lebanese mountains), *Jibneh trabolsyeh* (a crumbly white cheese similar to feta), *Areesh* (a curd cheese made with yoghurt and lemon juice), and *Halloum* (a slightly chewy, hard cheese that is sometimes flavored with black cumin seeds).

Meals usually end with fresh fruit, which Lebanon produces in abundance: red and white cherries, prickly pears, pomegranates, medlars, custard apples, jujubes, and mulberries, as well as all kinds of citrus fruit, melons, apricots, peaches, plums, grapes, and figs.

Pastries are usually eaten between meals with a cup of Turkish coffee. *Ba'lawah* (baklava) are made in many shapes and sizes and filled with chopped almonds, walnuts, pine nuts, cashews, or pistachios. *K'nafeh* (shredded-wheat pastries) are filled with chopped nuts or fresh cheese. Both *ba'lawah* and *k'nafeh* are coated in *ater* (a sugar syrup flavored with rose water and orange-flower water). Other traditional desserts include *tamriyeh* (little envelopes of paper-thin pastry with a sweet semolina filling scented with rose water) and *kellage* (sweet fritters filled with ashtah (clotted cream) that are made during Ramadan). *Kellage* is the name of the wafer-thin sheets of pastry used. *Ma-moul bil-joz* (walnut pastries), *rass bil-tamer* (date pastries), and *ka'k el seed* (ring-shaped biscuits) are all Easter specialties.

Israel has been called a country in search of a cuisine. The state of Israel was created a little over fifty years ago and is inhabited by immigrants from more than seventy countries. The Jews basically divide into two cultures: Ashkenazi (Jews from Northern and Eastern Europe and Russia), and Sephardic Jews (from Spain, North Africa, the Middle East, and as far away as Yemen, Ethiopia, and India).

Both cultures have brought their own culinary heritage. Since Jewish dietary laws forbid the mixing of meat and milk at one meal, there are a wide variety of dairy and vegetarian dishes. The Ashkenazi world brought Russian *borsht* (beetroot soup), *piroshki* (yeasted pastries filled with curd cheese, cabbage, potato, sauerkraut, or mushrooms), cheese *blintzes* (pancakes), *kreplach* (a kind of ravioli), and potato *kugel* (a potato pudding). They also introduced *challah* (egg bread) and bagels, *lekach* (honey cake), *babka* (a yeasted butter cake), and *plava* (sponge cake), as well as various cheesecakes and strudels.

Sephardic specialties include Moroccan couscous, Tunisian *breiks* (filo pastry cigars) with an egg or potato filling, Lebanese *sambousak* (spinach turnovers), Syrian *kibbeh*, and various sweet pastries and cakes that are usually filled with nuts or dried fruit and coated in sugar syrup.

Israel has also adopted many indigenous dishes as its own. The most famous is *falafel* (a chickpea rissole), which is sold by street vendors all over Israel. *Falafel* are stuffed inside pita bread with a variety of fresh and pickled salads and topped with tahini, as well as a hot chili sauce. Other Arab dishes include the ubiquitous *hummus bil-tahinah* (a chickpea and sesame seed paste), *dolmas* (stuffed vine leaves), and *kaʾak* (Arab flat bread topped with *zaʾatar* (a mixture of wild marjoram, thyme, oregano, and olive oil).

Israel grows an abundance of fresh fruit and vegetables. Dates, figs, pomegranates, and apples have been grown since biblical times. Israeli avocado, pears, and Jaffa oranges are world famous.

A few cheeses are made, mainly from goat's or ewe's milk. *Kachkaval*, a hard yellow cheese also known as *Kasseri*, is made in a few villages in the Golan Heights. *Labaneh*, a fresh white cheese made from drained yoghurt, is sometimes rolled into balls and stored in olive oil with rosemary and dried chilies.

The Egyptian civilization, which dates back more than six thousand years, is one of the oldest known to man. The Egyptians were the first people to bake bread and were eating a well-balanced diet when most of mankind was still hunting for food. Herodotus called Egypt "the gift of the Nile"— without the Nile, Egypt would just be another part of the Sahara Desert. The rich, fertile Nile Valley produces fruit, vegetables, and grains, especially wheat, barley, corn, rice, sugar cane, oranges, lemons, watermelons, and dates, all year round.

For centuries, the peasants, or *fellahin,* have lived on a diet based on vegetables, grains, legumes, fruits, sweet pastries filled with nuts, and coffee. Egyptians do not like their food hot and spicy, although *taʾliya* (a mixture of crushed garlic and coriander) is widely used to flavor most vegetable stews.

Ful medames (small brown broad beans flavored with garlic and cumin) is the national dish. The beans are dressed with olive oil and lemon juice and served with *aiysh baladi* (whole-wheat Arab bread) and various pickled salads. *Falafel* (broad-bean rissoles) have been made in Egypt since the days of the pharaohs. Another popular dish is *bissara*, a thick broad-bean soup flavored with onion, garlic, cumin, mint, and *melokhia* (a green leafy vegetable that can be eaten fresh or dried). Dried *melokhia* leaves are often added to soups to give them a thicker, more glutinous consistency. Egyptians also love egg dishes, especially *eggah*, a thick omelet similar to the Italian frittata that is served cut in wedges like a pie.

Desserts and pastries include the ubiquitous *ba'lawa* and *k'nafeh*, *zalabia* (little pastry fritters soaked in sugar syrup that are similar to the Greek *loukoumades)*, and *balouza* (a kind of jelly flavored with rose water and topped with chopped almonds or pistachios). *Balouza* should not be confused with *basbouza*, a semolina and almond cake coated in lemon-flavored sugar syrup. Another refreshing dessert is *koshaf* (a dried fruit salad with almonds and pine nuts).

> *"Insects, leaves, flowers, petals, seeds, roots, and galls. China, India, Java, Egypt, black Africa, the gardens and valleys of Morocco, blending perfume foreign to our European senses. Spices virulent with all the wildness of the countries where they have ripened, sweet from loving cultures of the gardens where they have flowered. Here is all the fascination of your dark kitchens, the odor of your streets. Spices are the soul of Fez."*
> —Madame Guinaudeau, *Traditional Moroccan Cooking*

North African cooking, perhaps more than any other in the Mediterranean, has been molded by a long history of invasions and occupations. The indigenous people of the *Magreb* (the coastal strip along the southern shores of the Mediterranean that make up the modern states of Morocco, Algeria, Tunisia, and Libya) were the Berbers, a light-haired, fair-skinned people, who are thought to originate in Asia Minor. The Berber diet was based on wheat, lentils, broad beans, goat's milk, and honey. *Kesksou* (couscous), the most famous dish of North Africa, was invented by the Berbers.

In the first millennium B.C., the Phoenicians set up trading posts along the coast of North Africa and founded Carthage near modern-day Tunis. Although the Carthaginians planted wheat, olives, and vines in the fifth century B.C., it was the Romans who developed agriculture on a grand scale, building aqueducts and canals as far away as Numidia in eastern Algeria. They built such vast estates of wheat fields that Carthage became known as the granary of Rome.

In the sixth century A.D., the Romans were overthrown by the Vandals, followed by the Byzantines. After the death of Mohammed in A.D. 631, the Arab Muslims overran North Africa and converted the people to Islam. The Arabs were great agriculturists and re-established Roman irrigation systems that had been destroyed by the vandals. They built new underground canals in Tunisia and Morocco using techniques they learned from the Persians.

New vegetables were introduced as well as all kinds of citrus fruit, rice, and sugar. In the eighth century, the Arabs swept across the Straights of

Gibraltar and invaded Spain, where they remained until they were expelled by the Spanish Inquisition in 1492. Spanish Moors and Jews fled *Al-Andalus* (the old word for Moorish Spain) and sought refuge in the *Magreb,* bringing with them a rich culinary heritage after seven hundred years in Spain. They encouraged the use of olives and olive oil in cooking instead of the Berber *smen* (a kind of clarified butter). They brought new vegetables and fruits: eggplants, carrots, turnips, quinces, apricots, peaches, and cherries, as well as new vegetables from the New World—tomatoes, potatoes, and chili peppers. Exotic spices (cumin, cinnamon, saffron, turmeric, and cloves) were introduced and *warka* (a paper-thin pastry similar to *filo* pastry).

In the sixteenth century, much of the *Magreb,* (except Morocco) came under Ottoman rule. The Ottoman culinary influence is still apparent today. Tunisian *brik* and Algerian *bourek* both derive from the Turkish *börek.* Sweet pastries such as *baklava* and *ktaif* have obvious Turkish origins.

In the nineteenth century, Algeria, followed by Tunisia, became a French protectorate. (The French did not gain control of Morocco until 1912, at the same time that the Italians snatched Libya from the Ottomans.) The French were nicknamed *"Pied-Noirs"* (Black Feet) on account of their heavy black boots. Later *"Pied-Noirs"* came to refer to anyone of Italian, Spanish, or Portuguese origin—many of whom were Sephardic Jews—who lived in the Magreb. When Morocco, Algeria, and Tunisia became independent, many *"Pied-Noirs"* returned to live in France, bringing their adopted North African cooking with them, which had some influence in introducing the French to new exotic flavors and new ways of cooking.

Moroccan cooking has been called one of the world's greatest cuisines. Spices play an important part of most savory dishes. Saffron, ginger, cinnamon, turmeric, and sweet and hot peppers are used to flavor most savory dishes. Meals usually begin with a colorful array of raw, cooked, or puréed salads that rival the *mezze* of the Middle East. Simple salads of grilled or fried vegetables dressed with olive oil, garlic, preserved lemons, fresh coriander, and parsley; are little dishes of finely grated radishes; or carrots and apples scented with orange-flower water; or bowls of lentils or chickpeas dressed with olive oil, lemon juice, grated ginger, cumin, and garlic round out each meal.

The Fast of Ramadan is usually broken with a nourishing chickpea or lentil soup called *harira. Harira* has many variations. *Harira kerouiya* (a kind of gruel flavored with mint, lemon juice, mastic, and caraway seeds) is highly prized for its digestive qualities. Another nourishing soup is *bessara,* a broad-bean soup that is often served in winter as a meal on its own with some *khobz* (Moroccan bread) on the side.

Kesksou (couscous) is the national dish. The word couscous not only refers to the fine grains of semolina with which it is made, but also to the finished dish. The Berbers originally ate couscous with *smen* (a pungent aged butter flavored with herbs) and a bowl of milk. Today, couscous is served in a variety of ways. In fact, there are probably as many couscous dishes as there are cooks.

All kinds of vegetables (peppers, eggplant, zucchini, artichokes, okra, peas, potatoes, dried beans, or chickpeas) are made into *maraks* or *tajines* (stews) with onions, garlic, fruits, olives, or nuts, and flavored with fresh coriander and flat-leaf parsley and an exotic mix of spices. *Tajines* are named after the round earthenware pot with a conical lid in which they are cooked, but take note—most Moroccan *tajines* include some meat, fish, or poultry. Another Moroccan specialty is *briouats*, deep-fried triangular or cigar-shaped pastries made with *warka* (paper-thin pastry similar to *filo* pastry) that may be sweet or savory. Savory fillings include spinach or Swiss chard with onions, garlic, and cumin, or rice and coarsely ground almonds. Sweet *briouats* filled with pounded dates or figs, or almond paste are usually served for festivals, marriages, or other special occasions.

Like most North Africans, Moroccans have a sweet tooth. Rich sweets and cakes are not usually served at the end of a meal, but at any time during the day with a glass of mint tea. Traditional pastries include *m'hanncha* (the serpent), a coiled pastry made with *warka* and filled with almond paste flavored with orange-flower water and dusted with powdered sugar and cinnamon, and *kaab el ghzal* (literally, gazelle's horns), crescent-shaped pastries filled with dates or almonds. *Shebbakia* (deep-fried pastries in the shape of rosettes that are dipped in honey and coated in sesame seeds) are usually served during Ramadan. *Jabane* is Moroccan nougat.

Algerian cooking is less spicy than that of Morocco and Tunisia although the Algerians are fond of *dersa* (a hot sauce made with garlic, ground caraway seeds or cumin, and sweet and hot pepper, that is usually served with vegetables or fried eggs). Traditional salads include *h'miss* (a chopped roast pepper and tomato salad) and *badendjel m'charmel* (roast eggplant dressed with olive oil, vinegar, garlic, and ground caraway seeds). Soups—*chorba*, *djari*, or *harira*—are usually rich in vegetables and legumes. Several kinds of pasta are made, including *rechta* (egg noodles) and *trida* (little pasta squares), as well as rice, couscous, and *berkoukes* and *m'hamsa*, both of which are similar to couscous but with a large grain. *Mesfouf* is a sweet couscous with raisins or dates.

Algerians are fond of eggs and pancakes, especially *m'hadjeb* (a savory pancake filled with fried onions, tomatoes, garlic, and hot peppers). Egg dishes include *bayd maqli bil dersa* (fried eggs with hot sauce), and *chakchouka* (a delicious vegetable stew that is cooked with eggs that has many variations). Other vegetable dishes of note are *khalota*, a spicy vegetable stew reminiscent of the Provençal ratatouille, and *yamma wicha* (eggplant simmered with chickpeas, fresh coriander, cinnamon, and rice).

Briks or *boureks* are delicious savory pastries made with paper-thin sheets of pastry called *dioul* that are similar to the Moroccan *warka*. *Briks* are often filled with spinach, Swiss chard, potatoes, egg, or cheese, and spices, and deep-fried.

Meals usually end with fresh or dried fruit, a bowl of fruit salad scented with orange-flower water, or perhaps a light milk pudding or cream. Traditional pastries such as *knidlette* (little tarts filled with almond paste), *sfendj* (ring-shaped doughnuts), and *kaak bel qaress* (lemon cakes) are usually prepared for religious festivals and special occasions. *Bradj* (date-filled pastries) are often served with *leben* (a kind of buttermilk).

The cooking of Tunisia and Libya are influenced by Italian and Ottoman cuisines. All kinds of pasta dishes are made, especially in Libya, with sauces highly seasoned with chili, cinnamon, fresh coriander, and parsley. *Rishtit kas kas* are homemade egg noodles with a chickpea sauce. Tunisians like their food hot and spicy. *Harissa* comes in varying strengths from hot to fiery. *Mezze* or *kemia*, as they are called in Tunisia, include a variety of raw and cooked salads. The most well-known are *mzoura* (a cooked carrot salad spiced with *harissa* and cumin and *salada mechouia* (a roast pepper and tomato salad).

Breiks (deep-fried savory or sweet pastries) are the pride of the Tunisian kitchen. *Breiks* are similar to the Algerian *boureks* and Moroccan *briouats* except they are prepared with a paper-thin pastry called *malsouka* that is made with semolina instead of flour. One of the classic fillings for *breiks* is a whole egg, but they may also be filled with potatoes, cheese, or tuna fish. Sweet *breiks* are usually filled with date or almond paste, dusted with sugar, and served hot or cold.

In Tunisia, couscous is usually served with *harissa* or *hhlou*, a sweet and sour condiment made with dried apricots, chestnuts, or pumpkin. *Qalib kesksou*, a Libyan dish, consists of couscous topped with a beaten egg, tomato sauce, and grated cheese and baked in the oven. Other Libyan specialties include *roz bil-tamar* (rice with dates and pistachios) and *sansafil maghli* (salsify fritters).

Tunisian pastries and cakes clearly demonstrate the mix of Italian and Ottoman influences, especially *boka di dama* (an almond sponge cake), manicotis (deep-fried pastries coated in sugar syrup), and *scoudilini* (a sponge cake dredged in sugar syrup and filled with a rich almond cream). *Scoudilini* is a Passover specialty of Sephardic Jews who originally came from Livorno. Libyan pastries include *lugmat el quadi* (doughnuts coated in honey) and *dableh* (deep-fried pastries similar to Moroccan *shebbakia*). *Halva ditzmar* is a rich sweetmeat made with dates, figs, walnuts, honey, aniseed, and grated chocolate.

SPAIN

ANDALUSIA   THE LEVANT
CATALONIA   THE BALEARIC ISLANDS

*"For Spain is a mystery and I am not at all convinced
that those who live within the peninsular and were born
there understand it much better the I, but that we all
love the wild, contradictory, passionately beautiful land
there can be no doubt."*
—James Michener, *Iberia*

Spain is a country of extremes—of climate, terrain, and temperament. Spaniards have hot tempers, high spirits, and a strong sense of individuality. It is a unique land cut off from the rest of Europe by the Pyrenees. As the travel author Jan Morris writes: "Whichever way you enter her, from Portugal, France, Gibraltar, or the open sea, instantly you feel a sense of separateness, a geographical fact, exaggerated by historical circumstance."

Throughout its history, Spain has been a melting pot of cultures: Iberian, Celtic, Phoenician, Roman, Arabic, Berber, Jewish, and many others. In the first millennium B.C., the Phoenicians settled along its southern shores and called the land "Shapan," the Hidden Land (sometimes translated as "the Land of Rabbits") from which Espana is derived. Although the Carthaginians first introduced the olive and the vine to Spain, it was the Romans who planted olives on a grand scale. Spain produced such vast quantities of olive oil, wine, wheat, and raisins that Baetica (the Roman name for modern-day Andalusia) became one of the richest provinces of the Roman Empire.

In A.D. 711, the Arab Muslims (sometimes called the Moors) crossed the straits of Gibraltar and swept through Spain, gaining control of most of the land, except for a few states in the north. Arab rule lasted over seven hundred years. The Arab influences were profound on all aspects of Spanish culture, art, architecture, literature, philosophy, and especially its cuisine.

The Moors introduced a wide range of new foodstuffs: oranges, lemons, eggplant, asparagus, artichokes, spinach, figs, dates, apricots, pomegranates, almonds, pistachios, rice, and sugar, as well as new spices from the orient: cinnamon, nutmeg, cumin, aniseed, ginger, sesame, coriander, and saffron. New irrigation systems were set up—aqueducts, underground canals, waterwheels, and windmills. Rice was cultivated along the coast, especially around Valencia. Orchards of apples, peaches, cherries, and citrus fruit were planted. New sweetmeats were introduced and fine pastries soaked in honey and flavored with rose and orange-blossom water.

Spain prospered and Cordoba, the seat of the Caliphate, became the most cultivated city in Europe, next to Constantinople. The Jews also thrived under Arab rule. Jews have lived in Spain since the destruction of the First Temple by the Babylonians in 586 B.C. They called the land *Sepharad*, which means "Spain" in Hebrew. Before the Arab conquest of Spain, the Jews had suffered a hundred years of persecution by the Visigoths, but under Muslim rule, many Jews rose to prominence as poets, philosophers, scientists, financiers, doctors of medicine, and statesmen. However, in 1492, after Ferdinand and Isabella defeated the last Moors in the Kingdom of Granada, the Jews, except the *conversos*, were expelled from Spain, taking their language and their culture with them. Most fled to North Africa and the eastern Mediterranean, especially Constantinople and Thessalonika. Many of their descendants today still speak *Ladino* or Judesmo—a language that evolved from medieval Spanish mixed with Hebrew, Arabic, Greek, and Turkish—and cook dishes that date back to fifteenth-century Spain.

It was no coincidence that Columbus discovered America in the same year of the Christian reconquest of Spain. Columbus was sent by Ferdinand and Isabella to seek out new trade routes to Asia in order to avoid trading with the Muslim Middle East. The discovery of the New World brought the introduction of a whole range of new foodstuffs to Spain: potatoes, tomatoes, maize, squash, all kinds of beans, sweet and hot peppers, avocados, and chocolate.

After the accession of the Hapsburgs to the Spanish throne in the sixteenth century, Spain became the most powerful country in the world, ruling Austria, the Netherlands, the Kingdoms of Naples and Sicily, with colonies in North and Central America and most of South America. As a result, Spain had one of the world's richest and most varied cuisines.

Unfortunately when the Spanish throne was bequeathed to a Bourbon king in 1759, French cooking was adopted by the Spanish court and the upper classes, and Spanish cooking was considered inferior. However, traditional Spanish cooking was never totally eclipsed. In the nineteenth century, a new element, tapas, was introduced into the Spanish culinary heritage. Tapas means "lid" or "cover." Originally, a slice of bread was placed over a glass of sherry or wine to keep off dust or flies in summer. Later a piece of cheese was added to make it more appetizing. Tapas bars originated in Seville, but today they are found all over Spain.

Today Spanish cooking is regional cooking. The Mediterranean cuisines of Andalusia, The Levant, Catalonia, and the Balearic Islands have little in common with the cooking of Galicia or Asturias in the north. Andalusian cooking is based on olive oil, garlic, and plenty of vegetables. The most famous dish is "gazpacho," a chilled vegetable soup or liquid salad. Originally gazpacho was made with olive oil, garlic, wine vinegar, and bread, all pounded together in a mortar and thinned with water. Later chopped tomatoes and peppers were added. Today there are many versions. Jose Carlos Capel gives at least sixty recipes for gazpacho in his book on Andalusian cooking. Andalusians love fried vegetables, especially potatoes, eggplant, zucchini, and peppers, which are usually served as a separate course. Flavors reflect the Arab influence: *habas a la andaluza* (broad beans simmered with onions, tomatoes, and cumin), *acelgas a la sevillana* (Swiss chard with raisins and pine nuts), and *alcachofes a la sevillana* (sautéed artichokes and potatoes in a garlic and saffron sauce). Malaga wine and sherry from the Bodegas of Jerez-de-la-Frontera are widely used in cooking.

Eggs are prepared in a variety of ways—boiled, fried, shirred, scrambled with all kinds of vegetables, and of course, made into tortillas. The Spanish tortilla or omelet, like its relative the Italian frittata, is round and flat like a pancake and usually contains potatoes or some other vegetable. The *tortilla andaluza de cebolla* is made with onions cooked until they are very soft and caramelized. *Tortilla sevillana* includes onions, tomatoes, red peppers, and mushrooms.

The Moorish influence is reflected in the wide variety of sweet pastries and desserts rich in honey and nuts such as *pestiños* (deep-fried pastries flavored with anise and white wine) and *alfajores* (almond and honey sweetmeats that are made in Sidona for Christmas). Other traditional desserts include *yemas de San Leandro* (candied egg yolks made by nuns of the convent of San Leandro in Seville) and *tocino de cielo* (roughly translated as "heavenly bacon"), a kind of cream caramel rich in egg yolks.

Several fine ewe's milk cheeses are made in Andalusia: *Queso de Grazalema* (a hard cheese similar to *Manchego*), *Queso de los Pedroches* (a soft cheese produced near Cordoba), and *Moro* (a soft, creamy cheese made in the province around Seville).

The Levant, Land of the Sunrise, is made up of the provinces of Valencia, Castellon de la Plana, Alicante, and Murcia. Valencia is the birthplace of paella. Paella is named after the shallow, round iron pan in which it is cooked. Although paella is traditionally made with fish, some versions (such as *paella huertana)* are made only with vegetables. Other rice dishes include *moros y christianos* (Moors and Christians), which is made with black beans and white rice, and *arroz con acelgas* (rice with Swiss chard).

Along the flat coastal strip lies the fertile *huertas* (market gardens) of Valencia, which produces a wealth of vegetables and fruits: broad beans, peas, green beans, asparagus, onion, garlic, olives, capers, melons, peaches, apricots, plums, cherries, pears, Muscat grapes, lemons, grapefruit, and of course, Valencia oranges. Elche in Alicante has the only date grove in Europe. Almonds also flourish and appear in many desserts and sweetmeats. The most famous confection is *turron* (nougat), which is made in Jijona and Alicante.

Cheeses from Valencia include *Tronchon* (a semi-hard cheese made with goat's and ewe's milk) and *Queso fresco Valenciano* or *Puzol*, as it is sometimes called (a fresh goat's cheese).

Further south, the *huertas* of Murcia produce early spring vegetables and salad greens. The region is famous for its fine tomatoes and peppers, both of which appear in *tortilla murciana* (a thick omelet that sometimes includes eggplant).

Catalonia lies in the northeast corner of Spain, between the French and Andorran border, and Valencia. The Catalans are a fiercely independent people who have retained their own language and culture. At the height of its power in the fifteenth century, Catalonia, together with the Kingdom of Aragon, ruled much of the Mediterranean coast from the Levant to Provence, as well as Corsica, Sardinia, The Kingdoms of Naples and Sicily, and the Duchy of Athens.

The Catalan cuisine is the oldest in Spain. The first gastronomic text, the *Libri de Sent Sovi*, appeared in Catalan in 1324. It was followed by Rubert de Nola's *Libre de Coch*, which was first printed in 1477 and contains recipes that are still prepared in Catalonia today.

Catalan cuisine has much in common with Provençal cooking. It is based on four sauces: allioli (a garlicky mayonnaise), *picada* (a thick paste made with toasted almonds and hazelnuts and flavored with saffron), *sofregit* (a rich tomato and onion sauce), and *samfaina* (which is made with onion, tomatoes, peppers, zucchini, and eggplant and resembles the Provençal ratatouille. Another popular sauce is *romesco*, which originated in Taragona. *Romesco* is made with sautéed almonds, bread crumbs, tomatoes, and sweet and hot peppers.

Catalonia is olive oil and wine country, both of which were introduced by the Romans. The Romans also taught the Catalans the art of leavening bread. Catalan meals usually begin with *pa amb tomaquet*, slices of country bread (toasted or not) that are rubbed with garlic and tomatoes and sprinkled with olive oil. Catalans love fried, stuffed, and roasted vegetables—especially peppers, eggplant, and all kinds of mushrooms. They are also fond of pasta (many Italians emigrated to Barcelona in the early nineteenth century), especially *canalons* (cannelloni) and *fideus* (short, thin vermicelli that is not cooked, like pasta, in a pot of boiling water, but sautéed in olive oil in a shallow pan and cooked like *paella* with hot water slowly added until it is absorbed). *Fideus* is thought to derive from the Arabic word *fada*, meaning "to overflow."

Desserts include the ubiquitous *crema catalana* (a rich custard cream topped with caramelized sugar similar to the French *crème brulée*) and *menjar blanc* (a chilled almond pudding which the French also claim as their own under the name of blancmange). *Mel i mato* is a dish of fresh white cheese similar to Italian ricotta that is sweetened with honey.

The Balearic Islands have a long history of invasions by Romans, Vandals, Byzantines, Moors, and Barbary pirates. Even the English occupied Minorca in the eighteenth century. The islands have many cultural links to Catalonia, which is reflected in their language—a dialect of Catalan—and their cuisine. Mallorca's most famous dish is probably *sopa mallorquinas*, a dry bread and cabbage soup that is rich in tomatoes, onions, and garlic and prepared in a *greixoneira*, a shallow earthenware pot with a rounded base similar to a wok. Mallorcans make various savory tarts called *cocas* which are similar to *pizze*, but without the cheese. *Cocarois* are spinach turnovers with raisins and pine nuts.

Pastries and confections often include almonds. *Gato* (a moist almond cake) is traditionally made for Christmas and for various fiestas. One of Mallorca's most famous desserts is *gelat d'ametilla* (an almond sorbet). *Greixonera de Brossat* is an almond cheesecake made with *Requeson* cheese flavored with cinnamon and lemon rind.

The cooking of Menorca is less spicy than that of Mallorca. Menorca is famous for its fine vegetables, especially onions, leeks, tomatoes, cabbage, and potatoes. Bread is a staple and held in high esteem. Traditionally, the most important dish of the poor was *oliaigua*, a simple garlic soup made with onions, garlic, olive oil, parsley, and water. Today there are many variations, made with tomatoes, leeks, cabbage, asparagus, cress, or eggs. *Oliaigua* was once eaten for breakfast, lunch, and supper with plenty of *pan casero* (homemade bread).

Like Mallorcans, Menorcans have a sweet tooth. Numerous pastries and cakes are made including *estrellas* (sugar cookies), *buñuelas* (doughnuts), *carquinols* (almond biscuits), *congret* (a kind of sponge cake made with mashed potatoes), and *amargas*, an almond sweetmeat that is traditionally made for Christmas.

No part of the world can be more beautiful
than the western and southern coasts of Turkey.
—Freya Stark, *Alexander's Path*

Turkey lies on the northeast corner of the Mediterranean astride two continents—Europe and Asia. The Turks are proud of their history and proud of their cultural heritage. Turkey has a wealth of classical monuments and biblical sites. It is a land of tremendous contrasts, with its rugged mountains and wooded hillsides that drop sharply down to the sea, the strange volcanic landscape of Cappadocia and the rolling steppes of Central Anatolia. Turkey is surrounded by the sea on three sides: the Black Sea and the Sea of Marmara to the north, the Aegean to the west, and the Mediterranean to the south.

Turkey has a long and turbulent history. It is home to the oldest town known to man—at Catal Hoyuk near Konya around 7500 B.C. where irrigation was first used and where animals were probably first domesticated. Around 200 B.C. the Hittites—an Indo-European people from the Balkans—swept across the land and established their first empire in Anatolia. The Hittites were followed by the Phrygians, Lydians, Persians, the armies of Alexander the Great, and the Romans. After the Roman Empire was divided into eastern and western parts, Constantine moved the seat of the Eastern Roman Empire in 330 A.D. to Byzantium, which he renamed Constantinople. Later, after Constantine's death, the empire became known as the Byzantine Empire. Byzantine rule lasted more than seven hundred years.

Turkish cooking is a reflection of Turkish history. The Turks were descendants of nomadic Turkic tribes from Central Asia. Little is known of their diet except that it included unleavened bread or pastry made of wheat flour, and various milk products and cheeses. One dish, *manti* (a kind of ravioli similar to the Chinese wonton that an early Turkic tribe, the Uyghurs, adopted from their Chinese neighbors), is still eaten in Turkey today. Other dishes that originated in Central Asia are *togyar çorbasi* (a yoghurt soup thickened with wheat flour), *cörek* (a ring-shaped bun), early forms of *börek* (savory pastries), and *tarhana* (a kind of dough or soup base made with fermented wheat flour and dried curds). *Güveç*, a kind of vegetable stew cooked in an earthenware pot, is another pre-Anatolian dish. The name is thought to derive from *kömeç* or *gömmeç*, meaning "buried"—presumably because the earthenware pot was buried in ashes until its contents were cooked.

The essence of Turkish cooking was already established in the Seljuk Period (1071–1299 A.D.). The Seljuks, one of the most powerful Turkic clans, ruled Persia and much of the eastern Islamic world before they invaded Anatolia in the eleventh century. Rice *pilav*, *yahni* (vegetable stews), and stuffings that included dried fruit and nuts were all adopted from the Persians. The Greeks introduced the Turks to olive oil and showed them how to bake round loaves of bread. The thirteenth-century Sufi poet, Rumi, often mentions food in his writings, notably *tutmac* (a dish of lentils and noodles that was popular all over Anatolia until the nineteenth century, but is little known today), wheat soup, *bulgur* (cracked wheat), a wide range of vegetables and fruit, pickles, *ekmek* (bread), savory pastries coated in honey, *halva* or *halvah* made with grape juice or almonds, and *zerde* (a saffron-flavored rice pudding).

The Ottoman Period was a great influence not only on Turkish cuisine, but on the cooking of the whole of the eastern Mediterranean. The Ottoman Empire lasted for over six hundred years. At its height, it stretched from the Danube, across the Balkans to Syria, Egypt, and much of North Africa. Ottoman cooking was primarily developed in the Palaces of the Sultans, especially the Topkapi Palace in Istanbul, where chefs, assisted by a host of apprentices, specialized in the preparation of every classification of food: soups, vegetable dishes, *pilav*, bread, sweet and savory pastries, syrups and jams, *helva*, yoghurt, and even pickles. The preparation of these dishes was not just restricted to the palaces, but was also familiar to most of the population of the Ottoman cities. By the mid-seventeenth century, forty-three food guilds (*esnaf*) had been set up in Istanbul to organize the preparation and selling of foods, including cheese and *börek* makers, pastry cooks, bakers, fritter makers, yoghurt makers, pickle makers, oil merchants, butter merchants, grocers, and fruit merchants with a separate guild of watermelon sellers, many of whom are still in existence today.

Contemporary Turkish cooking is based on the use of fresh ingredients served in season. Mint, dill, and flat-leaf parsley are the favorite herbs. Cumin, allspice, cinnamon, *kirmizi biber* (sweet or hot pepper), and *sumak*—with its characteristic tart, lemony flavor—are the predominant spices used in the Turkish kitchen.

Meals usually begin with a selection of *meze* (appetizers) and salads. *Meze* derives from the Arabic word *mezaq*, meaning the taste or savor of a thing. *Meze* include bit-size cubes of *beyaz peynir* (white cheese) marinated in olive oil, *mercimek koftesi* (small balls of mashed lentils and bulgur), *fasulye piyasi* (a white bean salad), *tomatesli patlicanli tavasi* (fried eggplants in a tomato and garlic sauce), and *ezme* (a dish of almost any puréed vegetable mixed with olive oil and vinegar or garlic and yoghurt). *Meze* are usually served with *raki* (an anise-flavored drink distilled from grapes).

The Turkish cuisine has a vast repertoire of vegetable dishes. Vegetables are stuffed, made into fritters, or gently stewed in olive oil or *zeytinyağli*. Classic dishes include *imam bayildi* (literally, "the priest fainted"), a dish of eggplants stuffed with onions, tomatoes, garlic, and parsley and dressed with so much olive oil that the priest was overcome, *kabak mucveri* (zucchini and white cheese fritters), and *zeytinyagli yaprak dolmasi* (vine leaves stuffed with rice, currants, pine nuts, and herbs and cooked in olive oil).

All kinds of rice *pilav* are made, especially with eggplant, zucchini, tomatoes, peas, currants and pine nuts, carrots, and chickpeas. *Pilav* is also made with *bulgur* (cracked wheat) instead of rice. *Börek* (savory pastries) are made with *yufka* (thin sheets of dough similar to *filo* pastry) as well as various puff and flaky pastries. Fillings include spinach, white cheese, potato and onion, pumpkin, zucchini, mushroom, and green lentils.

Bread is a staple, especially *pide* (a soft round bread with a hollow pouch). *Pide* is sometimes stuffed with cheese or vegetables. In the region around Antalya, *pide* is often spread with *hibes* (a paste made with crushed chickpeas, yoghurt, red pepper, and onions). *Misir ekmegi* (cornbread) is popular in eastern and central Anatolia. *Simit* (ring-shaped rolls coated in sesame seeds) are sold by street vendors all over Turkey.

Some traditional desserts include a variety of sweet pastries coated in sugar syrup with such evocative names as *kiz memesi kadayif* (young girls' breasts), *kadin gobeği* (ladies' navels), and *dilber dudaği* (beauty's lips). *Aşure* is a sweet rice pudding made with whole wheat, legumes, nuts, and dried fruit that used to be made to celebrate Noah's salvation from the flood. Today it is eaten on the tenth day of Muharren to commemorate the martyrdom of Mohammed's grandsons, Hasan and Huseyin. Turks are fond of all kinds of *kompostosu* (fruit compôtes) and *muhallebiler* (chilled milk puddings) that are flavored with almonds, pistachios, coconut, and rose and orange-flower water.

APPETIZERS AND SALADS

La femme est comme la salade, il lui plaît d'être remuée.
Woman is like a salad, it pleases her to be stirred.
—French proverb

Meals throughout the Mediterranean usually begin with a selection of little cooked dishes or salads that are designed to stimulate the appetite. Flavorings change from country to country. In North Africa, appetizers—called *aadrou* in Tunisia or *kemia* in Algeria—are usually highly seasoned with garlic, chili, cumin, or coriander. Salads are often unexpectedly light and refreshing such as the Moroccan *salata bi-khissou was tufah* (a grated carrot and apple salad that is flavored with orange-flower water). In Albania, Greece, and Turkey, vegetables and salads are often served with a creamy yoghurt sauce flavored with mint or dill. Tahini appears in many Middle Eastern dips and salads. Of course, all around the Mediterranean, salad dressings are made with fruity extra virgin olive oil, lemon juice, or wine vinegar.

Many other dishes in this book, especially fritters and croquettes, can also be served as appetizers—just use smaller quantities. Serve them the Mediterranean way—with a glass of *ouzo, raki, pastis,* or sherry.

CHRISTMAS CAPONATA

Caponata di Natale

Caponata is Sicily's most famous antipasto. It is usually made with fried eggplant simmered in a sweet and sour sauce with olives and capers, but at Christmas time, when eggplants are out of season, it is made with celery instead. The word caponata is said to derive from *capon* or *cappone* (a kind of cracker flavored with oil and vinegar that sailors used to eat on board ship instead of bread).

6 stalks celery
2 tablespoons extra virgin olive oil
¼ cup blanched almonds
¼ cup sultanas
¼ cup green olives, pitted and chopped
2 tablespoons capers
3 tablespoons red wine vinegar
1 tablespoon sugar

Trim the ends of the celery and slice them thinly. Heat the olive oil in a large frying pan and add the celery. Cover and simmer for 10 to 15 minutes or until the celery is tender.

Toast the almonds in a 300°F oven for 15 minutes or until they are golden. Chop finely and add to the celery, together with the sultanas, olives, and capers. Cover and simmer for 5 minutes. Add the vinegar and sugar and cook, uncovered, for 5 minutes or until the flavors are blended and the vinegar has evaporated. Serve at room temperature. Serves 4.

ARTICHOKES BARIGOULE

Artichauts à la Barigoule

This famous Provençal dish is named after a variety of mushroom called *barigoulo* or *barigoule*. Originally artichokes prepared *à la barigoule* were cooked, like mushrooms, over hot coals. Today there are many variations. Sometimes they are simply cooked with onions and thyme. Or the artichokes may be stuffed with a mixture of bread crumbs, chopped mushrooms, and garlic. In this recipe, they are simmered in a little white wine on a bed of carrots and onions.

12 small purple artichokes
½ lemon
5 tablespoons extra virgin olive oil
l large onion, finely chopped
2 carrots, diced into small pieces
salt
freshly ground black pepper
2 garlic cloves, finely chopped
2 tablespoons flat-leaf parsley, finely chopped
1 bay leaf
a pinch of thyme
½ cup dry white wine
½ cup water

Cut off the stalks of the artichokes and remove any tough outer leaves. Slice off the top of the remaining leaves about halfway down and remove the chokes with a teaspoon. Rub the cut parts with a piece of lemon to prevent them from discoloring.

Pour 3 tablespoons olive oil in a casserole large enough to hold the artichokes in one layer. Add the onion and carrots. Place the artichokes on top. Dribble over the remaining olive oil and season with salt and black pepper. Cook, covered, over a gentle heat for 15 minutes or until the carrots and onions start to turn golden. Add the remaining ingredients and bring to a boil. Cover and simmer for 1 hour or until the artichokes are tender and most of the liquid is evaporated. Serves 4 to 6.

WILD ASPARAGUS WITH SPINACH AND HARD-BOILED EGG SAUCE

Šparoge Divlje s Umakom od Špinata

Wild asparagus has a more astringent flavor than the cultivated variety but is equally delicious. In this recipe from Istria, it is served with mayonnaise enriched with spinach, hard-boiled eggs, herbs, and a little sour cream.

2 pounds wild or cultivated asparagus
2 ounces spinach
1 hard-boiled egg
2 egg yolks
about 2 tablespoons lemon juice
2 tablespoons fresh chives, chopped
2 tablespoons flat-leaf parsley, finely chopped
2 tablespoons sour cream
salt
freshly ground black pepper

Trim the ends of the asparagus with a sharp knife and remove any fibrous inedible parts from the lower stalks. Steam for 15 to 20 minutes or until tender.

Meanwhile wash the spinach carefully and cook in a covered saucepan over a moderate heat for 5 minutes. The water clinging to the leaves is sufficient to prevent scorching. Drain, squeeze dry, and chop finely.

Separate the yolk from the white of the hard-boiled egg and place in a mixing bowl with the raw egg yolks and a few drops of lemon juice. Mix well together. When the mixture becomes very thick, thin it with a few drops of lemon juice. When the oil is used up, stir in the spinach, finely chopped egg white, herbs, and sour cream. Season with salt and black pepper.

Arrange the asparagus on individual plates and serve with the sauce on the side. Serves 4.

EGGPLANT AND PEPPER RELISH

Pindžur

This dish makes a very good appetizer or snack with some crusty bread on the side. In Croatia, it is usually stored in sterilized jars topped with a layer of olive oil for use throughout the winter.

1 pound eggplant
1 pound red bell peppers
½ pound tomatoes
1-2 red chili peppers, to taste
1 small onion
3 tablespoons extra virgin olive oil
1 tablespoon red wine vinegar
2 garlic cloves, crushed
salt

Place the eggplant, peppers, tomatoes, and onion on a well-oiled baking sheet and bake in a preheated 375°F oven 15 minutes to 1 hour until the skins are blackened all over and the flesh is tender. When they are softened, remove from the oven and set aside to cool. Scoop out the flesh of the eggplant and mash with a fork. Place the peppers under cold water and wash off the blackened skins. Cut in half and remove the core and seeds. Keep your hands away from your face when handling the chili pepper.

Cut the tomatoes in half, scoop out the flesh, and remove the seeds. Cut the onion in half and remove the flesh. Chop the peppers, tomatoes, and onion finely or you can chop them coarsely in a food processor. Add to the eggplant purée, together with the olive oil, vinegar, and garlic. Mix well and season with salt. Transfer to a serving dish and chill thoroughly before serving. Serves 4.

Eggplant and Yoghurt Salad
Yoğurtlu Patlicanl Salatasi

The exact amount of olive oil, lemon juice, and garlic can be varied to taste. If a little of the blackened skin of the eggplant is mixed in with the flesh by mistake, it only adds to the slightly smoky flavor of the dish. Serve as part of a *meze* with some pita bread on the side.

2 medium eggplants, about 1¼ pounds
¼ cup shelled walnuts, finely ground in a blender or food processor
4 tablespoons yoghurt
2–3 cloves garlic, crushed
2 tablespoons finely chopped fresh mint leaves
3 tablespoons extra virgin olive oil
2 tablespoons lemon juice
salt
freshly ground black pepper
8 black olives

Place the unpeeled eggplants over a gas burner or charcoal grill over a high flame. Turn from time to time until the skins are blackened all over and the eggplants are tender. Remove from the flame and allow to cool slightly. Peel the eggplants and set aside to cool.

Squeeze any excess moisture out of the eggplants and chop coarsely. Place in a bowl and mash them thoroughly with a fork. If you like, you can purée the eggplant in a food processor. Stir in the walnuts, yoghurt, garlic, mint, olive oil, and lemon juice and blend well. Season with salt and black pepper. Transfer to a serving dish and chill thoroughly. Garnish with black olives and serve. Serves 4.

AVOCADO AND CHICKPEA DIP
Avocado Hummus

Israel is famous for its avocado pears. In recent years, they have been incorporated into one of Israel's few traditional dishes, *hummus* (chickpea dip). If you use dried chickpeas, they need a long soaking—about 48 hours. Drain and cook them in plenty of unsalted water for 2 to 6 hours—the exact time depends on their age. If you are using canned chickpeas, drain them well and rinse thoroughly under cold water to remove the salt. Avocado hummus may be served with pita bread or with a selection of raw vegetables such as carrots, celery, spring onions, cucumbers, or sweet peppers, cut into sticks about 4 inches long.

1 large ripe avocado pear
½ pound cooked and drained chickpeas, liquid preserved
about 6 tablespoons lemon juice
4 tablespoons tahini
1–2 garlic cloves, crushed
salt
paprika
8 black olives

Cut the avocado pear in half and remove the pit. Scoop out the flesh and place in a blender or food processor with the chickpeas, lemon juice, tahini, garlic, and a little of the preserved liquid. Process until smooth and creamy, adding a little more water if necessary. Season with salt to taste. Transfer to a serving platter, sprinkle with paprika, and garnish with black olives. Serves 4 to 6.

STUFFED VINE LEAVES

Yalanci Dolma

Stuffed vine leaves are made all over the Balkans and the Middle East. In Turkey, they are filled with a tasty mixture of rice, currants, pine nuts, and herbs. *Yalanci* means "imitation" because the "real" ones contain meat.

7 ounces preserved vine leaves
¾ cup long-grain rice
¼ cup currants
¼ cup pine nuts
½ cup extra virgin olive oil
1 medium onion, finely chopped
1 clove garlic, finely chopped
1 teaspoon sugar
a handful of fresh mint leaves, finely chopped
a handful of flat-leaf parsley, finely chopped
½ teaspoon cinnamon
½ teaspoon allspice
juice of half of a lemon
½ teaspoon salt
freshly ground black pepper
lemon wedges

Unroll the vine leaves and boil in plenty of water for 2 minutes. Remove with a slotted spoon and drain in a colander.

To prepare the filling, heat 3 tablespoons of olive oil in a heavy-based pan and cook the onions and garlic over moderate heat for 2 minutes. Add the sugar, 1 tablespoon lemon juice, salt, and 1 cup of boiling water. Cover and simmer for 5 to 10 minutes or until the water is absorbed. The rice should only be partially cooked.

Line the pan with a few vine leaves. Take one vine leaf and lay flat on a work surface, smooth side down, with the stem towards you. Place a heaping teaspoon of the filling onto the center of the leaf near the stem end. Fold the stem over the filling, then fold over each side to enclose the filling. Roll up not too tightly, like a cigar.

Arrange the dolmas in the pan, side by side, with their stem side down. Pour in the remaining olive oil and lemon juice, and enough boiling water to just cover the dolmas. Put an inverted plate on top to prevent the dolmas from unrolling during cooking. Cover the pan and simmer for 50 minutes, adding a little more water if necessary. There should only be a tablespoon or two of liquid in the pan when the dolmas are cooked. When cool, transfer to a serving dish and serve cold with lemon wedges. Makes about 30 dolmas.

HOT GOAT CHEESE WITH TOMATO AND PISTOU

Labro caud à la poumo d'amour et pistou

In this recipe from Provence, rounds of French bread are topped with melted goat cheese and *pistou*—a relative of the famous Italian basil and garlic sauce, *pesto*. They make a delicious snack or appetizer served with a glass of red wine.

4 tomatoes, sliced
4 slices of French bread
8 ounces Fourme de Labro, or similar goat cheese, sliced
a small bunch of basil
2 garlic cloves
about 2 tablespoons extra virgin olive oil
salt
freshly ground black pepper

Arrange the tomatoes on top of the French bread and cover with slices of goat cheese. Place the basil and garlic in a mortar and crush with a pestle.

Dribble over enough olive oil to make a smooth purée. Season with salt and black pepper. Spread a little of the purée on top of the cheese. Place the slices of bread under a hot grill for 3 to 4 minutes or until the cheese is melted. Serve at once. Serves 4.

CROSTINI WITH BLACK OLIVE CAVIAR
Crostini con crêma di olive neri

This recipe comes from Tuscany, where it is often nicknamed "poor man's caviar." It consists of a mixture of puréed black olives, artichoke bottoms, capers, and chili. Sometimes half a small zucchini is substituted for the artichoke bottom.

2 cups Gaeta black olives, pitted
1 tablespoon capers
½ red or green chili pepper, cored, seeded, and finely chopped
1 cooked artichoke bottom
4–5 tablespoons extra virgin olive oil
4–6 slices of whole-meal bread

Place the olives, capers, chili pepper, artichoke bottom, and 2 tablespoons olive oil in a blender or food processor and process to a smooth purée, adding a little more olive oil if necessary.

Remove the crusts of the bread and cut into quarters. Brush lightly with the remaining olive oil and toast in a preheated 400°F oven for 6 to 8 minutes or until golden. Spread the caviar over the crostini and serve. Serves 4 to 6.

CAULIFLOWER WITH PARSLEY AND TAHINI SAUCE

Arnabeet ma Ba'Doones bil-Tahineh

This is a very popular *meze* in Lebanon. Steamed cauliflower florets are served with a rich green sauce made with parsley, tahini, lemon juice, and garlic. New potatoes or slices of cooked beetroot may be served the same way.

1 medium cauliflower
½ cup tahini
juice of 2-3 lemons, to taste
about ⅓ cup water
2 cloves garlic, crushed
½ cup flat-leaf parsley, very finely chopped
salt

Trim the ends of the cauliflower and break into florets. Steam for 8 minutes or until the cauliflower is just tender, but still retains its crispness.

To make the sauce, put the tahini in a mixing bowl and slowly pour in a little lemon juice, stirring constantly. The mixture will start to thicken. Thin it with a little water. Repeat until the sauce has a smooth creamy consistency. Stir in the garlic and parsley and mix well. Season with salt. Serve with the cauliflower florets. Serves 4.

EGGPLANT PATTIES

Melitzanokeftedes

These delicious little patties come from the island of Rhodes in the Dodecanese, but variations are made all over Greece. Sometimes the cheese is omitted and a little grated onion and oregano is added instead. The Greeks have a wide repertoire of vegetable patties made with tomatoes, potatoes, chickpeas, zucchini, leeks, or *horta* (wild greens). The preparation is basically the same. The vegetables are chopped, mashed, or grated, and mixed with flour or bread crumbs and perhaps a little egg or grated cheese. They are then formed into patties and fried in hot oil.

2 small eggplants, about 1 pound
2 tablespoons freshly grated Kefalotyri or Parmesan cheese
½ cup fresh bread crumbs
½ cup flat-leaf parsley, finely chopped
1 egg yolk
salt
freshly ground black pepper
flour
oil for deep frying

Wash the eggplants and bake in a preheated 375°F oven for 30 minutes or until they are tender. Remove from the oven. When they are cool enough to handle, scoop out the flesh and chop finely. Place in a mixing bowl and drain away any excess liquid. Add the grated cheese, bread crumbs, parsley, and egg yolk and mix well. Season with salt and black pepper. Shape into small patties about 2 cm in diameter. Roll in flour and flatten slightly. Deep fry in hot oil until golden on both sides. Drain on paper towels. Serve hot or at room temperature. Serves 4.

SICILIAN PEPERONATA

Peperonata

Sicilian *peperonata* or *pipirunata* as it is called in the local dialect is spicier than its Florentine counterpart and includes potatoes, green olives, and chili.

4 red, green, or yellow peppers
½ pound new potatoes
4 tablespoons extra virgin olive oil
2 medium onions, sliced
1 small red chili pepper, cored, seeded, and finely chopped
1 pound ripe plum tomatoes, peeled, seeded, and chopped
¼ cup green olives, pitted and sliced
2 tablespoons red wine vinegar
salt

Slice the peppers in half and remove the cores and seeds. Cut into strips. Peel the potatoes and slice them thinly. Heat the olive oil in a large frying pan and cook the onions and chili over a moderate heat for 5 minutes. Add the potatoes and peppers.

Cover and cook over gentle heat for 20 minutes or until the vegetables are tender. Add the tomatoes and olives and cook, uncovered, over moderate heat until the sauce is thickened. Pour in the vinegar and season with salt to taste. Simmer for 4 minutes to blend the flavors. Serve hot or at room temperature. Serves 4.

FRIED CHEESE SLICES

Saganaki

This dish is named after the two-handled frying pan in which it is cooked. Choose a fairly hard, cheese such as Kefalotyri or *Parmesan*. *Saganaki* is a popular *meze* in most Greek tavernas, where it is usually served with a glass of *retsina* (resinated wine).

½ pound Kefalotyri or Parmesan cheese
flour
4 tablespoons butter or olive oil
1 lemon, cut into wedges

Cut the cheese into slices about 1 centimeter thick. Dip lightly in flour.

Heat the butter in a heavy-based frying pan and fry the cheese slices until they are golden on both sides and the cheese has just started to melt. Serve with lemon wedges on the side. Serves 4.

WILD MOUNTAIN GREENS IN OLIVE OIL

Horta Tou Vounou

Horta (wild mountain greens) are found all over Greece. They usually consist of slightly bitter leafy vegetables such as chicory, dandelion, or *vlita* (a member of the amaranth family). The greens are usually cooked in a pan of boiling water until they are tender, then liberally dressed in luscious green olive oil and served with lemon wedges. I prefer to cook the greens in just enough water to prevent them sticking to the pan in order to retain their high vitamin content. A mixture of spinach, Swiss chard, mustard greens, turnip tops, sorrel, beet greens, or rocket may be substituted for the wild mountain greens.

2 pounds mixed greens such as spinach, dandelion, rocket, etc.
3 or 4 tablespoons water
about ½ cup extra virgin olive oil
salt
freshly ground black pepper
lemon wedges

Trim the ends of the greens and wash them thoroughly. Cook in a covered saucepan with the water for 5 to 7 minutes or until they are tender. Drain away any excess water. Squeeze dry and chop coarsely. Transfer to a serving dish and dress with olive oil. Season with salt and black pepper. Serve with lemon wedges on the side. Serves 4 to 6.

NORTH AFRICAN EGGPLANT AND TOMATO SALAD

Salata Badendjel Tomatem

This tasty cooked salad consists of fried eggplants in a light tomato sauce flavored with cumin, paprika, and fresh coriander. It is usually served at room temperature, but it is also very good served hot as a side dish.

2 or 3 small eggplants, about 1 to 1¼ lbs
⅓ cup extra virgin olive oil
1 small onion, finely chopped
4 ripe plum tomatoes, peeled, seeded, and chopped
2 tablespoons flat-leaf parsley, finely chopped
2 tablespoons fresh coriander, finely chopped
½ teaspoon cumin
½ teaspoon paprika
salt
freshly ground black pepper

Trim the ends of the eggplants and dice them into **half**-inch pieces. Heat the olive oil in a large frying pan and cook the onion over moderate heat until it starts to soften. Add the eggplants and stir well so they are evenly coated in oil.

Cover and cook over a gentle heat until the vegetables are tender and starting to turn golden. Add the tomatoes, herbs, and spices and season with salt and black pepper. Simmer, uncovered, for a further 7 or 8 minutes, or until the sauce is thickened. Serve at room temperature. Serves 4.

Butter Beans in Olive Oil with Garlic and Coriander

Fassoulyah bil-zeit

This dish is a popular in Lebanon. Broad beans can be served the same way.

½ pound dried butter beans
4 tablespoons extra virgin olive oil
3 medium onions, finely sliced
4 garlic cloves, finely chopped
½ bunch fresh coriander, very finely chopped
salt
freshly ground black pepper

Soak the beans overnight and drain. Bring to a boil in plenty of unsalted water. Cover, and simmer for 1 to 1½ hours or until they are tender. Drain well.

Heat the olive oil in a saucepan and cook the onions and garlic over a gentle heat for 10 minutes or until they are very soft. Add the beans and season with salt and black pepper. Cook for 10 more minutes or until the onions start to turn golden. Two minutes before the end of cooking, stir in the coriander. Serve cold. Serves 4 to 6.

CATALAN BROAD-BEAN SALAD WITH FRESH MINT

Amanida de Faves amb Menta Fresca

Amanida is the Catalan word for "salad." It derives from "amanir," meaning "to season." This *amanida* is very popular in early spring when young tender broad beans are in season.

1 pound shelled fresh broad beans or frozen baby broad beans
3 lettuce leaves, shredded
1 green tomato, peeled and diced
1 green onion, finely chopped
⅓ cup extra virgin olive oil
2 tablespoons red wine or sherry vinegar
1 teaspoon whole-grain mustard
1 garlic clove, crushed
1 tablespoon fresh mint, finely chopped
2 teaspoons fresh tarragon
salt
freshly ground black pepper

Place the broad beans in a saucepan with 1 pint water and bring to a boil. Cover and simmer for 15 minutes or until the beans are tender. Drain and set aside to cool slightly.

Place the lettuce in a salad bowl and add the warm beans, tomato, and green onion. Make a dressing with the olive oil, vinegar, and mustard and stir in the garlic and herbs. Season with salt and black pepper. Pour over the salad, toss lightly, and serve. Serves 4.

SALAD OF WILD HERBS

E Salado Fero

Centuries of poverty have made the people of Provence avid collectors of food from the wild. In early spring, they look for wild asparagus and mushrooms—especially morels. In summer, they search for wild strawberries. In the fall, they collect pine nuts, chestnuts, filberts, all kinds of mushrooms, and wild blueberries. Winter is the season for wild herbs, which are not only delicious, but also very good for your health.

Here is a selection of the herbs they most often choose: wild chicory (*Cichorium intybus*), wild lettuce (*Lactuca perennis*), young tender dandelion leaves (*Taraxacum officinale*), lamb's lettuce, purslane, salad burnet, fennel, borage, and purple goat's beard that has long, thin, green leaves resembling leeks. You can make up your own combinations according to what is available. Rocket, parsley, basil, chives, red chicory, and watercress make very good additions.

½ pound mixed fresh herbs
1 hard-boiled egg yolk
3 tablespoons extra virgin olive oil
1 tablespoon red wine vinegar
1 garlic clove, crushed
salt
freshly ground black pepper

Wash the herbs carefully and break into bite-sized pieces. Place in a salad bowl. Mash the hard-boiled egg yolk in a bowl and blend in the olive oil, vinegar, and garlic to make a smooth creamy sauce. Season with salt and black pepper. Pour over the herbs, toss lightly, and serve. Serves 4.

MOROCCAN CARROT AND APPLE SALAD

Salata bi-Khissoo wa Tufah

This light, refreshing salad may be served at the beginning or the end of a meal.

1 pound carrots
3 apples, peeled
3 tablespoons extra virgin olive oil
juice of ½ lemon
1 tablespoon orange-flower water
salt
freshly ground black pepper

Grate the carrots and apples finely and place in a salad bowl. Make a dressing with the olive oil and lemon juice and stir in the orange-flower water. Season with salt and black pepper. Pour over the salad and toss lightly. Chill thoroughly before serving. Serves 4.

CUCUMBER AND WHITE CHEESE SALAD

Salatalik

The small unwaxed cucumbers that are found in Middle Eastern stores are best for this recipe. *Beyaz peynir* is a fresh white cheese that is made all over Turkey. It is usually made from cow's milk. After it has dried out, it is stored in salted water for up to a year to mature. If it is unavailable, feta cheese may be used instead.

2 or 3 small or 1 large cucumber
1 cup crumbled *beyaz peynir* or feta cheese
a handful of fresh mint, finely chopped
a handful of fresh dill, finely chopped
a handful of flat-leaf parsley, finely chopped
6 tablespoons extra virgin olive oil
2 tablespoons lemon juice
1 teaspoon red wine vinegar
salt
freshly ground black pepper
16 black olives

Trim the ends of the cucumbers and slice them very thinly. Place in a salad bowl and sprinkle the cheese and herbs over the top.

Make a dressing with the olive oil, lemon juice, and vinegar, and season with salt and black pepper. Pour over the salad, toss lightly, and garnish with black olives. Serves 4.

FENNEL AND GREEN-OLIVE SALAD
Slata Bisbès

Fennel is highly prized in Tunisia, not only for its pleasant aniseed flavor, but also for its excellent digestive qualities. If any leaves are attached to the fennel bulb, they can be chopped and added to the dressing to enhance the flavor.

2 or 3 fennel bulbs
¼ cup green olives, pitted and sliced
3 tablespoons extra virgin olive oil
1 tablespoon lemon juice
1 tablespoon flat-leaf parsley, finely chopped
1 tablespoons fresh mint, finely chopped
salt
freshly ground black pepper

Remove the outer leaves and stalks from the fennel bulbs. Trim the bases and cut into thin slices. Place in a salad bowl with the green olives.

Make a dressing with the olive oil, lemon juice, and herbs, and season with salt and black pepper. Pour over the salad, toss lightly, and serve. Serves 4.

ALGERIAN ROAST PEPPER AND TOMATO SALAD

H'miss

This traditional salad from Constantine is usually served with some crusty Arab bread on the side.

3 red bell peppers
1–2 red chili peppers, to taste
3 ripe tomatoes
4 garlic cloves
3 tablespoons extra virgin olive oil
salt
12 black olives

Roast the peppers, tomatoes, and unpeeled garlic under a hot grill until they are blackened all over. The garlic and chiles will take less time than the other vegetables. Slip the garlic pulp out of their skins. Peel and seed the tomatoes.

Wash the peppers under cold water and remove the skins. Chop all the vegetables finely. Place them in a bowl with the olive oil and mix well. Season with salt to taste. Transfer to a serving dish and garnish with black olives. Serve at room temperature. Serves 4.

ROAST PEPPER AND
YOGHURT SALAD

Biberli Cacik

This salad is usually made with *sivri biber*—long thin tapering green peppers that resemble large chiles. The taste of *sivri biber* varies from mild to hot. If they are unavailable, a combination of bell peppers and chilies may be used instead.

12 *sivri biber* or 4 green bell peppers
1–2 chili peppers, to taste
1½ cups thick yoghurt
2 or 3 garlic cloves, crushed
1 tablespoon extra virgin olive oil
a handful of fresh mint leaves, finely chopped
1 tablespoons fresh dill, finely chopped
salt

Roast the peppers and chiles under a hot grill until they are blackened all over. Wash under cold water and remove the skins. Cut in half and remove the cores and seeds. Slice very thinly. In a bowl, beat the yoghurt with the garlic, olive oil, mint, and dill. Add the peppers and chiles and season with salt. Chill thoroughly before serving. Serves 4.

LAMB'S LETTUCE, ROCKET, AND BORLOTTI BEAN SALAD

Matavilz, Rucola e Fasoi

This salad comes from the region of Venezia Giulia near the border of Croatia, where lamb's lettuce is often called by its dialect name of *matavilz*. If you want to use canned borlotti beans, drain away any excess liquid and wash the beans thoroughly under cold water to remove the salt.

¼ pound lamb's lettuce
¼ pound rocket
½ pound cooked and drained borlotti beans
1 medium purple onion, thinly sliced
⅓ cup extra virgin olive oil
2 tablespoons red wine vinegar
2 garlic cloves, finely chopped
salt
freshly ground black pepper

Wash the lamb's lettuce and rocket thoroughly and break into bite-sized pieces. Place in a salad bowl with the borlotti beans and onion. Make a dressing with the olive oil, vinegar, and garlic and season with salt and black pepper. Pour over the salad, toss lightly, and serve. Serves 4.

MUSHROOM AND LAMB'S LETTUCE SALAD

Insalata di Funghi e Valeriana

This salad comes from the Veneto. Lamb's lettuce has a pleasant, lemony taste that contrasts nicely with the mushrooms and the Parmesan cheese.

½ pound small white mushrooms
4 ounces lamb's lettuce
¼ cup freshly grated Parmesan cheese
5 tablespoons extra virgin olive oil
2 tablespoons lemon juice
1 garlic clove, crushed
salt
freshly ground black pepper

Trim the ends of the mushrooms and slice them thinly. Place in a salad bowl with the lamb's lettuce and sprinkle with Parmesan cheese. Make a salad dressing with the olive oil, lemon juice, and garlic and season with salt and black pepper. Pour over the salad, toss lightly, and serve. Serves 4.

TUNISIAN SALAD WITH PURSLANE
Salata Tounsiya bil Bindelika

Salata Tounsiya (Tunisian salad) is based on chopped tomatoes, onion, and sweet and hot peppers. Sometimes diced apple, cucumber, or radishes are added, or finely chopped parsley or purslane. It is usually garnished with black olives, chiles, sliced hard-boiled eggs, and *jibna* (a fresh white cheese similar to feta).

2 eggs
3 large firm tomatoes, peeled
2 green peppers, cored and seeded
1 or 2 chili peppers, to taste
1 medium purple onion, chopped
½ bunch purslane, chopped
3 tablespoons extra virgin olive oil
1 tablespoon red wine vinegar
2 tablespoons fresh mint leaves, finely chopped
salt
16 black olives
¼ pound *jibna* or feta cheese, cut into strips

Hard-boil the eggs. Remove the shells and cut into slices. Cut the tomatoes into quarters and remove the seeds. Dice the tomatoes and peppers into small pieces.

Place in a salad bowl with the onion and purslane. Make a dressing with the olive oil, vinegar, and mint, and season with salt. Pour over the salad and toss lightly. Serve on individual plates and garnish with slices of hard-boiled egg and cheese. Serves 4.

MALLORCAN SUMMER SALAD

Enciam amb Trempo

In Mallorca, *enciam* can mean "lettuce" or a mixed salad. Ingredients vary according to the season. In summer, salads often include a little diced apple or pear, green tomatoes, sliced beets, and a selection of wild or cultivated herbs and greens such as chicory, purslane, rocket, or nasturtium flowers.

3 green tomatoes
2 green peppers, cored, seeded, and diced
1 apple, peeled and diced
1 slightly under-ripe pear, peeled and diced
1 small purple onion, chopped
a handful of purslane or rocket, finely chopped
2 tablespoon capers
3 tablespoons extra virgin olive oil
1 tablespoon red wine vinegar
salt
freshly ground black pepper

Place the tomatoes, peppers, apple, pear, onion, purslane, and capers in a salad bowl. Make a dressing with the olive oil and vinegar, and season with salt and black pepper. Pour over the salad, toss lightly, and serve. Serves 4.

PROVENÇAL CHICKPEA SALAD
Salade De Pois Chiches à la Provençale

Dried chickpeas need a long soaking (up to 48 hours) before cooking. If you are in a hurry, canned chickpeas may be used instead.

1½ cups dried chickpeas
1 medium onion, peeled and quartered
1 bay leaf
2 hard-boiled egg yolks
⅓ cup extra virgin olive oil
2 tablespoons red wine vinegar
1 teaspoon whole-grain mustard
2 garlic cloves, finely chopped
2 tablespoons fresh chives, finely chopped
a pinch of thyme
salt
freshly ground black pepper
4 shallots, thinly sliced into rounds
a handful of flat-leaf parsley, finely chopped

Soak the chickpeas for 24 hours and drain. Place in a pan with the onion and bay leaf and cover with plenty of water. Bring to a boil. Cover and simmer for 2 to 3 hours or until tender. Meanwhile prepare the dressing.

Mash the egg yolks in a bowl and add the olive oil, vinegar, mustard, garlic, chives, and thyme. Mix well and season with salt and black pepper. Drain the chickpeas and remove the bay leaf. Place the hot chickpeas in a salad bowl with the shallots and parsley. Pour over the dressing, toss well, and serve warm. Serves 4 to 6.

Green Lentil and Spinach Salad
Salata adas Khoubiza

This salad is deliciously spicy and exotic. Serve it with some Arab bread and a bowl of mixed olives on the side.

1 cup green lentils
½ pound spinach
5 tablespoons extra virgin olive oil
1 medium onion, chopped
juice of 1 lemon, to taste
2 garlic cloves, crushed
1 teaspoon grated ginger
1 teaspoon cumin
1 teaspoon ground coriander
salt
freshly ground black pepper

Soak the lentils for 1 hour and drain. Place in a pan and cover with water. Bring to a boil. Cover and simmer for 1 hour or until they are tender. Drain well.

Meanwhile wash the spinach and cut into 1-inch strips. Cook in a covered saucepan over moderate heat for 5 minutes, or until it is just tender. The water clinging to the leaves is sufficient to prevent scorching. Heat 2 tablespoons olive oil in a large frying pan and cook the onion over moderate heat until it is softened.

Stir in the spinach and simmer for 2 minutes. Transfer to a serving dish and add the drained lentils. Make a dressing with the remaining olive oil, lemon juice, and garlic and stir in the ginger and spices. Season with salt and black pepper. Pour over the lentils and spinach and toss well. Serve warm or at room temperature. Serves 4 to 6.

Syrian Potato Salad

Batata Salata

I love potato salads, especially when they are dressed with luscious green olive oil and lemon juice. This one from Syria includes tomatoes, purple onions, black olives, mint, and parsley, which gives it a lovely flavor.

2 pounds waxy potatoes
4 tomatoes, peeled and diced into half-inch pieces
2 medium purple onions, chopped
a handful of flat-leaf parsley, finely chopped
a handful of fresh mint, finely chopped
½ cup black olives, pitted
6 tablespoons extra virgin olive oil
2 tablespoon lemon juice
salt
freshly ground black pepper

Scrub the potatoes and bring to a boil in lightly salted boiling water for 20 minutes or until they are tender. Drain and peel when they are cool enough to handle. Dice into medium pieces and place in a serving bowl with the tomatoes, onions, herbs, and black olives. Make a dressing with the olive oil and lemon juice and season with salt and black pepper. Pour over the salad while it is still warm. Toss lightly and serve. Serves 6.

PIQUANT TOMATO SALAD

Domates Salatasi

The addition of chili peppers and fresh mint make this an unusual, highly spiced tomato salad. It is very good served with slices of *beyaz peynir* (a fresh white cheese made that is usually with cow's milk) and some crusty bread on the side.

4 large tomatoes sliced
1 purple onion, thinly sliced
1–2 chili peppers, cored, seeded, and very finely sliced
3 tablespoons extra virgin olive oil
1 tablespoon lemon juice
a few sprigs fresh mint, finely chopped
16 Kalamata black olives

Place the tomatoes on a serving dish with the onions and chili peppers. Make a salad dressing with the olive oil, lemon juice, and mint and season with salt. Pour over the tomato salad. Garnish with black olives and serve. Serves 4.

RICE TABBOULEH

Tabbouleh bil-Rezz

Tabbouleh is prepared all over Lebanon. It is usually made with a mixture of bulgur (cracked wheat), chopped herbs, tomatoes, and onion, but sometimes it is prepared with rice. Traditionally *tabouli* is eaten scooped up with small lettuce leaves, white cabbage, or fresh vine leaves.

½ cup basmati rice
1 teaspoon butter
¾ cup boiling water
salt
1 pound firm ripe tomatoes, diced into small pieces
1 large bunch (about ½ pound) flat-leaf parsley
1 small bunch (about 2 ounces) fresh mint
1 small onion, finely chopped
2 green onions, thinly sliced
5 tablespoons extra virgin olive oil
juice of 1–2 lemons, to taste
¼ teaspoon cinnamon
¼ teaspoon allspice
freshly ground black pepper
1 head of Little Gem lettuce

Place the rice in a sieve and rinse thoroughly under cold water. Drain well. Heat the butter in a small heavy-based pan and cook the rice for 1 or 2 minutes, stirring constantly so that each grain is coated in butter. Pour in the boiling water and season with salt to taste. Cover and simmer for 10 to 12 minutes or until the water is absorbed and the rice still has a strong bite. Place in a large salad bowl and cover with the tomatoes. Place a clean tea towel over the top and leave for about 30 minutes to absorb the tomato juice.

Meanwhile wash the parsley and mint and dry thoroughly. Cut away most of the stalks and chop very finely. Add to the rice and tomatoes together with onions and green onions. Make a dressing with the olive oil and lemon juice and add the spices. Season with salt and black pepper. Pour over the *tabbouleh* and toss well. Serve with the Little Gem lettuce, cut into quarters. Serves 4.

SOUPS

La femme fait la soupe et la soupe fait l'homme.
The woman makes the soup and the soup makes the man.
—French proverb

S oup has always played an important role in the Mediterranean diet. As most Mediterranean lands were once very poor, soup was often served as the main course of a meal.Sometimes soup was served for breakfast, lunch, and dinner.

Most Mediterranean soups are rich in vegetables, legumes, and grains. The French *soupe* as well as the Catalan *sopa* and the Italian *zuppa* are always based on vegetables and served either accompanied by some bread or served poured over slices of bread or toast. The Italian *minestrone* and the North African *chorba*—both rich in vegetables and legumes—are usually thickened with pasta or rice.

Dark-green leafy vegetables are much loved throughout the Mediterranean. Spinach, Swiss chard, beet tops, cabbage, parsley, coriander, basil, or bunches of wild herbs and greens appear in many of the recipes in this chapter. Not only do they greatly enhance the flavor of a soup, they are also very rich in vitamins and minerals. It is no wonder that most Mediterranean people believe that soup is the best food to restore good health.

RED GAZPACHO, SEVILLE STYLE

Gazpacho Rojo Sevillano

Andalusia is famous for its gazpacho, a kind of liquid salad or soup. The name originally referred to a mixture based on bread, garlic, olive oil, vinegar, and salt that was ground with a mortar and pestle. Some cooks say that the name gazpacho derives from the Spanish Arabic word *kaz*, meaning "food eaten from a wooden bowl." Others claim that it comes from the old Portuguese word *caspa*, meaning "fragments" or "leftovers." The suffix "acho" is derogatory, which suggests that it was originally humble food of the poor.

Gazpachos vary enormously in both color and texture. Basically they are red, white, or green. *Gazpacho ajo blanco* is a smooth white gazpacho based on ground almonds or pine nuts, garlic, and bread. Red gazpachos, like this one from Seville, include tomatoes, red peppers, and cucumbers. Green gazpachos, which are popular in the region around Huelva, are usually made with green onions, peppers, cucumbers, and herbs such as parsley, basil, mint, or coriander.

2 ounces stale bread, crusts removed
3 tablespoons extra virgin olive oil
3 tablespoons sherry vinegar
2 garlic cloves, crushed
½ teaspoon salt
¼ teaspoon cayenne pepper
pinch of cumin
1 small purple onion, chopped
1 pound ripe tomatoes, peeled, seeded, and chopped
½ cucumber, peeled, seeded, and chopped
2 red peppers, cored, seeded, and chopped
2 ½ cups ice water

For the garnish:
4 tablespoons red peppers, cored, seeded, and finely chopped
4 tablespoons finely chopped cucumber
4 tablespoons finely chopped purple onion
2 tablespoons finely chopped fresh mint leaves

Soak the bread in water and squeeze dry. Place in a blender or food processor with the olive oil, vinegar, garlic, salt, and spices and process to a smooth cream. Add the onion, tomatoes, cucumber, and peppers and half of the ice water and continue to process the vegetables until smooth. Pour into a soup tureen and add the remaining water. Chill thoroughly before serving. Place the garnishes in small dishes and serve with the gazpacho. Serves 4.

GARLIC SOUP

Soupe d'Ail

Variations of garlic soup are made all over southern France. This one from the Roussillon is thickened with egg yolks and served poured over slices of toast.

5 cups water
1 head garlic, unpeeled
2 sprigs fresh thyme
2 tablespoons extra virgin olive oil
salt
freshly ground black pepper
2 egg yolks
4 slices of bread, lightly toasted

Bring the water to boil with the garlic and thyme and simmer for 20 minutes. Remove the garlic and peel. Place the flesh in a bowl and mash with a fork. Gradually add the olive oil and mix well. Return to the soup. Remove the thyme and season with salt and black pepper.

Beat the egg yolks in another bowl and gradually add a ladleful of the soup. Mix well and stir back into the soup. Simmer for a few minutes, but do not let it boil or the soup will curdle. Place the slices of toasts in individual bowls and pour over the soup. Serve at once. Serves 4.

Dalmatian Cabbage, Potato, and Pea Soup

Folša Juha

This simple vegetable soup from the island of Brač is called *folša* or "false," presumably because the real one contains meat. It is very quick and easy to prepare and is a very good example of the simplicity of Dalmatian cooking. The finished soup should be fairly thick.

4 tablespoons extra virgin olive oil
1 medium onion, chopped
2 carrots, coarsely grated
2 medium potatoes, peeled and diced into small pieces
¼ green cabbage, shredded
¾ cup fresh shelled peas, or frozen petit pois
1 quart water
salt
freshly ground black pepper

Heat the olive oil in a large pot and cook the onion over a moderate heat for 3 minutes. Add the carrots, potatoes, and cabbage and continue to cook for another 5 minutes.

Add the peas and water and bring to a boil. Cover and simmer for 35 to 40 minutes or until the vegetables are tender and the soup is fairly thick. Season with salt and black pepper and serve hot. Serves 4.

PROVENÇAL JERUSALEM ARTICHOKE SOUP

Soupo de Patatoun

This smooth, creamy soup is very popular along the Côte d' Azur at the end of winter when Jerusalem artichokes are at their best.

1 pound Jerusalem artichokes
3 tablespoons extra virgin olive oil
1 large onion, thinly sliced
½ pound potatoes, peeled and diced
5 cups of water
a grating of nutmeg
salt
freshly ground black pepper
2 tablespoons flat-leaf parsley, finely chopped

Scrub the Jerusalem artichokes and peel them thinly, cutting away any stringy roots or tips. Heat the olive oil in a large saucepan and cook the onion over moderate heat until it is translucent.

Add the Jerusalem artichokes and potatoes and simmer for 5 minutes, stirring once or twice so the vegetables cook evenly. Add the water and bring to a boil. Cover and simmer for 20 minutes or until the vegetables are tender.

Force through a sieve or puree in a blender. Return to the pan and heat thoroughly. Season with nutmeg, salt, and black pepper. Serve hot, garnished with parsley. Serves 4.

DALMATIAN POTATO SOUP

Juha od Krumpira

This velvety smooth soup is delicately flavored with onion, tomato, and basil.

1 pound potatoes
2 tablespoons extra virgin olive oil
1 large onion, chopped
4 ripe plum tomatoes, peeled, seeded, and chopped
1 bay leaf
5 cups water
2 tablespoons butter
2 tablespoons flat-leaf parsley, finely chopped
1 tablespoons fresh basil leaves, chopped
salt
freshly ground black pepper

Peel and dice the potatoes. Heat the olive oil in a large pot and cook the onion over a moderate heat until it is translucent. Add the potatoes, tomatoes, bay leaf, and water, and bring to a boil. Cover and simmer for 30 minutes.

Remove the bay leaf. Force the soup through a sieve or purée in a blender. Return to the pot and heat thoroughly. Add the butter, parsley, and basil, and season with salt and black pepper. Simmer for 5 minutes and serve hot. Serves 4.

Pumpkin Soup

Balkabaği Çorbasi

This soup is also made in Croatia, where they omit the spices and garnish the soup with sour cream instead of yoghurt.

1 small pumpkin, about 2 pounds
2 tablespoons butter
1 tablespoon extra virgin olive oil
2 medium onions, chopped
1 leek, white part only, thinly sliced
5 cups water
1 teaspoon cinnamon
½ teaspoon allspice
salt
freshly ground black pepper
4 tablespoons, thick, creamy yoghurt

Slice the pumpkin into quarters. With a sharp knife, cut off the skin and remove the seeds and pith. Dice the flesh into large pieces. Heat the butter and olive oil in a large pot and cook the onions and leeks over moderate heat until they are softened. Add the pumpkin, spices, and water and bring to a boil. Cover and simmer for 30 minutes. Force through a sieve or purée in a blender. Return to the pot and heat thoroughly. Season with salt and black pepper. Serve hot in individual soup bowls and garnish with a spoon of yoghurt. Serves 4.

PUMPKIN SOUP
WITH RICE AND SPINACH
Zuppa di Zucca

This unusual soup comes from the borders of Lombardy and the Veneto. Traditionally, Italian *zuppe* are served poured over slices of bread, but in this case the soup is usually served with some crusty bread on the side.

½ small pumpkin, about 1 pound
2 tablespoons extra virgin olive oil
1 medium onion, chopped
1 leek, white part only
3 medium potatoes, peeled and diced
4 cups vegetable stock or water
2½ cups milk
1 bay leaf
a sprig of thyme
a grating of nutmeg
salt
freshly ground black pepper
¼ cup arborio rice
¼ pound spinach
4 tablespoons butter
freshly grated Parmesan cheese

Slice the pumpkin. Cut off the skin and remove the seeds and pith.

Dice the flesh into small pieces. Heat the olive oil in a large saucepan and cook the onion and leek over a moderate heat until they are softened. Add the pumpkin, potatoes, stock or water, milk, and herbs and bring to a boil. Cover and simmer for 30 minutes or until the vegetables are tender. Season with nutmeg, salt, and black pepper.

Remove the bay leaf and thyme. Force through a sieve or purée in a blender.

Return to the pot, adding a little more water if the soup is too thick. Bring to a boil. Add the rice and cook for 20 more minutes or until the rice is tender but still firm.

Meanwhile, wash the spinach carefully and cook in a covered pan over a moderate heat for 5 minutes or until it is just tender. Drain well and chop coarsely.

Melt half of the butter in a frying pan and cook the spinach over a gentle heat for 3 or 4 minutes. Add to the soup. Stir in the remaining butter and serve hot with grated cheese on the side. Serves 4.

NETTLE SOUP

Soupo d'Ourtigo

Nettles are highly prized in Provence for their medicinal qualities. They are said to be good for the lungs as well as a cure for sore throats. They are also recommended as a general tonic, especially during the change of seasons. Remember to wear gloves when handling nettles. Once they are cooked, the hairy leaves lose their stinging properties. A similiar soup can be made with other green vegetables such as watercress, spinach, radish leaves, purslane, or parsley.

6 ounces nettles
3 tablespoons extra virgin olive oil
2 medium onions, sliced
1 pound potatoes, peeled and diced
5 cups water
½ cup crème fraiche
salt
freshly ground black pepper

Wash the nettles carefully and set aside. Heat the olive oil in a large saucepan and cook the onions over a moderate heat for 5 minutes. Add the nettles, potatoes, and water, and bring to a boil. Cover and simmer for 30 minutes. Force through a sieve or puree in a blender. Return to the saucepan and heat thoroughly. Stir in the crème fraiche and season with salt and black pepper. Serve hot. Serves 4.

WILD MUSHROOM SOUP

Sopa de Bolets

This classic Catalan soup is thickened with a *picada*, a mixture of ground toasted nuts, fried bread, olive oil, and garlic. If fresh wild mushrooms are not available, a mixture of field mushrooms and reconstituted dried wild mushrooms may be used instead.

1 pound mixed wild mushrooms
4 tablespoons extra virgin olive oil
1 Spanish onion, chopped
2 ripe plum tomatoes, peeled, seeded, and chopped
5 cups vegetable broth or water
salt
freshly ground black pepper

FOR THE *PICADA*:
15 blanched almonds
1 slice French bread about 1 inch thick (crust removed)
1–2 tablespoons extra virgin olive oil
3 garlic cloves, crushed
pinch of saffron powder

To make the soup, wash the mushrooms carefully and wipe dry. Cut them into 3 or 4 pieces according to their size. Heat the olive oil in a large pan and cook the onion over a gentle heat for about 10 minutes or until it starts to turn golden. Add the tomatoes and continue to cook until any liquid is evaporated and the tomatoes have been reduced to a pulp. Stir in the mushrooms. Cover and simmer for 15 minutes, stirring from time to time so the mushrooms cook evenly. Add the broth and bring to a boil. Simmer, uncovered, for 20 minutes. Season with salt and black pepper.

To make the *picada*, toast the almonds in a 350°F oven until they are golden. Chop coarsely. Heat 1 or 2 tablespoons olive oil in a small frying pan and fry the bread until it is golden on both sides. Drain on a paper towel and cut into small pieces.

Crush or grind the almonds, fried bread, garlic, and saffron with a mortar and pestle or in a food processor, until all the ingredients form a smooth, thick paste. Mix with a tablespoon or two of the soup into the *picada*, then stir the mixture back into the soup. Place a slice of bread on the bottom of 4 individual soup bowls. Pour the hot soup over the bread and serve. Serves 4.

TOMATO AND VERMICELLI SOUP

Chorba Zaria

Variations of this soup are found all over North Africa. Sometimes broad beans or chickpeas are added. Algerians often add a little ground caraway seed. In Morocco, turmeric and paprika usually replace the chili. A similar soup is also made in Provence, flavored with bay leaves and thyme instead of the spices, and served with a sprinkling of grated Gruyère cheese.

3 tablespoons extra virgin olive oil
1 large onion, chopped
3 garlic cloves, finely chopped
1–2 red chili peppers, cored, seeded, and finely chopped
1 cup canned plum tomatoes, forced through a sieve or
      puréed in a food processor
½ bunch flat-leaf parsley, finely chopped
6 cups water
4 ounces fine vermicelli or *capelli d'angeli* (angel hair)
salt

Heat the olive oil in a large pot and cook the onion over moderate heat until it is softened. Add the garlic and chili peppers and cook for 2 more minutes. Add the tomato purée and parsley and cook for a further 5 minutes. Pour in the water and bring to a boil. Simmer for 10 minutes. Increase the heat. When the soup is boiling, drop in the vermicelli and cook until it is tender but still firm. Season with salt and serve hot. Serves 4 to 5.

SORREL SOUP

Soupa me Xinithra

Sorrel has a sharp acidic flavor that makes a very tasty soup. When it is cooked in butter, sorrel quickly melts into a purée, so there is no need to force it through a sieve. This soup is usually served in Greece with some crusty bread on the side.

½ **pound sorrel**
3 tablespoons butter
3 tablespoons flour
5 cups hot water (or half water and half milk)
a grating of nutmeg
salt
freshly ground black pepper

Wash the sorrel carefully and remove the stalks and larger ribs. Heat the butter in a large saucepan and add the sorrel. Cover and cook over a gentle heat until the sorrel has softened into a purée. Stir in the flour and cook for 2 minutes.

Gradually add the hot water, stirring constantly, until the soup is slightly thickened. Simmer for 20 minutes. Season with nutmeg, salt, and black pepper. Serve hot. Serves 4.

Summer Vegetable Soup
Minestra D'estate

This delicious soup from Apulia is based on classic Mediterranean vegetables—eggplant, zucchini, peppers, tomatoes, and onions. Serve it with some crusty country bread and some freshly grated cheese on the side.

1 medium eggplant (about ½ pound)
½ pound zucchini
2 red, green, or yellow bell peppers
⅓ cup extra virgin olive oil
1 large onion, thinly sliced
2 celery stalks, diced
½ pound waxy potatoes, peeled and diced
½ pound ripe plum tomatoes, peeled, seeded, and chopped
4 cups water
2 tablespoons torn basil leaves
salt
freshly ground black pepper
freshly grated pecorino or Parmesan cheese

Peel and dice the eggplant. Trim the ends of the zucchini and cut into rounds. Cut the peppers into quarters and remove the cores and seeds. Cut into thin strips. Heat the olive oil in a large pot and cook the onion, celery, and potatoes over a low heat for 10 minutes, stirring from time to time so the vegetables cook evenly.

Add the eggplant, zucchini, and peppers, cover, and cook for a further 10 minutes. Add the tomatoes and cook, uncovered, for 10 more minutes. Pour in the water and bring to a boil. Cover and simmer for 15 to 20 minutes or until the vegetables are tender. The soup should be very thick, almost a stew. Add the basil and simmer for 2 or 3 minutes. Season with salt and black pepper. Serve hot with grated cheese on the side. Serves 4 to 6.

TUSCAN BLACK CABBAGE SOUP
Zuppa di Cavolo Nero

This soup is also called *le fette*—meaning "the slices" because it is always served poured over slices of bread. *Cavolo nero* (black cabbage) is a dark-leafed winter cabbage with a distinctive peppery taste. If it is unavailable, you can use Savoy cabbage, collards, or curly kale instead. In Tuscany, they usually stir a little freshly pressed olive oil into the soup just before serving to enhance the flavor.

1 pound Tuscan black cabbage
3 tablespoons extra virgin olive oil
1 large onion, thinly sliced
1 celery stalk, thinly sliced
1 carrot, diced
1 medium potato, peeled and diced
5 cups vegetable broth or water
salt
freshly ground black pepper
4 slices whole-wheat bread
2 garlic cloves, peeled, and cut in half
freshly grated Parmesan cheese

Wash the cabbage and remove the stalks. Cut into thin strips. Heat the olive oil in a large pot and cook the onion, celery, carrot, and potato for 3 minutes. Add the cabbage and broth and bring to a boil. Cover and simmer for 1 hour. Season with salt and black pepper.

Meanwhile place the slices of bread on a baking tray and toast in a preheated 375°F oven until they are golden. Remove from the oven and rub each slice with garlic. Place the slices of bread into individual soup bowls and pour the hot soup over them. Serve at once with grated cheese on the side. Serves 4.

WINTER VEGETABLE SOUP

Juha od Povrča

The vegetables used in this soup can be varied according to what is at hand. Celeriac, turnip, or parsley root all make good additions. Sometimes sorrel or spinach is used instead of the parsley.

2 tablespoons extra virgin olive oil
1 tablespoon butter
1 medium onion, chopped
1 leek, thinly sliced
2 carrots, diced
2 parsnips, peeled and diced
2 medium potatoes, peeled and diced
5 cups water
a grating of nutmeg
salt
freshly ground black pepper
3 tablespoons flat-leaf parsley, finely chopped

Heat the olive oil and butter in a large pot and cook the onion and leek over moderate heat until they are softened. Add the root vegetables and water and bring to a boil.

Cover and simmer for 30 minutes or until the vegetables are tender. Force through a sieve or purée in a blender. Return to the pot and heat thoroughly, adding a little more water if the soup is too thick. Season with nutmeg, salt, and black pepper. Stir in the parsley and serve hot. Serves 4.

MUSHROOM AND POTATO SOUP
Fugni e Patane

Fugni e patane means "mushrooms and potatoes" in the Apulian dialect. It is usually made with *funghi prataioli* (wild field mushrooms) that are similar to the French *rose de pré*, which are found in pasturelands in late summer and early autumn.

1 pound field mushrooms
4 tablespoons extra virgin olive oil
4 garlic cloves, finely chopped
a handful of flat-leaf parsley, finely chopped
1 tablespoon fresh oregano
10 ounces ripe plum tomatoes, peeled, seeded, and chopped
1 pound potatoes, peeled and diced
6 cups water
salt
freshly ground black pepper
4 to 5 slices whole-wheat country bread

Wash the mushrooms carefully. Cut in half and slice fairly thickly. Heat the olive oil in a large pot and cook the garlic and herbs over moderate heat for 1 or 2 minutes. Add the mushrooms and cook for 5 minutes or until they start to weep.

Add the tomatoes and continue to cook for 5 more minutes. Add the potatoes and water and bring to a boil. Cover and simmer for 30 minutes. Season with salt and black pepper. Serve hot with country bread on the side. Serves 4 to 5.

Zucchini, Tomato, and Rice Soup

Manistra od Tikvce i Rajčica

This delicious soup from Istria could not be easier to prepare. If you like, you can serve it with freshly grated Parmesan cheese on the side. It may also be served cold.

1 pound zucchini
4 tablespoons extra virgin olive oil
½ pound ripe plum tomatoes, peeled, seeded, and chopped
4 cups water
½ cup arborio rice
salt
freshly ground black pepper

Trim the ends of the zucchini and cut into rounds. Heat the olive oil in a large pot and cook the zucchini over moderate heat until they start to turn golden, stirring from time to time so they cook evenly.

Add the tomatoes and cook for 5 more minutes. Pour in the water and bring to a boil. Add the rice and seasoning and cook for 20 minutes or until the rice is tender but still firm. Serve hot. Serves 4.

ACQUACOTTA

Acquacotta

Acquacotta, literally "cooked water," has many variations. It was originally a simple soup for shepherds made with water, bread, and a few vegetables. Every region, almost every family, had its own recipe. Some people say that it originated in Grosseto, others that it dates back to Etruscan times. Today it is made all over central Italy from Tuscany to the Adriatic coast. Some versions include asparagus, zucchini, Swiss chard, or wild mushrooms. This recipe comes from Ascoli Piceno in the Marche, where it usually made with a variety of fresh herbs such as mint, chicory, or *oleapri*—a kind of wild spinach.

3 tablespoons extra virgin olive oil
1 medium onion, finely chopped
2 garlic cloves, finely chopped
1 celery stalk including the leaves, diced into very small pieces
1 small red chili pepper, cored, seeded, and finely chopped
2 tablespoons flat-leaf parsley, finely chopped
1 tablespoon fresh marjoram
3 ripe plum tomatoes, peeled, seeded, and chopped
6 cups vegetable stock or water
½ pound spinach, cut into strips
salt
4 slices whole-wheat bread, toasted
4 poached eggs
freshly grated pecorino or Parmesan cheese

Heat the olive oil in a large saucepan and cook the onion, garlic, celery, chili pepper, and herbs over a moderate heat for 3 minutes. Add the tomatoes and cook for 5 more minutes. Pour in the stock and add the spinach.

Bring to a boil. Cover and simmer for 20 minutes. Season with salt to taste. Place a slice of toast into 4 individual serving bowls and top with a poached egg. Pour over the hot soup and serve at once with grated cheese on the side. Serves 4.

CATALAN SPLIT PEA SOUP

Escudella de Pesols

This warming winter soup has a lovely flavor. Bright green split peas rather than the yellow variety are best for this recipe. They also need less soaking.

1½ cups split peas
4 tablespoons extra virgin olive oil
1 Spanish onion, chopped
1 celery stalk, diced
2 carrots, diced
6 cups water
salt
freshly ground black pepper
¼ cup short-grain rice
a handful of fresh mint, finely chopped

Soak the split peas for 1 hour and drain. Heat the olive oil in a large pot and cook the onion, celery, and carrots over a moderate heat for 3 minutes. Add the split peas and water and bring to a boil. Cover and simmer for 1 hour or until the peas are tender.

Force through a sieve or purée in a blender. Return to the pot, adding a little more water if the soup is too thick. Season with salt and black pepper. Increase the heat. When the soup is boiling, add the rice. Cook for 20 minutes or until the rice is tender, but still firm. Five minutes before the end of cooking, stir in the mint. Serve hot. Serves 4.

NORTH AFRICAN CHICKPEA SOUP
Leblabi

This velvety smooth chickpea soup is flavored at the end of cooking with a mixture of olive oil, lemon juice, garlic, cumin, and *harissa*. Serve it with some Arab bread on the side.

1½ cups dried chickpeas
7 cups water
6 tablespoons extra virgin olive oil
juice of 1 lemon
4 garlic cloves, crushed
1 teaspoon cumin
1 teaspoon harissa, see page 124
salt

Soak the chickpeas for 24 hours and drain. Rinse thoroughly and place in a large saucepan with the water. Bring to a boil. Cover and simmer for 2½ to 3 hours or until the chickpeas are tender. Force through a sieve or purée in a blender.

Return to the saucepan and heat thoroughly, adding more water if the soup is too thick. Meanwhile place the olive oil, lemon juice, garlic, cumin, and *harissa* in a bowl and mix well. Season with salt. Transfer to the bottom of a soup tureen. Pour the hot soup over the sauce and mix well. Serve at once. Serves 6.

LENTIL SOUP WITH LEMON AND CUMIN
Shorbet Adass Bil-Hamod

Variations of lentil soup are made all over the Middle East. Some recipes include rice or pasta. Others are strongly flavored with fresh coriander. This lentil soup includes Swiss chard and potato and is delicately flavored with lemon juice and cumin. It is usually served garnished with fried onions and a sprinkling of extra virgin olive oil

1 cup green or brown lentils
6 cups water
1 bunch Swiss chard, cut into thin strips
1 medium potato, peeled, and diced
juice of 1 to 2 lemons, to taste
1 teaspoon cumin
salt
freshly ground black pepper

FOR THE GARNISH:
6 tablespoons extra virgin olive oil
2 large onions, very thinly sliced

Soak the lentils for 2 hours and drain. Place in a large pot together with the Swiss chard and potato and bring to a boil. Cover and simmer for 1½ hours or until the lentils are tender. Add the lemon juice and cumin and seasoning to taste. To prepare the garnish, heat 4 tablespoons olive oil in a large pan and cook the onions over moderate heat until they are almost caramelized. Pour the hot soup into individual soup bowls and garnish with the fried onions and a sprinkling of extra virgin olive oil. Serves 4.

LENTIL SOUP WITH SPINACH

Faki Soupa me Spanaki

This soup comes from Macedonia where they like to season their food with hot red peppers. Spinach or wild greens are often added to lentil or bean soups in Greece as they enhance the flavor and texture.

1¼ cups brown lentils
6 tablespoons extra virgin olive oil
1 medium onion, chopped
1 celery stalk, diced
2 garlic cloves, finely chopped
1 to 2 chili peppers (to taste), cored, seeded, and finely chopped
2 ripe plum tomatoes
½ pound spinach, cut into strips
1 bay leaf
2–3 tablespoons red wine vinegar, to taste
salt
freshly ground black pepper

Soak the lentils in cold water for 2 hours and drain. Heat half of the olive oil in a large pot and cook the onion and celery over a moderate heat for 5 minutes. Add the garlic and chili and cook for 2 more minutes Add the lentils, tomatoes, spinach, and bay leaf and bring to a boil.

Cover and simmer for 1½ hours or until the lentils are tender, adding a little more water if necessary. Pour in the vinegar and remaining olive oil and season with salt and black pepper. Serve hot. Serves 4.

GREEK WHITE BEAN SOUP

Fassolada

Fassolada has been called the national dish of Greece. It was traditionally served on Wednesdays and Fridays (both fast days when the eating of meat was forbidden) accompanied by a bowl of black olives and a chunk of sourdough bread. Olive oil and lemon juice are always added at the end of cooking. The Greeks like to use large white beans called *gigantes*, but if they are unavailable, cannelini or butter beans may be used instead.

1 cup dried *gigantes*, cannelini, or butter beans
6 cups water
2 medium onions, chopped
1 garlic clove finely chopped
½ small red chili pepper, cored, seeded, and finely chopped
1 celery stalk, diced
1 carrot, diced
1 cup canned plum tomatoes, forced through a sieve
        or puréed in a food processor
a handful of flat-leaf parsley, finely chopped
6 tablespoons extra virgin olive oil
juice of 1 lemon, or to taste
salt
freshly ground black pepper

Soak the beans overnight and drain. Place the beans in a large pot with the water and bring to a boil. Add the onions, garlic, chili pepper, celery, carrot, tomato purée, and parsley. Cover and simmer for 1½ to 2 hours or until the beans are tender. Pour in the olive oil, lemon juice, and salt and black pepper to taste. Serve hot. Serves 4 to 6.

TUSCAN VEGETABLE AND BEAN SOUP WITH POLENTA

L' Infarinata

This warming peasant soup is a specialty of the Garfagnana, the mountainous region north of Lucca, near the borders of Tuscany and Liguria. *L'infarinata* literally means "made with flour"—in this case, *farina gialla* (yellow flour) or cornmeal.

½ cup dried cannelini beans
2 quarts water
4 tablespoons extra virgin olive oil
1 large onion, chopped
1 garlic clove, finely chopped
2 carrots, diced
1 celery stalk, diced
2 medium potatoes, peeled and diced
1 bunch black cabbage, cut into thin strips
1 cup polenta
salt
freshly ground black pepper
freshly grated Parmesan cheese

Soak the beans overnight and drain. Bring to boil in 2 quarts of water. Cover and simmer for 1½ hours or until the beans are tender. Heat the olive oil in a large saucepan and cook the onion, garlic, carrots, and celery over moderate heat for 5 minutes. Add the potatoes, cabbage, beans, and their cooking liquid, and enough water to make up to 2 quarts. Bring to a boil. Cover and simmer for 30 minutes or until the vegetables are tender.

Gradually pour in the polenta in a very thin stream, while stirring constantly to prevent lumps from forming. Cook over very low heat for 40 minutes. Season with salt and black pepper. Serve hot with Parmesan cheese on the side. Serves 6.

TUSCAN BEAN SOUP
Minestra di Fagioli alla Toscana

There are many variations of *minestra di fagioli* in Tuscany. This one includes rice and escarole. Escarole, or Batavian endive, as it is sometimes called, is a member of the chicory family. It has a pleasing, slightly bitter taste and is widely used as a salad green as well as for cooking. If it is unavailable, curly endive or rocket may be used instead.

1 cup dried cannelini beans
1¾ quarts water
a sprig of rosemary
4 tablespoons extra virgin olive oil
1 medium onion, finely chopped
2 garlic cloves, finely chopped
1 celery stalk, diced
a handful of flat-leaf parsley, finely chopped
1 cup canned plum tomatoes, forced through a sieve
     or puréed in a food processor
1 head of escarole, about 1 pound
½ cup arborio rice
salt
freshly ground black pepper
freshly grated Parmesan cheese

Soak the beans overnight and drain. Bring to a boil in 1¾ quarts of unsalted water with the rosemary. Cover and simmer for 1½ to 2 hours or until the beans are tender. Set aside and reserve the cooking liquid. Remove the rosemary. Force half of the beans through a sieve or purée in a blender with a little of the reserved cooking liquid.

Heat the olive oil in a large saucepan and cook the onion, garlic, celery, and parsley over moderate heat until the vegetables are softened. Add the tomatoes and continue to cook for 5 more minutes. Add the escarole, the cooked and puréed beans, and the reserved cooking liquid. Cover and simmer for 30 minutes. Pour in the rice and season with salt and black pepper. Raise the heat and cook for 15 to 30 minutes or until the rice is tender, adding a little more water if the soup is too thick. Serve hot with grated cheese on the side. Serves 6.

CORSICAN PEASANT SOUP

Soupe Paysanne Corse

This soup was traditionally served in Corsica as a main course with some crusty country bread and some *brocciu* cheese on the side, washed down, of course, with some full-bodied Corsican wine.

5 tablespoons extra virgin olive oil
1 medium onion, chopped
2 garlic cloves, finely chopped
2 medium potatoes, cooked and drained
¼ small green cabbage, shredded
1 cup cooked and drained *borlotti* or cranberry beans
1 cup ripe plum tomatoes, peeled and chopped
½ pound spinach or beet greens, cut into thin strips
6 cups water
salt
freshly ground black pepper
4 ounces egg noodles, broken into 2-inch lengths
freshly grated aged brocciu or Parmesan cheese

Heat the olive oil in a large pot and cook the onion, garlic, and potatoes over a moderate heat for 3 minutes. Add the cabbage and stir well.

Cook for a further 5 minutes. Add the beans, tomatoes, spinach and water and bring to the boil. Cover and simmer for 1½ to 2 hours. Increase the heat. When the soup is boiling, drop in the egg noodles and cook until tender but still firm. The soup should be very thick. Season with salt and black pepper. Serve hot with grated cheese on the side. Serves 4 to 6.

MINESTRONE GENOESE STYLE
Minestrone alla Genovese

There is no definitive recipe for this classic minestrone as the ingredients change from season to season, but it is always based on pasta, beans, a selection of vegetables, and pesto, the garlic and basil sauce that is the pride of the Genoese kitchen. The Genoese also like to add borage leaves when they are available, which gives the soup a distinctive flavor. Fresh or dried porcini mushrooms are another possible addition. Other vegetables not listed below that are sometimes used include cauliflower, cabbage, leeks, turnips, broad beans, pumpkin, and all kinds of squash.

1 celery stalk, diced
1 carrot, diced
2 medium potatoes, peeled and diced
1 small eggplant (about ¼ pound) peeled and cut into ½ inch pieces
2 small zucchini, trimmed and cut into rounds, then diced
2 ounces green beans, trimmed and cut into 2-cm lengths
½ cup shelled peas
2 ripe plum tomatoes, peeled, seeded, and chopped
1½ cup cooked and drained cannelini beans
1 bunch Swiss chard, spinach or beet greens, shredded
a handful of borage leaves (optional)
1¾ quarts water
1 cup soup pasta or vermicelli, broken into 1½ inch lengths
salt
freshly ground black pepper
6 tablespoons extra virgin olive oil
6 tablespoons pesto see below
freshly grated Pecorino Sardo or Parmesan cheese

Prepare all the vegetables and place in a pot with 1¾ quarts of water. Bring to a boil. Cover and simmer for 1¾ hours. Increase the heat. When the soup is boiling, drop in the pasta and season with salt and black pepper.

Pour in 4 tablespoons olive oil and cook for 10 to 15 minutes, or until the pasta is tender, but still firm. Remove from the heat. Stir in the pesto and the remaining olive oil. Serve hot with grated cheese on the side. Serves 6.

PESTO SAUCE:

a pinch of coarse sea salt
2 garlic cloves, peeled
1 tablespoon pine nuts
1 cup fresh basil leaves
3 tablespoons freshly grated Pecorino Sardo or Parmesan cheese
4–5 tablespoons extra virgin olive oil

Place the sea salt, garlic, and pine nuts in a large mortar, then crush with a pestle to make a smooth sauce. Add a small quantity of basil leaves and grind them against the sides of the mortar until they break apart.

Repeat until all the basil leaves have been used up and the mixture has formed a coarse paste. Add the grated cheese and slowly dribble in the olive oil, stirring with the pestle until the sauce is very smooth and creamy.

NORTH AFRICAN VEGETABLE SOUP
Chorba bil Khodra

There are many versions of this substantial soup. The vegetables vary according to the season, but it is usually strongly flavored with *harissa*—the fiery hot sauce that is so popular all over the Magreb. *Harissa* varies slightly from country to country. In Tunisia and Algeria, it is usually flavored with ground coriander and ground caraway seeds. Moroccans prefer to use cumin instead of caraway. Small jars or tubes of *harissa* can be found in most good supermarkets or Middle Eastern stores.

4 tablespoons extra virgin oil
1 medium onion, chopped
1 celery stalk, diced
1 carrot, diced
2 medium potatoes, peeled and diced
2 zucchini, trimmed and cut into rounds
½ cup shelled broad beans
1½ cups cooked and drained chickpeas
2 teaspoons *harissa* (see below)
1 teaspoon cumin
½ teaspoon paprika
1 pound ripe plum tomatoes, peeled, seeded, and chopped
1 large bunch flat-leaf parsley, coarsely chopped
1½ quarts water
salt
¾ cup soup pasta or vermicelli, broken into 1½-inch pieces
a handful of fresh coriander, coarsely chopped
lemon wedges

Heat the olive oil in a large pot and cook the onion, celery, carrot, and potatoes over gentle heat for 5 minutes. Add the zucchini, broad beans, chickpeas, *harissa*, and spices and stir well. Add the tomatoes, parsley, water, and salt and bring to a boil. Cover and simmer for 1½ hours.

Increase the heat. When the soup is boiling, add the pasta and cook for 10 to 15 minutes or until it is tender but still firm. Stir in the fresh coriander just before serving. Serve hot with lemon wedges on the side. Serves 6.

HARISSA:

Be warned—this fiery hot sauce should only be used in very small quantities. It will keep up to 3 weeks in the refrigerator.

½ cup dried hot red chili peppers
6–8 garlic cloves, peeled
1 teaspoon ground coriander
1 teaspoon ground caraway or cumin
¼ teaspoon salt
1–2 tablespoons water
extra virgin olive oil

Remove the seeds from the dried chili peppers and place in a bowl. Cover with water and soak for 30 minutes or until the chilies are soft. Drain and place in a mortar with the garlic, spices, and salt.

Pound with a pestle to a smooth paste. Gradually add a little water, by the teaspoonful, until the mixture is smooth and creamy. Spoon into a jar and cover with a layer of olive oil. Store in the refrigerator.

Chickpea and Lentil Harira

Harira

Harira is traditionally served in Morocco at sunset to break the fast of Ramadan, but it is also much appreciated on a cool winter evening. *Harira* is usually thickened with a *tedouira*—a mixture of flour (or dried yeast) and water that gives a velvety smooth texture to the soup.

¾ cup green or brown lentils
2 tablespoons extra virgin olive oil
2 tablespoons butter or ghee
1 Spanish onion, chopped
½ cup celery leaves or 1 celery stalk, diced
1 teaspoon turmeric
1 teaspoon cumin
¼ teaspoon ginger
¼ teaspoon cinnamon
¼ teaspoon powdered saffron
1½ cup cooked and drained chickpeas
1 pound ripe plum tomatoes, peeled, seeded, and chopped
1½ quarts water
salt
freshly ground black pepper
3 tablespoons flour
¼ cup vermicelli, broken into 1-inch pieces
1 small bunch flat-leaf parsley, finely chopped
a handful of fresh coriander, finely chopped
lemon wedges

Soak the lentils for 2 hours and drain.

Heat the olive oil and butter in a large pot and cook the onion and celery leaves over moderate heat until the onion is softened. Stir in the spices and cook for 1 minute. Add the lentils, chickpeas, tomatoes, and water and bring to a boil.

Cover and simmer for 1½ hours. Season with salt and plenty of black pepper. Mix the flour with a little cold water to make a smooth paste. Add a little of the hot soup to the flour mixture and pour back into the pot. Mix well.

Increase the heat. When the soup is boiling, add the vermicelli and cook for a further 10 minutes or until it is tender but still firm. Five minutes before the end of cooking, add the parsley and coriander.

Serve hot with lemon wedges on the side. Serves 6.

PASTA

A taera negra a fa bon gran.
Black earth makes good wheat.
—Genoese proverb

Although pasta is usually associated with Italy, it is also made in most countries around the Mediterranean, especially in Croatia, most of the Greek islands, Provence, and Catalan, Spain. Pasta is also much appreciated by the Turks. *Manti* (a kind of ravioli) was known in Turkey as early as the twelfth century. Pasta is also prepared in North Africa, especially in Libya (which was briefly under Italian rule) and Tunisia, where it is usually served with hot, spicy sauces.

To cook pasta, allow at least 4 quarts of water and 2 teaspoons salt to 1 pound of pasta. Cook the pasta until it is *al dente*—just tender, but still firm.

EGG NOODLES

Pasta All'Uova

Most cooks in Italy agree that the best *pasta all'uova* is produced using 90 to 100 grams flour (about ⅔ cup) to 1 egg. If the dough is too wet, add a little more flour. If it is too dry, add a teaspoon or so of water. The thickness can also vary. As a general rule, it is paper thin for lasagne and tagliatelle and slightly thicker for piccagge and fettucine.

2 cup sunbleached white flour
3 large eggs
½ teaspoon salt

Place the flour in a mound on a large wooden board or work surface and make a deep well in the center of the flour. Drop in 1 egg at a time and add the salt. Beat the eggs lightly with a fork and gradually add some of the flour. Then with your hands, slowly incorporate more flour until it forms a soft ball. Knead the dough well for about 10 minutes, or until it is smooth and elastic.

Wrap the dough in a damp cloth and allow it to rest for 20 to 60 minutes. Then divide it in half. Keep one half of the dough wrapped. With a long thin rolling pin, roll out the remaining dough on a floured work surface, making quarter turns to form a rectangle. Stretch and roll the dough repeatedly until it is very thin.

Repeat with the other half of dough. If you are making ravioli, use it right away. If making long pasta, allow the dough to dry out for 15 minutes, or until it is no longer sticky, before cutting. Makes about 1 pound.

GREEN NOODLES WITH BORAGE

Taggiaen Verdi

In Liguria, green noodles are often made with a mixture of borage and spinach, which gives them a distinctive flavor. They are usually served with a mushroom and tomato sauce, but they are also very good simply dressed with melted butter, Parmesan cheese, and a grating of nutmeg.

DOUGH:
2 ounces borage
¼ pound spinach
2¼ cups unbleached white flour
2 eggs
½ teaspoon salt

MUSHROOM AND TOMATO SAUCE:
1 ounce dried porcini mushrooms
3 tablespoons extra virgin olive oil
½ small onion, finely chopped
1 garlic clove, finely chopped
2 tablespoons flat-leaf parsley, finely chopped
1 teaspoon fresh marjoram
¼ cup dry white wine
3 cups ripe plum tomatoes, peeled, seeded, and chopped
salt
freshly ground black pepper
2 tablespoons butter
freshly grated Pecorino Sardo or Parmesan cheese

To make the noodles, wash the borage and spinach well and cook in a covered saucepan for 7 to 8 minutes or until tender. The water clinging to the leaves is sufficient to prevent scorching. Drain well and squeeze dry. Chop finely.

Place the flour in a mound on a large wooden board and make a deep well in the centre. Place the chopped vegetables, eggs, and salt in the well and gradually work in some of the flour. Then, with your hands, slowly incorporate more flour until it forms a soft ball, adding a little more flour if it is too soft. Knead the dough for about 10 minutes and proceed as for *pasta all uova* on page 129.

Roll the dough out very thinly and leave to dry out for 15 minutes. Roll up and cut into ¼-inch-wide noodles. Unfold and spread them out on a large cloth to dry out.

To make the sauce, soak the mushrooms in warm water for 30 minutes or until softened. Drain and chop coarsely. Heat the olive oil in a large frying pan and cook the onion, garlic, and herbs over moderate heat for 2 or 3 minutes. Add the mushrooms and cook for 5 minutes or until tender. Pour in the wine, raise the heat, and cook until it is evaporated. Add the tomatoes and cook for a further 10 minutes or until the sauce starts to thicken.

Cook the noodles in plenty of lightly salted boiling water until they are tender but still firm. Drain and transfer to a heated serving bowl. Dot with butter and pour over the sauce. Toss lightly and serve with grated cheese on the side. Serves 4.

TUNISIAN EGG NOODLES
WITH TOMATOES AND PEPPERS
Reuchta bil Tomatem wa Filfil

Tunisians are fond of egg noodles, which are made in all shapes and sizes. The most common are *hlelem* (very fine noodles which usually appear in soups), *reuchta* (which vary from ¼ to 1 inch in width), and *noissars* (little square egg noodles). *Reuchta* are usually served with a hot spicy tomato sauce that often includes roast peppers or tiny peas.

DOUGH:

2 cups flour

3 eggs

½ teaspoon salt

SAUCE:

4 sweet red peppers

3 tablespoons extra virgin olive oil

1 medium onion, finely chopped

4 garlic cloves, finely chopped

1–2 small red chili peppers (to taste), cored, seeded, and chopped

2 tablespoons torn basil leaves

1 teaspoon paprika

1–2 teaspoons *harissa*, to taste (see page 124)

1 pound ripe plum tomatoes, peeled, seeded, and chopped

salt

1 tablespoons butter

To make the egg noodles, follow the directions for *pasta all'uova* on page 129. Roll the dough out very thinly and leave to dry for 15 minutes. Roll up and cut into ½-inch-wide noodles. Unfold and spread the noodles out on a large cloth to dry.

To make the sauce, roast the peppers under a hot grill until they are blackened all over. Wash under cold water and remove the skins. Cut into quarters and remove the core and seeds. Slice thinly.

Heat the olive oil in a large frying pan and cook the onion over moderate heat until it is softened. Add the garlic and chili and cook for 2 minutes. Add the basil, paprika, *harissa,* chopped tomatoes, and red peppers, and salt to taste. Cook, uncovered, over low heat for 15 minutes or until the vegetables are tender and the sauce starts to thicken.

Cook the egg noodles in plenty of lightly salted boiling water until they are tender but still firm. Drain and transfer to a heated serving bowl. Dot with butter and pour over the sauce. Toss lightly and serve at once. Serves 4.

PICCAGGE WITH ARTICHOKE SAUCE

Piccagge con Tocco di Articocche

This recipe comes from the Riviera di Ponente, which lies between Savona and the French border. *Piccagge* are long thin ribbons of pasta similar to fettucine that are only found in Liguria. This sauce is also very good served with rice.

DOUGH:
2 cups unbleached white flour
2 large eggs
3 tablespoons extra virgin olive oil
1–2 tablespoons dry white wine
½ teaspoon salt

ARTICHOKE SAUCE:
4 medium artichokes
½ lemon
4 tablespoons extra virgin olive oil
1 small onion, finely chopped
1 garlic clove, finely chopped
2 tablespoons flat-leaf parsley, finely chopped
½ cup dry white wine
salt
freshly ground black pepper
2 tablespoons butter
freshly grated Pecorino Sardo or Parmesan cheese

To make the *piccagge*, follow the directions for *pasta all'uova* on page 129, adding the olive oil and white wine with the eggs. Roll the dough out very thinly and leave to dry for 15 minutes. Roll up and cut into ¼-inch-wide noodles.

Cut off the tops of the artichokes and remove all the inedible leaves. Trim the stems. Slice the artichokes in half and remove the fuzzy chokes. Slice the remaining hearts very thinly. Rub all over with the lemon to prevent them from discoloring.

Heat the olive oil in a large frying pan and cook the onion, garlic, and parsley over moderate heat for 3 minutes. Add the artichokes, cover, and cook over gentle heat for

8 to 10 minutes. Add the wine and seasoning. When it is boiling, cover and simmer until the vegetables are tender and sauce is reduced.

Cook the *piccagge* in plenty of lightly salted boiling water until tender but still firm. Drain and transfer to a heated serving bowl. Dot with butter and pour over the sauce. Toss lightly and serve with grated cheese on the side. Serves 4.

FETTUCINE, PEAS, AND BROAD BEANS

Fettucine, Piselli, e Fave

This recipe comes from Le Marche where it is made in springtime with young tender peas and broad beans.

DOUGH:
2 cups unbleached white flour
3 eggs
½ teaspoon salt

PEA AND BROAD BEAN SAUCE:
3 tablespoons extra virgin olive oil
1 small onion, finely chopped
1 garlic clove, finely chopped
1 celery stalk, chopped
1 baby carrot, chopped
1 cup fresh shelled peas, or frozen *petit pois*
1 cup shelled and skinned broad beans, or frozen baby broad beans
½ cup dry white wine
5 ripe plum tomatoes, peeled, seeded, and chopped
salt
freshly ground black pepper
freshly grated pecorino or Parmesan cheese

To make the tagliatelle, follow the directions for *pasta all'uova* on page 129. Roll the dough out very thinly and leave to dry for 15 minutes. Roll up and cut into ¼-inch-wide noodles.

Heat the olive oil in a saucepan and cook the onion, garlic, celery, and carrot over gentle heat for 10 minutes without browning. Add the peas, broad beans, and wine and bring to a boil. Cover and simmer for 15 minutes or until the vegetables are tender and the liquid is evaporated. Add the tomatoes and continue to cook for 10 minutes or until the sauce is thickened.

Cook the tagliatelle in plenty of lightly salted boiling water until tender but still firm. Drain and transfer to a heated serving bowl. Pour over the hot sauce and serve with grated cheese on the side. Serves 4.

EGG NOODLES WITH WILD GREENS AND OLIVES

Macaronia me Horta

Wild greens such as *vlita*, a member of the amaranth family, *zachos* (sow thistle), and wild chicory are widely used in cooking all over Greece. Young tender dandelion leaves, sorrel, turnip tops, mustard greens, or rocket all make good substitutes.

DOUGH:
2 cups unbleached white flour
3 eggs
½ teaspoon salt

SAUCE:
2 tablespoons extra virgin olive oil
2 garlic cloves, finely chopped
1 small red chili pepper, cored, seeded, and finely chopped
1 pound wild greens, stalks removed, and coarsely chopped
2 ounces Elitses or Gaeta black olives, pitted and coarsely chopped

TOPPING:
freshly grated Kefalotyri or pecorino cheese

To make the egg noodles, follow the directions for *pasta all 'uova* on page 129. Roll the dough out very thinly and leave to dry for 15 minutes. Roll up and cut into ⅛-inch-wide noodles. Unfold and spread them out on a large cloth to dry.

To make the sauce, heat the olive oil in a large frying pan and cook the garlic and chili pepper for 1 minute. Add the greens and olives. Cover and cook over a moderate heat for 7 to 8 minutes or until the green are tender.

Meanwhile cook the noodles in plenty of lightly salted boiling water until they are tender but still firm. Drain and transfer to a heated serving bowl. Cover with the greens and toss lightly. Serve at once with grated cheese on the side. Serves 4.

Penne with Tomatoes, Mozzarella, Olives, and Capers
Penne alla Vesuviana

This recipe comes from the Bay of Naples, where it is made with the finest ingredients—pure white mozzarella made from buffalo's milk, Gaeta olives, capers preserved in salt (well rinsed), and San Marzano tomatoes. Traditionally, this dish is served without any grated cheese.

4 tablespoons extra virgin olive oil
3 garlic cloves, finely chopped
1 tablespoon fresh oregano
3 cups canned plum tomatoes, forced through a sieve
    or puréed in a food processor
¾ pound penne or other short macaroni
24 black Gaeta olives
2 tablespoons capers
½ pound mozzarella cheese, diced
2 tablespoons torn basil leaves
salt
freshly ground black pepper

Heat 3 tablespoons olive oil in a large frying pan and cook the garlic and oregano for 2 minutes. Add the puréed tomatoes and cook over a moderate heat for 10 minutes or until the sauce starts to thicken. Season with salt and black pepper.

Cook the penne in plenty of lightly salted boiling water until tender but still firm. Drain, and transfer to a heated serving bowl. Pour over the remaining olive oil and add the olives, capers, diced mozzarella, and basil. Toss lightly and serve at once. Serves 4.

MACARONI WITH WILD MUSHROOMS
Maccarons amb Bolets

This dish from Catalonia is usually made with *rossinyols* (*Cantharellus gambosa*)—wild mushrooms that are similar to the French chanterelle. If they are not available, any other quality mushroom may be used instead.

1 pound chanterelles or other quality mushrooms
4 tablespoons extra virgin olive oil
1 medium onion, finely chopped
handful of flat-leaf parsley, finely chopped
1 pound ripe plum tomatoes, peeled, seeded, and chopped
a grating of nutmeg
salt
freshly ground black pepper
¾ pound short macaroni, such as ziti or penne
freshly grated Manchego or pecorino cheese

Wash the mushrooms and cut them into 2 or 4 pieces. Heat the olive oil in a large frying pan and cook the onion over a moderate heat until it is translucent. Add the parsley and cook for another 2 minutes. Add the mushrooms and continue to cook, uncovered, until they are tender and any liquid they have given off has evaporated. Add the tomatoes and cook for 10 minutes or until the sauce starts to thicken. Season with nutmeg, salt, and black pepper.

Cook the macaroni in plenty of lightly salted boiling water until it is tender but still firm. Drain and transfer to a heated serving bowl. Pour over the sauce, toss lightly, and serve at once with grated cheese on the side. Serves 4.

Whole-wheat Noodles with Green Beans and Pesto

Trenette Avvantaggiate con Fagiolini e Pesto

Trenette avvantaggiate are a specialty of Genoa. They are long flat egg noodles about ¼-inch-wide that are made with a mixture of whole wheat and white flour. They are usually served with green beans and pesto. Sometimes a couple of peeled and diced potatoes are added in which case the green beans are reduced by about one third.

DOUGH:
1⅓ cup unbleached white flour
⅔ cup whole wheat flour
3 eggs
½ teaspoon salt

SAUCE:
¾ pound green beans
2 tablespoons butter
1 recipe Pesto Sauce (see page 122)
freshly grated Pecorino Sardo or Parmesan cheese

To make the egg noodles, combine the flours and place on a large wooden board or work surface. Proceed to make the *pasta all'uova* on page 129. Roll the dough out very thinly and leave to dry out for 15 minutes. Roll up and cut into ¼-inch-wide noodles.

Trim the green beans and cut them in half. Bring a large pot of lightly salted water to the boil. Add the green beans and cook for 8 to 9 minutes, or until they are almost cooked. Add the egg noodles and continue to cook until they are tender but still firm. Drain and transfer to a heated serving bowl. Dot with butter and pour over the pesto sauce. Toss lightly and serve with grated cheese on the side. Serves 4.

ORECCHIETTE WITH POTATOES AND ROCKET
Orecchiette con Patate e Ruchetta

This dish comes from Apulia where more potatoes are grown than in any other region of Italy. The combination of potatoes and pasta is surprisingly light and well worth trying.

3 tablespoons extra virgin olive oil
2 garlic cloves, finely chopped
1 small red chili pepper, cored, seeded, and chopped
2 tablespoons torn basil leaves
1 tablespoon fresh oregano
1½ pounds ripe plum tomatoes, peeled, seeded, and chopped
salt
freshly ground black pepper
½ pound waxy potatoes, peeled and diced
1 bunch rocket, trimmed and cut into strips
¾ pound orecchiette
freshly grated pecorino or Parmesan cheese

Heat the olive oil in a large frying pan and cook the garlic, chili, basil, and oregano for 2 minutes. Add the tomatoes and season with salt and black pepper. Cook, uncovered, over moderate heat for 10 minutes or until the sauce is thickened.

Cook the potatoes in a large pot of lightly salted water until they are half cooked. Add the rocket and orecchiette and continue to cook until the pasta is tender but still firm. Drain and transfer to a heated serving bowl. Pour over the sauce, toss lightly, and serve with grated cheese on the side. Serves 4.

CATALAN PASTA, COUNTRY STYLE
Fideus Campesinos

Fideus or *fideos* are short strands of pasta, 1 to 2 inches long, similar to vermicelli. Unlike most pasta, they are not cooked in a large pot of water and drained. Instead, they are cooked like paella or risotto until they are tender and all the liquid is absorbed. This method of preparing pasta is also found in parts of Greece and Turkey, where it was probably introduced by Sephardic Jews after they fled the Inquisition.

1 pound zucchini
4 tablespoons extra virgin olive oil
2 garlic cloves
2 tablespoons flat-leaf parsley, finely chopped
5 ripe plum tomatoes, peeled, seeded, and chopped
¼ cup black olives, pitted and sliced
½ teaspoon paprika
½ cup dry white wine
3½ cups water
¼ teaspoon powdered saffron, dissolved in a little hot water
salt
freshly ground black pepper
4 cups vermicelli, broken into 1½-inch lengths

Trim the ends of the zucchini and slice them thinly. Heat the olive oil in a large casserole or paella pan and cook the garlic and parsley over moderate heat for 1 minute. Add the zucchini and continue to cook until they are golden on both sides.

Add the tomatoes, black olives, and paprika and cook until the sauce is reduced. Add the wine, water, and saffron liquid, and season with salt and black pepper. Bring to a boil. Add the vermicelli and simmer for about 10 minutes or until it is tender and all the liquid is absorbed. Stir often to make sure the vermicelli does not stick to the pan. Serves 4.

EGG NOODLES, BORLOTTI BEANS, AND POTATOES

Tagliatelle alla Contadina

In this recipe from Tuscany, the tagliatelle are cooked together with borlotti beans and potatoes and served with a light tomato and onion sauce with grated cheese on the side.

¾ cup dried borlotti beans
1–2 sage leaves
a sprig of rosemary
½ pound waxy potatoes, peeled and diced
1 pound egg noodles
1–2 tablespoons butter
freshly grated Parmesan cheese

TOMATO AND ONION SAUCE:
2 tablespoons extra virgin olive oil
2 garlic cloves, finely chopped
1 small onion, finely chopped
2 tablespoons flat-leaf parsley, finely chopped
1 tablespoon fresh marjoram
1½ pounds ripe plum tomatoes, peeled, seeded, and chopped
salt
freshly ground black pepper

Soak the beans in cold water overnight and drain. Bring to a boil in plenty of unsalted water with the sage and rosemary. Cover and simmer for 1½ to 2 hours or until the beans are tender. Drain well and remove the rosemary.

To make the tomato sauce, heat the olive oil in a large frying pan and cook the garlic, onion, and herbs over a moderate heat for 5 minutes or until the onions are softened. Add the tomatoes and season with salt and black pepper. Cook for a further 15 minutes or until the sauce is thickened.

Meanwhile cook the potatoes in plenty of lightly salted boiling water. Five minutes before the end of cooking, add the borlotti beans and the egg noodles and cook until they are tender but still firm. Drain and transfer to a heated serving bowl. Dot with butter and pour over the hot sauce. Toss lightly and serve at once with grated cheese on the side. Serves 4 to 5.

LINGUINE WITH OVOLI MUSHROOMS AND WALNUT SAUCE

Linguine con Ovoli e Salsa di Noci

Ovoli mushrooms (*Amanida caesarea*) are highly prized in Italy for their fine flavor. They usually grow under oak or chestnut trees and are easily distinguished by their bright orange caps. Although they are generally eaten raw, they do occasionally appear in sauces for pasta, like this one from Liguria.

¾ pound *ovoli* or other quality mushrooms
2 ounces freshly shelled walnuts
1 garlic clove, crushed
a handful of flat-leaf parsley, finely chopped
¼ cup freshly grated Parmesan cheese
6 tablespoons extra virgin olive oil
3 or 4 tablespoons water
salt
freshly ground black pepper
1 pound linguine
2 tablespoons butter

Trim the ends of the mushrooms and cut them into fairly thick slices.

To make the walnut sauce, place the walnuts, garlic, and parsley in a mortar and pound with a pestle to form a coarse paste. Alternatively, you may place the ingredients in a blender or food processor. Add the Parmesan cheese and mix well. Gradually dribble in the olive oil and enough water to make a smooth, creamy sauce. Season with salt and black pepper.

Cook the mushrooms in a large pot of lightly salted boiling water until they are half cooked. Add the linguine and cook until tender but still firm. Drain and transfer to a heated serving dish. Dot with butter and pour over the sauce. Toss lightly and serve at once. Serves 4.

Egg Noodles with Potatoes and Cabbage
Tagliatelle con Patate e Cavoli

This traditional peasant dish from Tuscany could not be easier to prepare. The egg noodles are cooked together with the potatoes and black cabbage and served dressed with fruity extra virgin olive oil and grated cheese.

1 pound Tuscan black cabbage
½ pound waxy potatoes, peeled and diced
1 pound egg noodles
⅓ cup extra virgin olive oil
freshly ground black pepper
freshly grated Parmesan cheese

Remove the ribs from the black cabbage and cut into thin strips.

Bring the potatoes and cabbage to a boil in a large saucepan of lightly salted boiling water. Cook for 15 minutes. Add the egg noodles and cook until tender but still firm.

Drain and transfer to a heated serving bowl. Pour over the olive oil and season with plenty of black pepper. Toss lightly and serve with grated cheese on the side. Serves 4.

LASAGNETTE WITH MUSHROOMS, BROAD BEANS, AND EGGPLANT

Lasagnette coi Funghi, Fave, e Melanzane

This dish has a lovely combination of textures and flavors. Lasagnette are egg noodles about half an wide. They are sometimes called *taglierini* in Sicily.

2 small eggplants, about 1 pound
salt
extra virgin olive oil
2 garlic cloves, finely chopped
1 tablespoon fresh oregano
1½ small red chili pepper, cored, seeded, and chopped
½ pound mushrooms, sliced
1½ pounds ripe plum tomatoes, peeled, seeded, and chopped
16 black olives, pitted and sliced
1 tablespoon capers
1 cup fresh shelled and skinned broad beans, or frozen baby broad beans
1 pound egg noodles
freshly grated pecorino or Parmesan cheese

Trim the ends of the eggplants and dice into ½-inch pieces. Place in a colander and sprinkle with salt. Set aside for 1 hour to release bitter juices. Fry in hot oil. Drain on paper towels and keep warm.

Heat 3 tablespoons olive oil in a large frying pan and cook the garlic, oregano, and chili for 1 minute. Add the mushrooms and cook until they are tender. Add the tomatoes and cook over moderate heat for 10 minutes or until the sauce starts to thicken. Add the olives and capers and simmer for a further 5 minutes. Bring the broad beans to boil in a large pan of lightly salted boiling water. Cook for 10 minutes. Add the egg noodles and cook until they are tender, but still firm. Drain and transfer to a heated serving bowl. Pour over the sauce and toss lightly. Top with the fried eggplant and serve with grated cheese on the side. Serves 4.

ORZO WITH LENTILS

Fakomatso

This dish is a cross between a stew and a pasta dish. It is made with lentils and *orzo* (small pellets of pasta a little larger than a grain of rice). The orzo are not cooked like pasta in a separate pan of boiling water. Instead, they are simmered with the lentils in an onion and tomato sauce until they are tender.

1½ cups small brown lentils
6 tablespoons extra virgin olive oil
2 large onions, finely chopped
4 ripe plum tomatoes, peeled, seeded, and chopped
1 quart water
¾ cup orzo
salt
freshly ground black pepper

Soak the lentils for 2 hours and drain. Heat the olive oil in a pan and cook the onions over a moderate heat until they start to turn golden. Add the tomatoes and cook for a further 5 minutes. Add the lentils and 1 quart of water and bring to a boil. Cover and simmer for 50 to 60 minutes, or until the lentils are tender. Add the orzo and seasoning. Simmer for a further 20 minutes, adding a little more hot water, if necessary, to prevent them from sticking. Serve hot. Serves 4.

EGG NOODLES WITH FRESH WHITE CHEESE

Beyaz Peynirli Makarna

This dish can be made in just about as much time as it takes to cook the noodles. It is especially good served with a large leafy salad and a bowl of black olives on the side. *Beyaz peynir* is a fresh white cheese that is usually made with cow's milk. If it is unavailable, feta cheese may be used instead.

½ pound egg noodles
3 tablespoons butter
6 ounces *beyaz peynir* or feta cheese, crumbled

Cook the noodles in plenty of lightly salted water until they are tender but still firm. Drain. Melt the butter in a large pot and add the egg noodles. Stir well. Add the cheese and cook over a gentle heat for 2 or 3 minutes or until the pasta is heated through and the cheese is melted. Serve at once. Serves 2 to 3.

CHEESE RAVIOLI FROM ALBONA

Krafi de Albona

Krafi de Albona is the old Italian dialect name for these cheese-filled ravioli from Albona in Istria. The touch of sweetness goes very well with the dressing of melted butter and grated cheese. *Pujine* is a fresh white cheese similar to ricotta.

DOUGH:

2 cups unbleached white flour

3 eggs

½ teaspoon salt

FILLING:

1½ cups ricotta or *pujine* cheese

1 egg

2 tablespoons raisins

2 teaspoons sugar

a grating of nutmeg

SAUCE:

½ cup butter, melted

freshly grated Parmesan cheese

To make the filling, place the ricotta, egg, raisins, sugar, and nutmeg in a bowl and mix well. To make the ravioli, follow the directions for egg noodles on page 129. Roll the dough out to 2 very thin rectangles of equal size. Place a teaspoonful of the filling over one of the sheets at regular intervals about 2 inches apart. Cover with the other sheet of dough. Using your fingertips, press well around each mound. Cut the ravioli into 2 inches squares with a pastry knife or ravioli wheel.

Line them up on a lightly floured board or tray, making sure they do not touch, and leave for 15 minutes to dry. Cook the ravioli in plenty of lightly salted boiling water for 5 or 6 minutes or until they are just tender. Remove with a slotted spoon and transfer to a heated serving dish. Pour over the melted butter and serve at once with grated cheese on the side. Serves 4.

SARDINIAN RAVIOLI WITH EGGPLANT
Agnolotti alla Sarda

These delicious little ravioli are filled with a mixture of roasted eggplant, fresh Pecorino cheese, egg yolks, and ground walnuts. They are usually served with a light tomato and basil sauce and grated cheese. If fresh Pecorino is unavailable, ricotta may be used instead.

DOUGH:
1½ cups semolina or unbleached white flour
2 eggs
¼ teaspoon powdered saffron dissolved in a little warm water
a pinch of salt

FILLING:
1 medium eggplant about ½ pound
extra virgin olive oil
¾ cup fresh Pecorino or ricotta cheese
2 egg yolks
¼ cup freshly shelled walnuts, finely ground in a blender
3 tablespoons freshly grated Pecorino Sardo or Parmesan cheese
salt
freshly ground black pepper

TOMATO AND BASIL SAUCE:
2 tablespoons extra virgin olive oil
2 garlic cloves, finely chopped
1 pound ripe plum tomatoes, peeled, seeded, and chopped
a handful of fresh basil leaves, coarsely chopped

To make the pasta, follow the directions for *pasta all'uova* on page 129 adding the saffron liquid with the eggs.

To make the filling, bake the eggplant in a preheated 375°F oven for 40 minutes or until it is tender. Remove from the oven and cut in half. Scoop out the flesh and mash with a fork. Combine the fresh Pecorino Sardo cheese and egg yolks in a bowl. Add the mashed eggplant, walnuts, and grated cheese and mix well. Season with salt and black pepper. To make the sauce, heat the olive oil in a large frying pan and cook the garlic over moderate heat until it starts to turn golden. Add the tomatoes and cook for a further 10 minutes or until the sauce starts to thicken. Add the basil and seasoning to taste and simmer for 1 or 2 more minutes.

Roll the dough out to two very thin rectangles of equal size. Place teaspoonfuls of the filling over one sheet of dough at regular intervals about 1½ inches apart. Cover with the other sheet of dough. Using your fingertips, press well around each mound. Cut the ravioli into 1½-inch squares with a pastry or ravioli wheel. Line them up on a lightly floured board or tray, making sure they do not touch, and leave for 10 to 15 minutes to dry.

Cook the ravioli in plenty of lightly salted water for 4 to 5 minutes or until they are just tender. Remove with a slotted spoon and transfer to a heated serving dish. Pour over the sauce and serve at once. Serves 3 to 4.

CORSICAN RAVIOLI

Raviolis

In Corsica ravioli is usually stuffed with a mixture of fresh *brocciu* cheese, spinach, and wild herbs such as *frigula* (borage), *insalatone* (lamb's lettuce), or *puleghin* (wild mint). If *brocciu* is unavailable, pecorino may be used instead.

DOUGH:
2 cups unbleached white flour
3 eggs
½ teaspoon salt

FILLING:
½ pound spinach
¼ pound lamb's lettuce
¼ pound borage
1 cup ricotta
l egg
¼ cup freshly grated dried *brocciu* or pecorino cheese
2 tablespoons finely chopped mint

SAUCE:
l recipe "Tomato and Basil Sauce" (see page 150)
freshly grated aged brocciu or pecorino cheese

Wash the spinach, lamb's lettuce, and borage and cook in a covered saucepan for 5 to 7 minutes over moderate heat or until they are tender. Squeeze dry and chop coarsely. Combine the chopped greens with the ricotta, egg, grated cheese, and mint in a mixing bowl and season with salt and black pepper. Blend well.

To make the dough, follow the directions for *pasta all'uova* on page 129. Allow the dough to rest and roll out into two very thin sheets. Place teaspoonfuls of the filling over one sheet of the dough at regular intervals about 2-inches apart. Cover with the other sheet of dough and press well around each mound. Cut the ravioli into 2 inch squares with a pastry or ravioli cutter. Line them up on a lightly floured board or tray in one layer and leave for 15 minutes to dry.

Cook the ravioli in plenty of lightly salted boiling water for 4 to 5 minutes or until they are just tender. Transfer to a heated serving bowl. Pour over the hot tomato sauce and serve at once with grated cheese on the side. Serves 4.

PUMPKIN RAVIOLI FROM LIGURIA
Pansôti di Zucca

Pansôti means "pot-bellied" in Ligurian dialect. They are usually triangular in shape and contain slightly more filling than most ravioli—about 1 heaping teaspoonful. They are also very good served with pesto.

DOUGH:
2¼ cups unbleached white flour
3 eggs
1–2 teaspoons dry white wine

FILLING:
1 pound cooked pumpkin
½ cup ricotta
1 egg yolk
¼ cup freshly grated Parmesan cheese
a grating of nutmeg
salt
freshly ground black pepper

SAUCE:
½ cup butter, melted
Freshly grated Parmesan cheese

To make the pasta, follow the directions for *pasta all'uova* on page 129, adding the wine with the eggs. To make the filling, combine the cooked pumpkin, ricotta, egg yolk, and Parmesan cheese in a bowl. Mix well and season with nutmeg, salt, and black pepper.

Roll the dough out into thin sheets, one at a time. Cut the first sheet into 2¼-inch squares and place 1 heaping teaspoonful of the filling in the centre of each square.

Fold over diagonally to make triangles. Using your fingertips, press along the edges to seal. Repeat with the remaining sheets of dough. Line the *pansôti* up on a lightly floured board or tray, making sure they do not touch, and leave for 15 minutes to dry.

Cook the *pansoti* in plenty of lightly salted boiling water for 5 to 6 minutes or until they are just tender. Remove with a slotted spoon and transfer to a heated serving dish. Pour over the melted butter and serve at once with grated cheese on the side. Serves 4.

Baked Macaroni with Eggplant
Ma'karoni bil-Batinjan

This dish consists of layers of cooked macaroni, fried eggplant, tomato sauce, and grated cheese. In Lebanon, they use *Kashkavan* or (Romanian Kashkaval)—a hard yellow cheese that is usually made from ewe's milk. If it is unavailable, Greek *Kasseri* or Gruyère cheese may be used instead.

2 large eggplants, about 1½ pounds
salt
vegetable oil for frying
3 tablespoons extra virgin olive oil
1 medium onion, finely chopped
2 garlic cloves, finely chopped
a few thyme leaves
1½ pounds ripe plum tomatoes, peeled, seeded and chopped
freshly ground black pepper
¼ pound short macaroni, such as penne or ziti
1½ pound *Kashkaval, Kasseri,* or Gruyère cheese, grated

Trim the ends of the eggplants and cut into rounds about ¼ inch thick. Sprinkle with salt and set in a colander for 1 hour to release the bitter juices. Wash off the salt and pat dry. Fry in hot olive oil until golden on both sides. Drain on a paper towel.

Heat the olive oil in a large frying pan and cook the onion, garlic, and thyme over a moderate heat until it is softened. Add the tomatoes and continue to cook, uncovered, for 15 minutes or until the sauce starts to thicken.

Cook the macaroni in plenty of lightly salted boiling water until it is tender but still firm. Arrange a layer of fried eggplant in the bottom of a well-oiled shallow baking dish. Cover with a layer of macaroni and tomato sauce and sprinkle over some grated cheese. Repeat until all the layers are used up, ending with the grated cheese on top. Bake in a preheated 350°F oven, until the top is golden and the sauce is bubbling. Serves 4.

BAKED ORECCHIETTE WITH WILD MUSHROOMS
Orecchiette con i Funghi

Orecchiette are the most popular form of pasta in Apulia. They are shaped like concave disks or little ears. In this recipe, they are dressed with a wild mushroom and tomato sauce. Mozzarella and grated cheese, and baked in the oven until the cheese is melted and the top is golden.

¾ pound mixed wild mushrooms
¼ extra virgin olive oil
1 small onion, finely chopped
2 garlic cloves, finely chopped
2 tablespoons flat-leaf parsley, finely chopped
1 tablespoon fresh oregano
1½ pounds ripe plum tomatoes, peeled, seeded, and chopped
salt
freshly ground black pepper
1 pound orecchiette
½ pound mozzarella, diced
1 cup freshly grated pecorino or Parmesan cheese

Wipe the mushrooms with a damp cloth to remove any dirt or grit, and cut into fairly thin slices. Heat the olive oil in a large frying pan and cook the onion, garlic, parsley, and oregano over a moderate heat for 3 minutes. Add the mushrooms and continue to cook until they start to give off their juices. Add the tomatoes and continue to cook for 15 minutes or until the sauce starts to thicken. Season with salt and black pepper.

Cook the orecchiette in plenty of lightly salted boiling water until tender but still firm. Drain and transfer to a well-oiled shallow baking dish. Pour over the tomato sauce and top with the mozzarella and ¾ cup grated cheese. Mix gently with a fork. Sprinkle over the remaining grated cheese and bake in a preheated 350°F oven until the cheese is melted and top is golden. Serves 4.

NIÇOISE BAKED POTATO GNOCCHI
Tian de Gnocchi a la Niçarde

In Provence, potato gnocchi are made with or without eggs. As a general rule, there is no need to add eggs if using waxy potatoes such as Desirée. Floury "old" potatoes such as King Edwards, however, usually need some egg in order to prevent them from falling apart.

GNOCCHI:
2 pounds floury potatoes
2 egg yolks
a grating of nutmeg
salt
freshly ground black pepper
about 1¾ cups unbleached white flour

TOMATO COULIS:
2 tablespoons extra virgin olive oil
4 shallots, finely chopped
2 garlic cloves, finely chopped
1 pound ripe plum tomatoes, peeled, seeded, and chopped
a few thyme leaves
a pinch of sugar
salt
freshly ground black pepper

TOPPING:
⅔ cup Gruyère cheese, grated

Scrub the potatoes and bring to a boil in lightly salted water for 20 minutes or until they are tender. Drain and remove the skins when they are cool enough to handle. Force through a sieve onto a lightly floured work surface or board. While the potatoes are still warm, add the egg yolks and mix well. Season with nutmeg, salt, and black pepper. Gradually work in just enough flour to make a soft dough. Too much flour will make the gnocchi heavy.

Roll the dough out into long cylinders about the thickness of your finger, then cut into 1-inch lengths. Press each *gnocco* against the prongs of a fork. This helps them to hold the sauce.

To make the sauce, heat the olive oil in a large frying pan and add the shallots and garlic. Cook over moderate heat for 3 minutes. Add the tomatoes, thyme, and sugar and cook for a further 10 minutes or until the sauce starts to thicken. Season with salt and black pepper. Cook the gnocchi in plenty of lightly unsalted boiling water. Salted water can make the gnocchi stick together. The gnocchi will float to the surface just before they are cooked.

Cook for 2 or 3 more minutes. Remove with a slotted spoon and transfer to a well-oiled shallow baking dish. Sprinkle with half of the Gruyère cheese and pour over the sauce. Mix gently with a fork. Sprinkle over the remaining grated cheese and bake in a preheated 350°F oven for 15 to 20 minutes or until the top is golden. Serves 4.

DALMATIAN LASAGNE

Lazanje u Pećnici

Lasagne is one of the many pasta dishes that the Dalmatians adopted from the Italians. In this recipe, it is layered with Swiss chard, *pujine* cheese, béchamel and tomato sauce, and grated cheese. *Pujine* is a fresh white cheese similar to ricotta.

DOUGH:
2 cups unbleached white flour
3 eggs
¼ teaspoon salt

FILLING:
1 pound Swiss chard or spinach
1 recipe béchamel sauce (see page 213)
1 recipe Tomato and Basil Sauce (see page 150)
1½ cups ricotta or *pujine* cheese
1 cup freshly grated Parmesan cheese

To make the lasagne, follow the directions for *pasta all'uova* on page 129. Allow it to rest, then roll out thinly. Cut into rectangles about 4½ by 7 inches.

To make the filling, wash the Swiss chard and cut away the stalks. Cook in a covered saucepan over moderate heat for 5 minutes, or until the Swiss chard is tender. The water clinging to the leaves is sufficient to prevent scorching. Drain and chop coarsely.

Cook 6 sheets of lasagne at a time in plenty of lightly salted boiling water for 3 or 4 minutes, or until just tender. Remove with a slotted spoon and rinse under cold water. Lay the lasagne flat on a towel. Repeat until all the lasagne are cooked.

Arrange a layer of lasagne over the bottom of a well-oiled shallow baking dish. Spoon a little ricotta over the lasagne and cover with a layer of chopped Swiss chard. Spoon over a little béchamel sauce and then some tomato sauce. Sprinkle some grated cheese over the top. Repeat the layers until all the ingredients are used up, finishing with lasagne, béchamel sauce, and grated cheese. Bake in a preheated 350°F oven for 30 to 40 minutes or until the top is golden and the sauce is bubbling. Serves 4 to 6.

RICE AND COUSCOUS

A kettle will not boil without its lid.
—Turkish proverb

Rice is a staple in most of the Mediterranean countries. It was first introduced to the Middle East from Asia around 1000 B.C., then the Arabs spread it across North Africa to Sicily and Spain in the eighth century.

Each country prepares rice in its own way. In Turkey and most of the Middle East, there is a preference for long-grain rice that is cooked like a pilaf. In Spain and Italy, they like to use short-grain or medium-grain rice for paella and risotti. The exact time of cooking depends on the type of rice used and the way it is cooked.

Couscous is the national dish of all the countries of the Magreb—Morocco, Algeria, Tunisia, and Libya. It is made with semolina that is sprinkled with water and flour and hand-rolled until it forms granules. Traditionally, it is served for lunch on Fridays and for festivals and special occasions.

To prepare couscous the authentic way can be a lengthy process. First the couscous is placed in a wide shallow bowl, covered with water, and drained. It is then left for about 15 minutes to swell. The grains are then gently rubbed through the fingers to remove any lumps and transferred to the top of a *couscousière* to steam over boiling water or a stew. Once the steam has penetrated all the way through the couscous, it is returned to the bowl and sprinkled with cold water. The whole process is then repeated (sometimes up to seven times) until the couscous is very light and fluffy. A little *smen* (a kind of clarified butter), butter, or olive oil is then mixed into the grain to enhance the flavor. It is then ready to serve.

Fortunately, most of the couscous available in this country are precooked and can be made very quickly and easily. Just follow the directions on the packet.

TUNISIAN RICE PILAF

Roz Klaya

In Tunisia, rice pilaf is usually delicately flavored with *spigol*—a spice mixture based on turmeric, paprika, and a little powdered saffron. Serve it as an accompaniment to vegetable stews or *tajines*.

2 tablespoons butter or extra virgin olive oil
1 small onion, finely chopped
1½ cups long-grain rice
2½ cups boiling vegetable broth or water
¼ teaspoon paprika
¼ teaspoon turmeric
a good pinch of powdered saffron
salt
freshly ground black pepper

Melt the butter in a heavy saucepan and cook the onion over a moderate heat until it is softened. Stir in the rice and cook for 2 minutes, or until the grains start to whiten. Add the boiling broth and spices and season with salt and black pepper. Lower the heat, cover, and simmer for 18 to 20 minutes or until the rice is tender and small craters have appeared over the surface of the rice. Remove from the heat and let stand for 5 minutes before serving. Serves 4.

Risotto with Wild Asparagus
Risotto con Asparagi di Campo

This delicate risotto comes from the Veneto, where wild asparagus is much appreciated for its fine flavor. If it is unavailable, choose young tender asparagus with thin green spears instead.

About 4 cups vegetable broth or water
¾ pound wild or thin green asparagus
2 tablespoons extra virgin olive oil
3 tablespoons butter
1½ cups arborio rice
½ cup dry white wine
salt
freshly ground black pepper
1 cup freshly grated Parmesan cheese

Bring the broth to boil in a saucepan and keep just under the simmering point.

Trim the ends of the asparagus and remove any fibrous, inedible parts from the lower stalks with a sharp knife. Cut into 1-inch lengths. Heat the olive oil and 1 tablespoon butter in a heavy saucepan and cook the asparagus over a gentle heat for 10 minutes, taking care that it does not brown. Stir in the rice and cook for 1 minute. Add the wine, raise the heat, and when it has completely evaporated, add a ladleful of broth. Cook, stirring constantly, until the liquid is almost evaporated.

Add another ladleful of broth and repeat until the rice is tender but still firm. The finished risotto should be slightly creamy. Remove from the heat and stir in the remaining butter and half of the Parmesan cheese. Season with salt and black pepper and serve at once with the remaining grated cheese on the side. Serves 4.

RICE PILAF WITH DATES AND ALMONDS

Roz bil Tamar

This traditional Bedouin dish is much loved in Libya, where it is often made for weddings and other special occasions.

2 tablespoons butter or ghee
1½ cups long-grain rice
2½ cups boiling water
salt
freshly ground black pepper

GARNISH:
3 tablespoons butter
⅓ cup blanched almonds, cut in half lengthwise
½ cup dates, pitted and cut in half lengthwise
1 teaspoon rose water

Melt the butter and stir in the rice. Cook over a moderate heat for 2 minutes. Add the boiling water and seasoning to taste. Cover and simmer for 18 to 20 minutes or until the rice is tender and small craters have appeared over the surface of the rice. Remove from the heat and let stand for 5 minutes.

To make the garnish, melt the butter in a large frying pan and cook the almonds over a moderate heat until they start to turn golden. Add the dates and cook for another 2 or 3 minutes. Remove from the heat and stir in the rose water. Transfer the rice to a heated serving dish and spoon the date and almond mixture over the top. Serve at once. Serves 4.

RICE WITH TOMATOES

Bourani

Bourani derives from the Persian *boorani*, which originally meant a "Persian salad." In Persia today it refers to various vegetables dishes with yoghurt. The dish was then adopted by the Turks, who added rice. When the Turks introduced it to Greece, the yoghurt was omitted.

3 tablespoons extra virgin olive oil
2 medium onions, finely chopped
l red bell pepper, cored, seeded, and diced into small pieces
3 garlic cloves, finely chopped
½ cup flat-leaf parsley, finely chopped
1 pound ripe plum tomatoes, peeled, seeded, and chopped
2 cups long-grain rice
3 cups boiling water
salt
freshly ground black pepper

Heat the olive oil in a heavy-based saucepan and cook the onions, red pepper, and garlic over a moderate heat for 5 minutes. Stir in the parsley and cook for a further 2 minutes. Add the tomatoes and continue to cook for 10 minutes or until the sauce is thickened. Add the rice and boiling water and season with salt and black pepper. Bring to a boil. Cover and simmer for 18 to 20 minutes or until the rice is tender and the liquid is absorbed. Serves 4.

RICE AND PEAS
Riži-biži

The Dalmatian version of this famous Venetian dish usually includes tomatoes. Sometimes toasted fennel seeds are added for additional flavor.

about 4 cups boiling broth or water
2 tablespoons extra virgin olive oil
1 small onion, finely chopped
2 tablespoons flat-leaf parsley, finely chopped
2 cups freshly shelled peas, or frozen *petit pois*
1 teaspoon sugar
2 canned plum tomatoes, forced through a sieve
        or puréed in a food processor
1½ cups arborio rice
salt
freshly ground black pepper
1 cup freshly grated Parmesan cheese

Bring the broth to a boil in a saucepan and keep just below the simmer point. Heat the olive oil in a heavy saucepan and cook the onion over moderate heat until it is softened. Add the parsley, peas, and sugar and simmer for 3 minutes.

Add the tomato purée and cook for a further 5 minutes. Add the rice and seasoning and stir well so each grain is well coated. Add a ladleful of broth and cook, stirring constantly, until the liquid is almost evaporated. Add another ladleful of broth and repeat until the rice is tender but still firm and the liquid is evaporated.

The finished risotto should be creamy. Remove from the heat and stir in the butter and half of the Parmesan cheese. Serve at once with the remaining cheese on the side. Serves 4.

RICE WITH SPINACH

Rezz bil-S'banegh

This dish is traditionally prepared for Lent in both Syria and Lebanon. It may be served hot or cold. If it is served cold, it is always made with extra virgin olive oil rather than butter.

2 pounds spinach
4 tablespoons extra virgin olive oil or butter
1 medium onion, finely chopped
1½ cups long-grain rice
a grating of nutmeg
¼ teaspoon allspice
salt
freshly ground black pepper
2½ cups boiling water
1 lemon, cut into wedges

Wash the spinach and cut into very thin strips. Heat the olive oil in a heavy saucepan and cook the onion over a moderate heat until it starts to turn golden. Add the spinach and cook for a further 5 or 6 minutes or until it is tender. Stir in the rice and spices and season with salt and black pepper.

Add the water and bring to a boil. Cover and simmer for 18 to 20 minutes or until the rice is tender but still moist. Remove from the heat and set aside for 5 minutes. Serve hot or cold with lemon wedges on the side. Serves 4.

CHICKPEA PILAF

Nohutlu Pilav

Legend has it that one of the great pashas of the Topkapi Palace would have golden nuggets made to look like chickpeas hidden in this pilaf. Any guest fortunate enough to find a golden chickpea would be allowed to keep it for good luck.

3 tablespoons butter or extra virgin olive oil
1 leek, white part only, thinly sliced
a handful of flat-leaf parsley, finely chopped
1½ cups long-grain rice
1 cup cooked and drained chickpeas
¼ teaspoon cinnamon
¼ teaspoon allspice
salt
freshly ground black pepper
2½ cups hot water

Melt the butter in a heavy saucepan and cook the leek and parsley over a moderate heat for 5 minutes. Stir in the rice and cook for 2 or 3 minutes or until the grains start to turn white. Add the chickpeas and spices and season with salt and black pepper. Pour in the hot water and bring to a boil.

Cover and simmer for 18 to 20 minutes or until the liquid is absorbed and small craters have appeared on the surface of the rice. Remove from the heat and let stand at the back of the stove for 5 minutes before serving. Serves 4.

CABBAGE AND RICE
Lahanorizo

This simple peasant dish was traditionally prepared on Wednesdays and Fridays when the eating of meat was forbidden by the Greek Orthodox Church. It is usually served with lemon wedges, but it is also very good sprinkled with a little grated Kefalotyri or pecorino cheese.

1 small green cabbage (about 2 pounds)
4 tablespoons extra virgin olive oil
1 medium onion, finely chopped
a handful of flat-leaf parsley, finely chopped
1 pound plum tomatoes, peeled, seeded, and chopped
salt
freshly ground black pepper
¾ cup long-grain rice
1½ cup boiling water
1 lemon, cut into wedges

Trim the bases of the cabbage and shred it coarsely. Heat the olive oil in a heavy saucepan and add the onion and cabbage. Cover and cook over moderate heat until the vegetables start to turn golden, stirring from time to time so they cook evenly. Add the tomatoes and simmer for 5 minutes.

Season with salt and black pepper. Add the rice and stir well. Add the water and bring to a boil. Cover and simmer for 18 to 20 minutes or until the rice is tender but still moist. Let stand for 5 minutes before serving. Serve with lemon wedges on the side. Serves 4 to 6.

RICE AND BROAD BEANS

Riso e Fave

This recipe is a specialty of Bari in Apulia, where it is often called by its dialect name of *graneriso e fafe*. Broad beans were a staple of the peasants of southern Italy for so many centuries that they were nicknamed *carne del poveri*—"the meat of the poor." Today they are often called the queen of vegetables.

About 4 cups vegetable broth or water
1½ cups shelled broad beans or frozen baby broad beans
3 tablespoons extra virgin olive oil
1 small onion, finely chopped
¾ cup canned plum tomatoes, forced through a sieve
    or puréed in a food processor
2 tablespoons torn basil leaves
1½ cups arborio rice
salt
freshly ground black pepper
2 tablespoons butter
freshly grated pecorino or Parmesan cheese

Place the shelled beans in a saucepan and cover with water. Bring to a boil. Cover and simmer for 20 minutes or until they are tender. Drain and set aside. Bring the stock or water to a boil in a saucepan and keep to just below the simmer. Heat the olive oil in another saucepan and cook the onion over moderate heat until it is translucent.

Add the beans and tomato purée and simmer for 10 minutes. Stir in the basil, rice, and a ladleful of hot stock. When the liquid is almost evaporated, add another ladleful of stock. Repeat until the rice is tender, but still firm. This will take about 25 minutes. Stir in the butter and season with salt and black pepper. Serve at once with grated cheese on the side. Serves 4.

RISOTTO WITH WILD MUSHROOMS
Risotto coi Funghi

You can use any combination of wild mushrooms—porcini, oyster mushrooms, morels or chanterelles—for this elegant risotto from the Veneto.

about 4 cups vegetable broth or water
¾ pound mixed wild mushrooms
3 tablespoons extra virgin olive oil
3 shallots, finely chopped
1 garlic clove, finely chopped
2 tablespoons flat-leaf parsley, finely chopped
1½ cups arborio or vialone rice
½ cup dry white wine
salt
freshly ground black pepper
1 cup freshly grated Parmesan cheese

Bring the broth to boil in a saucepan and keep just below the simmering point. Wipe the mushrooms with a damp cloth and remove any sand or grit. Slice fairly thinly. Heat the olive oil in a heavy saucepan and cook the shallots over moderate heat until they are softened. Add the garlic and parsley and cook for a further 2 minutes.

Add the mushrooms and cook for 10 minutes or until they are tender. Add the rice and stir well. Season with salt and black pepper. Pour in the wine, raise the heat, and cook until it is evaporated. Add a ladleful of broth and cook, stirring constantly, until the liquid is almost evaporated. Add another ladleful of stock and repeat until the rice is tender but still firm. The finished risotto should be slightly creamy. Remove from the heat and stir in the butter and half of the Parmesan cheese. Serve at once with the remaining Parmesan cheese on the side. Serves 4.

LEEKS AND RICE

Prassorizo

This simple country dish makes a very good light lunch or supper. Serve it with a dollop of Greek yoghurt or slices of feta cheese on the side.

2 pounds leeks
4 tablespoons extra virgin olive oil
1 medium onion, chopped
2 celery stalks, thinly sliced
½ small red chili pepper, cored, seeded, and finely chopped
4 ripe plum tomatoes, peeled, seeded, and chopped
1½ cups long-grain rice
2½ cups boiling vegetable broth or water

Trim the ends of the leeks, cut into 1½-inch lengths, and wash away any dirt that collects between the leaves. Heat the olive oil and cook the onion and celery over moderate heat for 3 minutes. Add the leeks and chili and stir well. Cover and cook over moderate heat for 10 minutes, or until the vegetables are softened.

Add the tomatoes and cook, uncovered, for a further 10 minutes or until the liquid is evaporated. Add the rice and stir well. Pour in the water and season with salt and black pepper. Bring to a boil, cover, and simmer for 15 to 20 minutes or until the rice is tender but still moist. Set aside for 5 minutes before serving. Serves 4.

NORTH AFRICAN STEAMED RICE WITH VEGETABLES

Roz Mefacuar bil-Khodra

In Tunisia and Libya, rice is often steamed, like couscous, in the top of a *couscousière*, while the vegetables are stewed underneath. If you do not have a *couscousière*, you can steam the rice in a colander lined with muslin, set inside a saucepan. The vegetables can be varied according to the season.

3 tablespoons extra virgin olive oil
1 large onion, chopped
2 garlic cloves, finely chopped
3 sweet red peppers, cored, seeded, and cut into strips
1 small red chili pepper, cored, seeded, and finely chopped
1 teaspoon *harissa*, see page 124
1 teaspoon paprika
½ teaspoon ground cumin
½ teaspoon ground coriander
1 pound ripe plum tomatoes, peeled, seeded, and chopped
1 cup cooked and drained chickpeas
1 cup hot water
2 medium zucchini, trimmed, and cut into ½-inch-thick rounds
1½ cups long-grain rice
2 tablespoons butter or ghee
salt
freshly ground black pepper

Heat the olive oil in the bottom of a *couscousière* or large saucepan and cook the onion, garlic, and peppers for 2 minutes. Add the *harissa*, spices, tomatoes, and chickpeas and stir well. Pour in the hot water and bring to a boil. Wash the rice and place in the top of a *couscousière*, or in a colander lined with muslin, set inside a saucepan. Cover with a tight-fitting lid. Reduce the heat and simmer for 20 minutes.

Add the zucchini to the stew and stir well. Cut the butter into small pieces and add to the rice. Season with salt and black pepper and fluff up with a fork. Continue to cook for a further 15 or 20 minutes or until the vegetables and rice are tender. Arrange the rice in the center of a heated serving dish and surround with the vegetable stew. Serves 4.

SAFFRON PILAF

Safranli Pilav

This pilaf is sometimes called *sari pilav* (yellow pilaf) because of its beautiful color. Sometimes the raisins and pine nuts are omitted.

2 tablespoons butter
1 medium onion, finely chopped
1½ cups long-grain rice
2½ cups hot water
¼ teaspoon saffron threads, soaked in 2 tablespoons water
3 tablespoons raisins
3 tablespoons pine nuts
½ teaspoon ground coriander
½ teaspoon allspice
a pinch of cloves
½ teaspoon salt
freshly ground black pepper

Melt the butter in a heavy saucepan and cook the onion over a moderate heat until it is softened. Stir in the rice and cook over a gentle heat until it starts to whiten. Pour in the water and add the saffron, raisins, pine nuts, spices, salt, and black pepper.

Bring to a boil. Cover and simmer for 15 to 20 minutes or until the liquid is evaporated and small craters have appeared on the surface of the rice. Remove from the heat and take of the lid of the saucepan. Place a napkin over the top and replace the lid. Let stand at the back of the stove for 5 minutes before serving. Serves 4.

RICE WITH PUMPKIN
Riso con la Zucca

This delicious, creamy risotto comes from the Veneto, where it is usually made with *zucca gialla* (yellow pumpkin). Sometimes the risotto is cooked in milk, or half milk and half water, instead of the broth.

4 cups vegetable broth or water, approximately
2 tablespoons extra virgin olive oil
1 tablespoon butter
1 small onion, finely chopped
1 pound pumpkin flesh, diced
1½ cups arborio rice
salt
freshly ground black pepper
3 tablespoons single cream
2 tablespoons flat-leaf parsley, finely chopped
½ cup freshly grated Parmesan cheese

Bring the broth to a boil in a pan and keep just below the simmering point. Heat the olive oil and butter in a heavy saucepan and cook the onion over moderate heat until it is softened. Add the pumpkin and stir well.

Cover and cook over gentle heat for 15 to 20 minutes or until the pumpkin is tender and reduced to a purée. Stir in the rice and season with salt and black pepper. Add a ladleful of stock and cook over gentle heat until most of the liquid is absorbed, stirring from time to time to prevent the risotto sticking to the pan.

Add another ladleful of stock and repeat until the rice is tender but still firm. Remove from the heat and stir in the cream, parsley, and ¼ cup grated cheese. Serve at once with additional grated cheese on the side. Serves 4.

GREEN RICE WITH WILD MUSHROOMS
Risotto Verde

This recipe comes from the Marche, where it is usually made with a mixture of wild herbs and greens such as rocket, chicory, dandelion, Swiss chard, spinach, beet greens, parsley, basil, marjoram, or oregano, and wild mushrooms.

About 4 cups vegetable stock or water
½ pound mixed herbs and greens
½ pound fresh *porcini* or other wild mushrooms
2 tablespoons extra virgin olive oil
1 small onion, chopped
1½ cups arborio rice
½ cup dry white wine
salt
freshly ground black pepper
2 tablespoons butter
1 cup freshly grated Parmesan cheese

Bring the stock to a boil in a saucepan and keep it just below the simmering point. Wash the herbs and greens carefully and cook in a covered saucepan over a moderate heat for 5 to 7 minutes or until they are tender. Drain and chop coarsely.

Wipe the mushrooms with a damp cloth and remove any sand or grit. Slice fairly thinly. Heat the olive oil in a heavy saucepan and cook the onion over a moderate heat for 3 minutes. Add the mushrooms and cook for a further 10 minutes or until they are tender. Stir in the rice and cook for a further 2 minutes. Pour in the wine. Raise the heat and cook until it is evaporated. Add the chopped greens and a ladleful of stock. Season with salt and black pepper.

Cook, stirring constantly, until the liquid is almost evaporated. Add another ladleful of stock and repeat until the rice is tender but still firm. The finished risotto should be slightly creamy and most of the liquid evaporated. Stir in the butter and half of the Parmesan cheese and serve with the remaining Parmesan cheese on the side. Serves 4.

RICE WITH VERMICELLI
Rezz bil Sha'riyeh

Rice with vermicelli is made all over the Middle East from Egypt to Turkey. The exact proportion of rice to vermicelli can vary. It is usually served with a vegetable stew and some yoghurt on the side.

1½ cups long-grain rice
3 tablespoons butter or extra virgin olive oil
½ cup vermicelli, broken into ½ inch lengths
2½ cups hot water
a pinch of cinnamon
½ teaspoon salt
freshly ground black pepper

Rinse the rice under cold water and drain well.

Heat the butter in a heavy saucepan and add the vermicelli. Cook over moderate heat until it is golden brown. Stir in the rice and cook for another 2 minutes or until the grains are well coated in butter. Pour in the stock and add the cinnamon, salt, and black pepper.

Bring to a boil. Cover and simmer for 15 to 20 minutes or until the rice and vermicelli are tender but still firm and the liquid is evaporated. Remove from the heat and take off the lid off the saucepan. Place a napkin over the top and replace the lid. Set at the back of the stove for 5 minutes before serving. Serves 4.

RICE CROQUETTES
Fritelle di Riso

These tasty croquettes from Modena are usually served with a simple salad of red chicory dressed with extra virgin olive oil and balsamic vinegar, and a glass of Lambrusco wine.

About 4 cups vegetable stock or water
1 tablespoon extra virgin olive oil
1 small onion, finely chopped
1¼ cups arborio rice
salt
freshly ground black pepper
1 tablespoon butter
¼ cup freshly grated Parmesan cheese
1 egg plus 1 egg white
dry bread crumbs
vegetable oil for frying

Bring the stock to a boil in a large saucepan and keep just below the simmering point. Heat the olive oil in a heavy saucepan and cook the onion over a moderate heat until it is softened. Stir in the rice and cook for 1 or 2 minutes. Add a ladleful of stock and cook, stirring constantly, until the liquid is almost evaporated. Add another ladleful of stock and repeat until the rice is tender and the liquid is evaporated.

Season with salt and black pepper. Stir in the butter and Parmesan cheese. Transfer to a mixing bowl and set aside to cool. Add the egg and mix well. Shape into croquettes the size of a walnut. Beat the remaining egg white until stiff. Dip the croquettes in the egg white and roll in bread crumbs. Deep-fry in hot oil until golden on both sides. Drain on paper towels and serve hot. Serves 4.

RICE AND EGGPLANT TIMBALE

Risu a Palermitana

This delicious *timballo* or pie from Palermo consists of layers of fried eggplant, risotto, tomato sauce, and grated cheese.

2 or 3 large eggplants, just over 2 pounds
salt
about 1 cup extra virgin olive oil
1 small onion, finely chopped
1 cup arborio rice
about 3 cups boiling vegetable broth or water
1 recipe Tomato and Basil Sauce (see page 150)
1 cup freshly grated Caciacavallo or pecorino cheese

Trim the ends of the eggplants and cut into rounds about a quarter-inch thick. Sprinkle with salt and set in a colander for 1 hour to release the bitter juices. Wash off the salt and pat dry. Fry in hot olive oil until golden brown on both sides. Drain on paper towels.

Heat 2 tablespoons olive oil in a heavy saucepan and cook the onion over moderate heat until it is translucent. Stir in the rice and cook for 1 minute, so each grain is well coated in oil. Add a ladleful of stock and cook, stirring constantly, until the liquid is almost evaporated. Add another ladleful of stock and repeat until the rice is tender and the liquid is absorbed.

Arrange a layer of fried eggplant in the bottom of a baking dish. Cover with ⅓ of the rice and spoon over one third of the tomato and basil sauce. Sprinkle one third of the grated cheese over the top. Repeat the layers until all of the ingredients are used up, ending with the grated cheese. Bake in a preheated 350°F oven for 25–30 minutes or until the top is golden and the sauce is bubbling. Serves 4.

VEGETABLE PAELLA
Paella de Verduras

Paella is named after the shallow, round metal or earthenware pan in which it is cooked. Paella originated in the region around Valencia, but today it is made all over Spain. Traditionally, it is cooked outdoors over an open fire, but it can also be made very well on top of the stove, if necessary, over two burners. Paella is always made with short-grain rice similar to arborio, which resembles the rice grown in Valencia.

5 tablespoons extra virgin olive oil
1 Spanish onion, chopped
2 garlic cloves, finely chopped
2 tablespoons flat-leaf parsley, finely chopped
1 cup shelled peas, or frozen *petit pois*
1 cup tiny green beans, trimmed and cut into 2-inch lengths
2 red peppers, cored, seeded, and diced
3 artichoke hearts, cooked and cut into quarters
2 large ripe tomatoes, peeled, seeded, and chopped
1 teaspoon paprika
2 cups short-grain or arborio rice
10 saffron threads, lightly toasted and dissolved in 2 cups
    of hot water
about 4½ cups boiling vegetable stock or water
1 cup dry white wine
salt
freshly ground black pepper

Heat the olive oil in a paella pan or large frying pan (about 15 inches in diameter) and cook the onion over moderate heat until it is softened. Add the garlic, parsley, peas, green beans, peppers, artichoke hearts, and tomatoes and cook for 5 minutes. Add the paprika and stir well. Add the rice and cook for 1 or 2 minutes so each grain is well coated. Combine the saffron liquid, stock, and wine and season with salt and black pepper.

Add about one third to the rice and bring to the boil. Cook over gentle heat until it has been absorbed. Add another third and repeat until the rice and vegetables are tender and the liquid is absorbed, adding a little more stock if necessary. Remove from the heat and let stand for 5 to 10 minutes before serving. Serves 4 to 6.

Saffron Couscous

Seksu

If saffron is not available, you can use turmeric instead. Couscous is also very good garnished with toasted almonds or pine nuts, chopped dates, or raisins that have been soaked in hot water and drained.

2 tablespoons butter or ghee
3 shallots, finely chopped
2 cups couscous
¼ teaspoon cinnamon
¼ teaspoon ground coriander
¼ teaspoon ginger
½ teaspoon powdered saffron
2¼ cups boiling water or vegetable broth
salt
freshly ground black pepper
2 tablespoons flat-leaf parsley, finely chopped

Melt the butter in a saucepan and cook the shallots over moderate heat until they are softened. Add the couscous, cinnamon, coriander, and ginger and stir well. Add the saffron dissolved in the boiling water and season with salt and black pepper. Remove from the heat.

Cover with a tight-fitting lid and let stand for 5 to 10 minutes. Fluff up with a fork and serve at once garnished with chopped parsley. Serves 4.

PUMPKIN COUSCOUS

Seksu Kar'a

This dish is spicy and exotic with just a hint of sweetness. Instant couscous makes it very quick and easy to prepare.

PUMPKIN STEW OR SOUP:
3 large carrots
1½ pound piece of pumpkin
3 tablespoons butter
2 medium onions, finely chopped
1 teaspoon ginger
1 teaspoon paprika
½ teaspoon cinnamon
½ teaspoon turmeric
a pinch of powdered saffron
4½ cups hot water
2 tablespoons sugar
¼ cup raisins
½ cup cooked and drained chickpeas
salt
freshly ground black pepper

COUSCOUS:
2 tablespoons butter
3 shallots, thinly sliced
2 cups couscous
salt
freshly ground black pepper
½ teaspoon powdered saffron
2¼ cups boiling water or vegetable broth

Cut the carrots in half lengthwise then cut into 3-inch lengths. Peel the pumpkin, remove the seeds, and cut into 3-inch chunks. Melt the butter in a large saucepan and cook the onions over a gentle heat until they are lightly browned and caramelized. Add the spices and water and bring to a boil. Add the carrots and sugar and simmer for 15 minutes.

Add the pumpkin, raisins, and chickpeas and seasoning to taste. Simmer for a further 15 minutes or until the vegetables are just tender. The stew should be fairly thin—almost a soup. About 10 minutes before the end of cooking, start to prepare the couscous.

Follow the directions for saffron couscous on page 183, omitting the spices. When it is ready to serve, fluff up with a fork and pile onto a large serving dish. Shape into a mound. Remove the cooked vegetables and chickpeas with a slotted spoon and arrange over the top. Serve at once with the soupy sauce on the side. Serves 4.

COUSCOUS WITH PEAS AND CARROTS

Asfuru

This simple dish comes from the Kabylie, the richest agricultural region in Algeria. It is always made with fruity extra virgin olive oil, rather than *smen* (a kind of clarified butter). If you like, you can add a teaspoon or two of sugar to the peas and carrots while they are cooking to bring out their sweetness. *Asfuru* is usually served with a glass of *leben* (a kind of fermented milk) or buttermilk on the side.

½ pound young tender shelled peas, or frozen *petit pois*
½ pound young tender carrots, diced
2¼ cups vegetable broth or water
2 cups couscous
3 tablespoons extra virgin olive oil
salt

Steam the vegetables over boiling water for 15 minutes or until they are tender. Bring the vegetable broth to a boil in a large saucepan. Add the couscous and stir well. Remove from the heat.

Cover with a tight-fitting lid and let stand for 5 to 10 minutes. Fluff up with a fork. Drizzle over the olive oil and season with salt. Transfer to a heated serving dish and shape into a mound. Serve at once. Serves 4.

COUSCOUS WITH SWEET AND HOT PEPPERS

Keksu bil-Filfil

Tunisian couscous is usually flavored with paprika, garlic, and chili, instead of the exotic mix of spices used in Morocco. The couscous grains are often spiced with *bharat*, a subtle mixture of spices made from dried rosebuds (*Rosa damascus*), cinnamon, cloves, and black pepper. Dried rosebuds are available in most Middle Eastern stores and in the herbal tea section of most health stores. If you like your food very spicy, you can garnish the couscous—as they do in Tunisia—with roasted chili peppers.

VEGETABLE STEW OR SOUP:
2 tablespoons extra virgin olive oil
1 medium onion, finely chopped
1 teaspoon paprika
1 teaspoon *harissa*, (see page 124)
1 tablespoon tomato paste, diluted in a little hot water
6 red or green sweet peppers, cored, seeded,
    and cut into quarters
½ cup cooked and drained chickpeas
2 medium potatoes, peeled and quartered
4 cups hot water
salt

GARNISH:
4–6 red chili peppers

COUSCOUS:
2 tablespoons butter or extra virgin olive oil
2 shallots, finely chopped
1 teaspoon *bharat* (see below)
2 cups couscous
2¼ cups boiling water or vegetable broth
salt

To make the vegetable stew, heat the olive oil in a saucepan and cook the onion over moderate heat for 2 minutes. Add the paprika and *harissa* and stir well. Add the diluted tomato paste, peppers, chickpeas, potatoes, and hot water and salt to taste. Bring to a boil and simmer for 20 minutes or until the vegetables are just tender. The stew should be fairly thin, like a soup.

To make the garnish, roast the chili peppers under a hot grill until they are blackened all over. Cut in half lengthwise and remove the core and seeds. Set aside.

About ten minutes before the end of cooking, start to prepare the couscous. Melt the butter in another saucepan and cook the shallots over a moderate heat until they are softened. Add the *bharat* and couscous and stir well. Pour in the boiling water and season with salt. Remove from the heat.

Cover with a tight-fitting lid and let stand for 5 to 10 minutes. Fluff up with a fork and pile onto a heated serving dish. Shape into a mound. Remove the vegetables and chickpeas from the stew with a slotted spoon and arrange over the couscous. Garnish with roasted chili peppers and serve at once with the remaining soupy sauce on the side. Serves 4.

BHARAT
10 dried rosebuds
1 tablespoon cinnamon
2 or 3 cloves
½ teaspoon freshly ground black pepper

Place the ingredients in a mortar and grind with a pestle until they form a fine powder. Store in an airtight jar.

MAIN COURSES

L'appetit est le meilleur des cuisiniers.
Appetite is the best cook.
        —French proverb

Every country around the Mediterranean has a vast repertoire of vegetable dishes that make very good main courses. Centuries of poverty as well as the shortage and expense of meat has led to the creation of a vast array of vegetarian dishes.

Many Mediterranean countries are Roman Catholic where the eating of meat is forbidden on Fridays and during Lent. The Greek Orthodox Church imposes an even larger calendar of feast days including Wednesdays, one week in June to celebrate St. Peter and St. Paul, 15 days in August prior to the Assumption of the Virgin Mary, and the 40 days before Christmas, which is why so many vegetarian dishes— especially pies—are made in Greece.

Virtually the same vegetables grow from one end of the Mediterranean to the other, so it is not surprising that these dishes have much in common. In most Mediterranean countries, eggplants, zucchini, tomatoes, and peppers are combined with eggs, cheese, or béchamel sauce. There is also the same love of stuffing vegetables with rice or bread crumbs, herbs, nuts, and seeds. Each country shares a fondness for savory pastries (often paper-thin) filled with a mixture of cooked vegetables, eggs, and fresh white cheese (ricotta in Italy, feta in Greece, *beyaz peynir* in Turkey, and *Jibneh* in Lebanon and North Africa). Many of the dishes found in the chapter on vegetables also make good main courses if served with some bread and cheese on the side.

Artichoke Parmigiana

Parmigiana di Carciofi

This dish from Campania is must for all artichoke lovers. It consists of fried artichoke bottoms topped with tomato sauce, *Fior di Latte* cheese, and grated Parmesan, and baked in the oven. *Fior di Latte* is a fresh cheese made from cow's milk that is similar to mozzarella. If it is not available, mozzarella may be used instead.

8 or 9 frozen artichoke bottoms, thawed
flour
2 eggs, beaten
vegetable oil for frying
1 recipe Tomato and Basil Sauce (see page 150)
6 ounces mozzarella or *Fior di Latte* cheese
¼ cup freshly grated Parmesan cheese

Dip the artichoke bottoms in flour and then in beaten egg. Fry in hot oil until golden on both sides. Drain on a paper towel. Arrange in the bottom of a well-oiled shallow baking dish and spoon over the tomato sauce.

Top each artichoke bottom with a slice of mozzarella cheese and sprinkle a little grated cheese over the top. Bake in a preheated 350°F oven for 20 minutes or until the cheese is melted and the sauce is bubbling. Serves 3 to 4.

CABBAGE STRUDEL

Savijača s Kupusum

Cabbage strudel makes a very good snack or light main course. As it is fairly low in protein, I like to sprinkle the top liberally with sesame seeds. Or you can serve it as they do in Croatia, with a bowl of yoghurt on the side.

About 6 tablespoons extra virgin olive oil
1 medium onion, finely sliced
1 small green cabbage (about 1½ pounds), shredded
¼ cup pine nuts, lightly toasted in a 300°F oven
¼ cup raisins
salt
freshly ground black pepper
3 sheets filo pastry, (16 x 12 inches), thawed
2 tablespoons sesame seeds

Heat 4 tablespoons of olive oil in a heavy saucepan and add the onion and cabbage. Stir well. Cover, and cook over gentle heat for 20 to 25 minutes, or until the vegetables are tender and starting to turn golden. Add the pine nuts and raisins and season with salt and black pepper. Set aside to cool.

Cover the work surface or table with a clean cloth. Lay a sheet of pastry over the cloth and brush lightly with some of the remaining olive oil. Place another sheet of pastry on top and repeat until all three sheets have been used up. Arrange the cabbage mixture over the third of the pastry closest to you. Carefully pick up the corners of the cloth closest to you and roll over once. Brush the top lightly with olive oil. Lift the cloth again and let the strudel roll over completely.

Brush the top lightly with olive oil. Pick up the cloth and the strudel and very carefully twist onto a well-greased baking sheet. Brush the top lightly with olive oil and sprinkle with sesame seeds. Bake in a preheated 350°F oven for 20 to 25 minutes or until the top is golden. Serve hot. Serves 4.

BAKED CHEESE BOREK

Peynirli Tepsi Börek

Turkish *böreği* (savory pastries) come in all shapes and sizes. They are usually made with *yufka* (a paper-thin pastry similar to filo), but some *böreği* are made with flaky or puff pastry. This *börek* is very light and puffy and makes a very good main course or snack served with a cup of tea or coffee. If *beyaz peynir* is unavailable, feta cheese may be used instead.

FILLING:
1½ cups *beyaz peynir* or feta cheese, crumbled
a handful of flat-leaf parsley, finely chopped
a handful of fresh mint leaves, finely chopped
a handful of fresh dill, finely chopped
2 eggs, lightly beaten
freshly ground black pepper
12 sheets filo pastry, about 12 x 16 inches, or *yufka*

COATING FOR THE PASTRY:
¾ cup yoghurt
6 tablespoons melted butter
2 eggs, lightly beaten

To make the filling, place the feta cheese in a mixing bowl and mash with a fork. Add the herbs and eggs and blend well. Season with black pepper. To make the coating mixture, combine the yoghurt, melted butter, and eggs in a bowl and mix well.

Place one sheet of the filo pastry over the bottom of a well-oiled baking dish and brush lightly with the coating mixture. Place another sheet of filo pastry on top and repeat until 4 sheets of pastry have been used. Pour half of the cheese filling over the top, making sure the whole surface is covered. Place a sheet of filo pastry over the top and brush lightly with the coating mixture.

Repeat until another 4 sheets of pastry have been used. Pour the remaining cheese filling over the top, making sure the whole surface is covered. Place a sheet of filo pastry on top and brush lightly with the coating mixture. Repeat until all the ingredients have been used up, ending with a generous layer of coating mixture. Bake in a preheated 350°F oven for 30 minutes or until the top is golden. Serve hot or cold. Serves 4 to 6.

Mallorcan Eggplant Mould

Granada d'Auberginies

This light pudding is made with a mixture of fried eggplant, tomatoes, and egg, topped with bread crumbs and baked in the oven. It is usually served with light tomato sauce, but it is also very good on its own.

2 large eggplants, about 1½ pounds
about ½ cup extra virgin olive oil
1 medium onion, finely chopped
1 pound ripe plum tomatoes, peeled, seeded, and chopped
2 tablespoons flat-leaf parsley, finely chopped
1 tablespoon fresh marjoram
3 eggs, lightly beaten
salt
freshly ground black pepper
about ½ cup dry bread crumbs

Peel the eggplants and dice them into ½-inch pieces. Heat ⅓ cup olive oil in a large frying pan and cook the onion over moderate heat until it is softened. Add the eggplants and stir well so they are well coated in oil. Cover and cook over a gentle heat for 10 minutes or until they are tender and starting to turn golden, stirring from time to time so the vegetables cook evenly.

Add the tomato and herbs and cook, uncovered, for another 10 minutes or until the sauce starts to thicken. Set aside to cool slightly. Transfer to a mixing bowl and add the eggs. Mix well and season to taste with salt and black pepper.

Grease a shallow baking dish and dust with bread crumbs. Pour in the eggplant mixture and sprinkle the remaining bread crumbs over the top. Dribble over the remaining olive oil. Bake in a preheated 375°F oven for 15 to 20 minutes, or until the top is golden. Serve hot or at room temperature. Serves 4.

EGGPLANT CAPONATA PIE

Pasticcio di Caponata

Eggplant *caponata* is usually served in Sicily as an antipasto, but it can also be made into a very tasty pie. Sometimes 1 or 2 chopped hard-boiled eggs are added instead of the pine nuts. It is usually served at room temperature.

SHORT-CRUST PASTRY:
3 cups whole-wheat pastry flour
½ teaspoon salt
6 ounces chilled, unsalted butter, cut into small cubes
3 or 4 tablespoons (or more) chilled white wine or water

FILLING:
2 large eggplants, about 1½ pounds
about ½ cup extra virgin olive oil
1 small onion, finely chopped
2 celery stalks, finely diced
1 cup canned plum tomatoes, peeled, seeded, and chopped
¼ cup green olives, pitted and sliced
¼ cup capers
¼ cup raisins
¼ cup pine nuts, lightly toasted in a 325°F oven
5 tablespoons red-wine vinegar
salt
freshly ground black pepper

To make the pastry, sift the flour and salt into a mixing bowl. Add the butter and rub in the flour with your fingertips until the mixture resembles coarse bread crumbs. Sprinkle over the wine. Work very quickly with your hand to form a soft ball, adding a little more wine if necessary. Wrap the dough in wax paper and set in a cool place for 1 to 2 hours before using.

To make the filling, dice the eggplants, unpeeled, into half-inch pieces. Heat ⅓ cup olive oil in a large frying pan and add the eggplants. Stir well so they are coated in oil. Cover and cook over gentle heat for 10 minutes or until they start to turn golden, stirring from time to time so they cook evenly.

Heat the remaining olive oil in another pan and cook the onion and celery over moderate heat until they are softened. Add the tomatoes and continue to cook, uncovered, for 8 to 10 minutes or until the sauce starts to thicken. Add the eggplant, olives, capers, raisins, and pine nuts and stir in the vinegar. Season with salt and black pepper. Simmer for 8 to 10 minutes to blend the flavors. Set aside to cool.

Meanwhile place the dough on a lightly floured work surface. Knead it briefly and divide into 2 parts, one slightly larger than the other. Roll the larger part into a circle about 12 inches in diameter. Carefully roll the dough around the rolling pine and unroll it onto a well-oiled flan case. Trim away any excess dough. Prick with a fork and pour in the *caponata* filling.

For the top crust, roll out the remaining dough into a circle about 11 inches in diameter. Place on top of the pie and trim away any excess dough. Press around the edges with your fingertips the top seal in the filling. Cut a few slits in the top to allow any steam to escape during baking. Bake in a preheated 375°F oven for 45 minutes or until the top is golden. Serve at room temperature. Serves 4.

BAKED EGGPLANT WITH TOMATOES AND FETA

Melitzanes Fournou me Tyri

This is the Greek version of Italy's well-known pie—*parmigiana di melanzane*. It is made with feta instead of mozzarella, which gives it a slightly different texture and taste.

2 pounds eggplants
salt
extra virgin olive oil for frying
1 recipe Tomato and Onion sauce (see page 143)
½ pound feta cheese, crumbled
½ cup freshly grated Kefalotyri or Parmesan cheese

Trim the ends of the eggplants, but do not peel them. Cut lengthwise into slices quarter-inch thick and sprinkle with salt. Set in a colander for 1 hour to release the bitter juices. Wash off the salt and pat dry with paper towels. Fry in hot olive oil until golden on both sides. Arrange one third of the eggplant slices in the bottom of a well-oiled shallow baking dish and cover with one third of the tomato sauce and top with one third of the feta cheese.

Sprinkle over one third of the grated cheese. Repeat the layers, ending with the feta cheese and the remaining grated cheese. Bake in a preheated 350°F oven for 30 minutes or until the top is golden and the sauce is bubbling. Serves 4.

COILED EGGPLANT AND CHEESE PASTRY

Tsaïzika

Tsaïzika is a Sephardic Jewish specialty from Larissa in central Greece, where it is traditionally served for the Sabbath dinner or lunch. Similar pastries are also found in various Jewish communities in Turkey, where they are called *kol boreği*. Tsaïzika is usually made into small individual coiled pastries, but one large pastry is much quicker and easier to prepare. Commercial filo, or *phyllo*, pastry is available in most Greek, Turkish, or Middle Eastern stores. It can be bought fresh or frozen. If you are using frozen filo pastry, it should be thawed in the refrigerator for about 2 hours before using.

FILLING:
2 medium eggplants, about 1½ pounds
2 tablespoons extra virgin olive oil
¾ cup feta cheese, crumbled
½ cup grated Kefalotyri or Parmesan cheese
2 eggs
a grating of nutmeg
salt
freshly ground black pepper

4 large sheets filo pastry, about 16 x 12 inches
3–4 tablespoons extra virgin olive oil

To make the filling, roast the eggplants under a hot grill until the skins are blackened all over and the flesh is tender. When they are cool enough to handle, scoop out the flesh. If a little of the blackened skin is mixed in, it only adds to the flavor. Place the flesh in a bowl and mash with a fork. Add the olive oil and mix well. Mash the feta cheese with a fork and add to the eggplant mixture together with the grated cheese and the eggs. Blend well and season with nutmeg, salt, and black pepper.

Place one sheet of filo pastry on a clean tea towel and brush lightly with olive oil. Cover with a second sheet of filo pastry and brush with oil. Place a quarter of the filling along the length of the pastry sheet nearest to you about 1 inch from the edge. Shape the filling into a long roll about 1½ inches thick. Fold over the edges to the right and left to seal the sides, then roll the pastry up like a log or strudel. Twist the log into a tight coil and place in the centre of a well-oiled baking sheet. Repeat with a second roll of pastry in the same way. Place the pastry rolls end to end and continue to roll it up like a snake, enlarging the pastry as you go. Brush the top with the remaining olive oil; and bake in a preheated 350°F oven for 30 minutes or until the top is golden. Serve hot or at room temperature. Serves 4 to 6.

NEAPOLITAN STUFFED EGGPLANT

Melanzane Ripiene alla Napoletana

Any book on Mediterranean cooking would be incomplete without at least one recipe for stuffed eggplants. This one from Naples is one of my favorites. The addition of olives and capers gives the stuffing a delicious flavor that contrasts nicely with the blandness of the mozzarella cheese.

4 small eggplants, about ½ pound each
about 6 tablespoons extra virgin olive oil
2 garlic cloves, finely chopped
a handful of flat-leaf parsley, finely chopped
1 tablespoon torn basil leaves
3 ripe plum tomatoes, peeled, seeded, and chopped
½ cup black Gaeta olives, pitted and slice
¼ cup capers
1 cup soft bread crumbs
salt
freshly ground black pepper
½ pound mozzarella cheese, thinly sliced
½ cup freshly grated Parmesan cheese

Place the eggplant in a saucepan of boiling water. Cover and simmer for 5 minutes. Remove and cut in half lengthwise. Scoop out the flesh, taking care not to damage the skins, to leave a shell about ⅛-inch thick. Chop the pulp coarsely. Heat the olive oil in a large frying pan and cook the garlic and herbs over moderate heat for 2 minutes. Add the chopped eggplants and stir well.

Cover and cook over gentle heat for 10 minutes or until they are tender and starting to turn golden, stirring from time to time so they cook evenly. Add the tomatoes, olives, and capers and continue to cook, uncovered, for 5 more minutes. Remove from the heat and stir in the bread crumbs. Season with salt and black pepper and mix well. Fill the eggplant shells with the mixture.

Top with slices of mozzarella cheese and sprinkle over a little grated cheese. Bake in a preheated 350°F oven for 30 minutes or until the tops are golden. Serve at once. Serves 4.

Mixed Greens Pie with Pine Nuts and Raisins

Torta d'Erbe, Pinoli e Uvetta

This *torta* or pie from Liguria is made with a mixture of herbs and greens such as spinach, borage, nettles, Swiss chard, beet greens, watercress, parsley, sorrel, or rocket. You can make up your own combination. *Quagliata,* or *prescinsena* as it is sometimes called, is a fresh cheese made in Liguria from cow's milk. If it is unavailable, ricotta may be used instead. The dough used for *torte* is very similar to the dough used for filo pastry, but it is not rolled out so thinly. If you like, you can use fresh or thawed filo pastry instead. In general 3 or 4 sheets of filo pastry is sufficient for the base and 3 or 4 sheets for the top.

PASTRY FOR TORTE:
2 cups unbleached pastry flour
½ teaspoon salt
2 tablespoons extra virgin olive oil
about ½ cup water or more

FILLING:
4 tablespoons extra virgin olive oil
1 pound mixed greens and herbs
¾ cup ricotta or *quagliata* cheese
2 eggs plus 1 yolk
¼ cup freshly grated Parmesan cheese
2 tablespoons raisins
2 tablespoons pine nuts, lightly toasted in a 300°F oven
1 tablespoon sugar
a grating of nutmeg
salt
freshly ground black pepper

To make the pastry, place the flour and salt in a mixing bowl and make a well in the center. Add the olive oil and enough water to make a smooth, elastic dough. The exact amount of water will depend on the absorbency of the flour. Shape the dough into 2 balls, one slightly larger than the other. Wrap in wax paper and let rest 1–2 hours in a cool place.

To make the filling, heat 3 tablespoons olive oil in a large saucepan and cook the greens and herbs over a moderate heat for 5 minutes or until they are tender. The water clinging to the leaves is sufficient to prevent scorching. Drain, squeeze dry, and chop coarsely. In a bowl, combine the ricotta, eggs, Parmesan cheese, raisins, pine nuts, and sugar. Mix well. Add the chopped greens and herbs and season with nutmeg, salt, and black pepper.

Roll the dough out into 2 circles about one-sixteenth of an inch thick. Place the larger circle over the bottom of a well-oiled baking sheet about 12 inches in diameter. Spread the filling over the top. Cover with the second sheet of dough. Press around the edges with your fingertip to seal in the filling. Brush the top lightly with the remaining olive oil and bake in a preheated 350°F oven for 30 minutes or until the top is golden. Serve hot. Serves 4 to 6.

LEEK PIE WITH OLIVES

Prassopita me Elies

There are many versions of *prassopita* in Greece. This one is made with béchamel sauce and black olives, which gives it a delicious savory flavor. I like to use Amfissa olives which have a slightly sweet taste, but any other black olives may be used instead.

FILLING:
3 pounds leeks, including the dark green tops
4 tablespoons extra virgin olive oil
1½ cups béchamel sauce, see page 213
½ cup grated Kefalotyri or Parmesan cheese
2 eggs plus 1 yolk
½ cup Amfissa or any other black olives, pitted and sliced
a grating of nutmeg
salt
freshly ground black pepper

½ pound filo pastry, thawed
about ⅓ cup extra virgin olive oil
2–3 tablespoons sesame seeds

To make the filling, trim the ends of the leeks and cut in half lengthwise. Wash carefully and remove any grit that collects between the leaves. Cut into 1-inch lengths. Heat the olive oil in a large saucepan and add the leeks. Cover and cook over moderate heat for 15 to 20 minutes, or until they are tender and starting to turn golden. Meanwhile prepare the béchamel sauce. Remove from the heat and set aside to cool slightly. Transfer to a mixing bowl and stir in the grated cheese, eggs, egg yolk, leeks, and olives. Season with nutmeg, salt, and black pepper.

Place a sheet of filo pastry over the bottom of a well-oiled baking dish and brush lightly with olive oil. Repeat until two-thirds of the pastry is used up. Spread the filling over the top. Place another sheet of pastry over the filling and brush lightly with oil. Repeat until all the pastry is used up. Brush the top lightly with oil and sprinkle over the sesame seeds. Bake in a preheated 350°F oven for 30 minutes or until the top is golden. Serve hot or at room temperature. Serves 6 to 8.

MUSHROOM CUTLETS

Cotolette di Funghi

This dish comes from the Veneto where it is usually made with porcini or *ovoli* mushrooms, but it is also very good with large field mushrooms. The cutlets consist of slices of Fontina cheese sandwiched between two mushroom caps that are dipped in batter and deep-fried. They are usually served with fried potatoes and a glass of red wine on the side.

16 large field mushrooms
about ½ pound fontina cheese
2–3 eggs, lightly beaten
salt
freshly ground black pepper
dry bread crumbs
oil for deep frying

Remove the caps from the mushrooms. Wash them carefully and wipe dry. Cut the cheese into slices about the same size as the mushrooms.

Place each slice between two mushroom caps. Dip in beaten egg, then bread crumbs, and deep-fry until golden on both sides. Drain on paper towels and sprinkle with a little salt and pepper. Serve hot. Serves 4 to 6.

Provençal Onion Quiche

Quiche Provençale

This creamy onion tart is delicately flavored with tomatoes and herbs. If you like, you can use half yoghurt and half single cream instead of the crème fraîche.

SHORTCRUST PASTRY:
1¾ cup unbleached pastry flour
¼ teaspoon salt
¼ pound chilled butter, cut into small cubes
1 egg yolk
1–2 tablespoons iced water

FILLING:
4 tablespoons extra virgin olive oil
1½ pounds onions, thinly sliced
3 garlic cloves, finely chopped
2 tablespoons flat-leaf parsley, finely chopped
1 bay leaf
a pinch of thyme
2 ripe plum tomatoes, peeled, seeded, and chopped
2 eggs
1 cup crème fraiche
salt
freshly ground black pepper

To make the pastry, sift the flour and salt in a mixing bowl. Add the butter and rub in the flour with your fingertips until the mixture resembles coarse bread crumbs. Add the egg yolk mixed with 1 tablespoon of iced water and sprinkle over the mixture. Work very quickly with your hand to form a soft ball, adding a little more water if necessary. Wrap the dough in wax paper and set in a cool place for 1 to 2 hours before using.

Place the dough on a lightly floured work surface and knead it briefly. Roll into a circle about 12 inches in diameter and eight of an inch thick. Carefully roll the dough around the rolling pin and unroll it onto a well-buttered 8- to 10-inch pie dish. Trim away any excess dough and flute the edges with a fork. Prick the bottom with a fork in a few places.

Cover the dough with a sheet of foil and fill with dried beans—this prevents the pastry from puffing up while baking. To partially bake the flan case, preheat the oven to 400°F and bake the pastry for 8 to 10 minutes. The pastry should have slightly shrunk away from the case. Take out of the oven and remove the tin foil and dried beans.

To make the filling, heat the olive oil in a large frying pan and cook the onions, garlic, and herbs over a gentle heat for 25 to 30 minutes, or until the onions are very soft and starting to turn golden. Add the tomatoes and season with salt and black pepper. Cook for 5 more minutes. Set aside to cool. Beat the eggs with the crème fraiche and add to the onion mixture. Pour into the partially baked flan case and bake in a preheated 375°F oven for 30 minutes or until the top is golden. Serve hot. Serves 4 to 6.

GRANDMOTHER'S LITTLE BUNDLES
Fagottini della Nonna

Fagottini (little bundles) are sweet or savory stuffed pancakes. In this recipe, they are filled with spinach and ricotta, topped with tomato sauce and grated cheese, and gratinéed in the oven.

PANCAKE BATTER:
1½ cups unbleached white flour
a pinch of salt
3 eggs
about 2 cups milk (or half milk, half water)
2 tablespoons extra virgin olive oil

FILLING:
¼ pound spinach
1 cup ricotta
1 egg
¼ cup freshly grated Parmesan cheese
a grating of nutmeg
salt
freshly ground black pepper

1 recipe Tomato and Basil Sauce, see page 150
¼ cup freshly grated Parmesan cheese

To make the pancakes, place the flour and salt in a bowl. Make a well in the center and drop in the eggs. Gradually add the milk, beating constantly, to form a batter the consistency of single cream. Allow to stand for 30 minutes before using.

Heat a little olive oil in a 6-inch heavy frying pan. When it is hot, pour in 2½ to 3 tablespoons batter. Quickly tilt the pan in all directions so the batter evenly covers the pan. Cook for about 1 minute on each side. Set aside and repeat until all the pancake batter is used up.

To make the filling, wash the spinach carefully and cook in a covered saucepan for 5 minutes or until tender. The water clinging to the leaves is sufficient to prevent scorching. Drain and chop coarsely. Set aside to cool.

Combine the ricotta, egg, and grated cheese in a bowl. Add the chopped spinach. Blend well. Season with nutmeg, salt, and black pepper. Spoon a little filling into the centre of each pancake and roll them up. Arrange the pancakes in a single layer in a well-greased shallow baking dish. Spoon over the Tomato and Basil Sauce and sprinkle the grated cheese over the top. Baked in a preheated 400°F oven for 15 minutes or until the pancakes are heated through and the cheese is melted. Serve hot. Serves 4 to 5.

LEBANESE STUFFED PEPPERS IN OLIVE OIL
Mehshi Flehfleh bil-Zeit

In Lebanon, vegetables cooked *bil-zeit* (in olive oil) are always made without meat. The stuffing usually contains split chickpeas, which have been soaked overnight and skinned. I prefer to use cooked and drained chickpeas, which have a much softer consistency. Sumac is a brownish purple spice with a tangy, lemony flavor that is widely used in cooking throughout the Middle East.

8 red, green, or yellow peppers
¾ cup long-grain rice
½ cup cooked and drained chickpeas
½ pound ripe tomatoes, peeled, seeded, and chopped
3 green onions, thinly sliced
½ cup flat-leaf parsley, finely chopped
½ cup fresh mint leaves, finely chopped
2 teaspoons sumac
½ teaspoon cinnamon
½ teaspoon allspice
juice of ½ lemon
⅔ cup extra virgin olive oil
salt
freshly ground black pepper

Slice the tops off the peppers and reserve. Remove the pith and seeds. To make the stuffing, wash the rice thoroughly and drain well. Place in a mixing bowl with the chickpeas, tomatoes, onions, herbs, and spices. Pour in the lemon juice and ½ cup olive oil and mix well. Season with salt and black pepper. Stuff the peppers three-quarters full with the mixture, leaving enough room for the rice to swell during cooking. Place the reserved caps on top.

Arrange side by side in a saucepan large enough to hold the peppers in one layer. Pack them tightly so they remain upright during cooking. Pour in enough hot water to come within 1½ inches of the tops of the peppers. Bring to a boil. Cover and simmer for 40 to 50 minutes or until the rice is tender and the peppers are soft. Set aside to cool slightly. Arrange on a serving dish and serve hot or at room temperature. Serves 4.

POTATO TORTINO
Tortino di Patate

A *tortino* is a kind of pie that is usually made without pastry. They are always made with chopped or puréed vegetables and make a very good light lunch or supper dish. This one from Naples is made with mashed potatoes, eggs, mozzarella, and Parmesan cheese.

2 pounds potatoes
6 tablespoons butter
2 large eggs
about ¼ cup milk
a grating of nutmeg
salt
freshly ground black pepper
6 ounces mozzarella cheese, sliced
⅓ cup freshly grated Parmesan cheese

Cook the potatoes in lightly salted boiling water for 20 minutes or until they are tender. Drain and peel when they are cool enough to handle. Force through a sieve into a mixing bowl and add 4 tablespoons butter, the eggs, and milk. Mix well and season with nutmeg, salt, and black pepper. The mixture should be fairly soft.

Grease a baking dish with the remaining butter and dust with half of the Parmesan cheese. Pour in half of the potato mixture and cover with slices of mozzarella. Pour in the remaining potato mixture and sprinkle the remaining Parmesan cheese. Bake in a preheated 350°F oven for 30 minutes or until the top is nicely browned. Serve hot. Serves 4.

POTATO LATKES

Latkes

Potato *latkes* or pancakes are one of the best known and delicious of Jewish specialties. Traditionally they were served for Channukah (the Festival of Lights) but today they are made in Israel throughout the year. They can be served as an appetizer, snack, or main course. Some cooks add a tablespoon or two of flour with the eggs.

1½ pounds potatoes
1 medium onion, finely grated
2 eggs, lightly beaten
salt
freshly ground black pepper
olive oil for frying

Peel the potatoes and grate them finely. Place them in a mixing bowl with the onions. Add the eggs and mix well. Season with salt and black pepper. Heat a thin layer of olive oil in the bottom of a heavy frying pan. Drop two or three heaping tablespoonfuls of the mixture at a time into the hot oil and flatten with a fork.

Cook over gentle heat until they are golden on both sides. Serve hot. Serves 4.

POTATO AND EGGPLANT MOUSSAKAS

Moussakas me Melitzanes me Patates

Moussakas is one of Greece's most famous dishes. It usually includes meat, but there are also many vegetarian versions. This one, made with eggplant and potatoes, is especially good. For a variation, you can substitute zucchini for the eggplants.

2 large eggplants, about 1½ pounds
salt
extra virgin olive oil for frying
1 pound waxy potatoes
1 large onion, chopped
1 tablespoon fresh oregano
1 pound ripe plum tomatoes, peeled, seeded, and chopped
¾ cup grated Kefalotyri or Pecorino cheese
6 tablespoons butter
4 tablespoons flour
2½ cups hot milk
a grating of nutmeg
salt
freshly ground black pepper
2 egg yolks

Trim the ends of the eggplants and cut into quarter-inch thick slices. Sprinkle with salt and set in a colander for 1 hour to release the bitter juices. Wash off the salt and pat dry with a paper towel. Shallow-fry in hot oil until golden on both sides. Drain on paper towels. Meanwhile cook the potatoes in plenty of lightly salted water for 20 minutes or until they are tender. When they are cool enough to handle, peel and slice fairly thinly.

Heat 3 tablespoons olive oil in a large frying pan and cook the onion over moderate heat until it is softened. Add the oregano and cook for 2 more minutes. Add the tomatoes and continue to cook for about 10 minutes or until the sauce starts to thicken. Set aside. Melt 4 tablespoons butter in a heavy saucepan and stir in the flour. Cook for 1 minute without browning.

Pour in a little hot milk and stir vigorously with a wooden spoon over moderate heat, until the mixture is free from lumps. Gradually add a little more milk until all the milk is incorporated and the sauce is very smooth and creamy. Season with nutmeg, salt, and black pepper. Simmer for 2 or 3 more minutes. Set aside to cool slightly. Add the egg yolks and blend well.

Arrange about one-third of the potatoes over the bottom of a well-oiled shallow baking dish. Cover with a third of the fried eggplant. Spoon over about one-third of the tomato and onion sauce and sprinkle with grated cheese. Repeat the layers ending with a layer of tomato and onion sauce and grated cheese. Pour the béchamel sauce over the top and sprinkle over the remaining grated cheese. Dot with the remaining butter. Bake in a preheated 350°F oven for 35 to 40 minutes or until the top is golden and the sauce is bubbling. Serve hot. Serves 4 to 6.

BECHAMEL SAUCE:
4 tablespoons butter
4 tablespoons milk
2½ cups hot milk
a grating of nutmeg
salt
freshly ground black pepper

Melt 4 tablespoons butter in a heavy saucepan and stir in the flour. Cook for 1 minute without browning. Pour in a little hot milk and stir vigorously with a wooden spoon over a moderate heat, until the mixture is free of lumps. Gradually add a little more milk until all the milk in incorporated and the sauce is very smooth and creamy. Season with nutmeg, salt and black pepper. Simmer for 2 to 3 more minutes.

POTATO KIBBEH BALLS
Kibbeh Batata

Vegetarian *kibbeh* are usually made with potatoes, pumpkin, or lentils and a mixture of *burghul*, nuts, herbs, and spices. They can prepared in numerous ways—boiled, baked, grilled, fried, or eaten raw. In this recipe, they are made into torpedo-shaped balls, stuffed with an onion and pine nut filling, flavored with pomegranate syrup, and deep-fried. Pomegranate syrup is made from the juice of sour pomegranates. It is highly prized in the Middle East for its sweet and sour flavor. If it is unavailable, you can use 1 or 2 teaspoons of lemon juice instead.

1 pound floury potatoes
½ cup fine *burghul* (cracked wheat)
¼ cup flour
1 tablespoon fresh basil, finely chopped
¼ teaspoon allspice
¼ teaspoon cinnamon
a grating of nutmeg
salt
freshly ground black pepper
oil for deep frying
1 to 2 lemons, cut into wedges, for serving

FILLING:
2 tablespoons extra virgin olive oil
1 medium onion, chopped
3 tablespoons pine nuts
1 teaspoon pomegranate syrup
pinch of cinnamon
pinch of allspice
salt
freshly ground black pepper

To make the *kibbeh*, soak the cracked wheat in a bowl of cold water for 15 minutes. Rinse thoroughly under cold water and drain well.

Boil the potatoes in plenty of lightly salted water for 20 minutes or until they are tender. Drain and remove the skins when they are cool enough to handle. Place in a mixing bowl and mash with a potato ricer. Add the cracked wheat, flour, basil, and spices and mix well. Season with salt and black pepper. Set aside.

To make the filling, heat the olive oil in a small frying pan and cook the onion over moderate heat until it is lightly browned. Add the pine nuts and cook until they start to turn golden. Stir in the pomegranate syrup and spices and season with salt and black pepper. Cook for 1 or 2 more minutes.

Moisten your hands with cold water and shape the potato mixture into balls the size of an egg. With your index finger, punch a hole into the top end of each ball. Place a teaspoonful of the filling into the hole, then seal shut with your fingers. Carefully shape the balls into a torpedo shape and deep fry in hot oil until golden. Serve hot with lemon wedges on the side. Serves 4.

POTATO AND SPINACH RISSOLES

Qofte Patatesh me Spinaq

These little rissoles are light and delicious. They are usually made with *djathë* (a fresh white cheese similar to Turkish *beyaz peynir* or Greek feta).

¼ pound spinach
1 pound floury potatoes
1 egg
1 cup grated feta cheese
salt
freshly ground black pepper
flour
extra virgin olive oil

Wash the spinach carefully and cook in a covered pan for 5 minutes or until it is tender. Squeeze dry and chop finely.

Cook the potatoes in lightly salted boiling water for 20 minutes or until they are tender. Drain and peel when they are cool enough to handle. Force through a sieve into a mixing bowl.

Add the eggs, cheese, and spinach and blend well. Season with salt and black pepper. Refrigerate for 1 hour. Shape into small rissoles about 1½ inches in diameter. Flatten them slightly and dredge in flour. Heat a little olive oil in the bottom of a heavy frying pan and fry the rissoles, in batches, until they are golden on both sides. Drain on paper towels. Serve hot. Serves 4 to 6.

Provençal Pumpkin Tian
Lou Tian de Cougourdo

All kinds of vegetables are made into *tians* in Provence, especially eggplants, spinach, artichokes, zucchini, and pumpkin. A *tian* is named after the shallow earthenware dish in which it is cooked. Like its relative, the gratin, the *tian* is usually topped with bread crumbs or grated cheese and baked in the oven until the top is nicely browned.

1 pumpkin, about 2 pounds
½ pound spinach
5 tablespoons extra virgin olive oil
2 medium onions, finely chopped
2 garlic cloves, finely chopped
2 tablespoons flat-leaf parsley, finely chopped
¼ cup arborio or short-grain rice
3 eggs, lightly beaten
⅓ cup freshly grated Parmesan cheese
a grating of nutmeg
salt
freshly ground black pepper

Peel the pumpkin, cut in half, and remove the seeds. Cut into cubes and steam for about 20 minutes, or until tender. Drain and purée in a food processor. Transfer to a mixing bowl. Wash the spinach carefully and cook in a covered saucepan for 5 minutes or until it is tender. Drain and chop finely. Stir into the pumpkin purée.

Heat 3 tablespoons olive oil in a heavy frying pan and cook the onions over a moderate heat until they are translucent. Add the garlic and parsley and cook for another 2 or 3 minutes. Add the pumpkin mixture and blend well.

Meanwhile, cook the rice in plenty of lightly salted boiling water for 10 to 15 minutes or until it is almost tender. Rinse under cold water to remove the starch. Add to the mixture together with the eggs and ¼ cup freshly grated Parmesan cheese. Blend well and season with nutmeg, salt, and black pepper. Pour into a well-oiled shallow baking dish and sprinkle the remaining grated cheese over the top. Dribble over the remaining olive oil. Bake in a preheated 350°F oven for 35 to 40 minutes or until the top is golden. Serve hot. Serves 4 to 6.

PUMPKIN AND MUSHROOM TORTINO
Tortino di Zucca

The Italian *zucca* refers to various large squash and gourds as well as pumpkin. They have thick, smooth, or knobby skins and flesh that varies from bright yellow to orangey-red. In Emilia-Romagna, where this recipe comes from, the *zucca* has a deep orange flesh with a slightly sweet flavor.

1 pumpkin, about 2 pounds
4 tablespoons butter
4 tablespoons extra virgin olive oil
½ pound mushrooms, thinly sliced
2 large eggs, lightly beaten
3 tablespoons single cream
¼ cup freshly grated Parmesan cheese
a grating of nutmeg
salt
freshly ground black pepper
about ¾ cup dry bread crumbs

Peel the pumpkin, cut in half, and remove the seeds. Cut into cubes and steam for 20 minutes or until tender. Force through a sieve or purée in a food processor. Transfer to a mixing bowl and add half of the butter. Heat half of the olive oil in a large frying pan and cook the mushrooms over a moderate heat until they are tender. Add to the pumpkin purée together with the eggs, cream, and the Parmesan cheese. Blend well and season with nutmeg, salt, and black pepper.

Grease a shallow baking dish with the remaining butter and dust it with bread crumbs. Pour in the pumpkin mixture and sprinkle the remaining bread crumbs over the top. Dribble over the remaining olive oil. Bake in a preheated 350°F oven for 30 minutes or until the top is nicely browned. Serve hot. Serves 4.

Spinach Pie with Sesame Seeds

Spanakopita me Sousami

Variations of *spanakopita* are made all over Greece. During Lent, the eggs and cheese are usually omitted and the pie is simply filled with spinach, spring onions, and dill. Sometimes a little béchamel sauce is added or a mixture of semolina and cream. On the island of Crete, it is often made with *mizithra* (a kind of cottage cheese made from the whey of goat's milk). In the villages, wild mountain greens such as dandelion, sorrel, or *vlita* (wild amaranth) is often substituted for the spinach, in which case the pie is called *hortopita*. This classic version of spanakopita is topped with sesame seeds, which not only increases the nutritional value, but also enhances the flavor.

2 pounds spinach
3 tablespoons extra virgin olive oil
6 green onions, thinly sliced
a handful of fresh dill, finely chopped
1 cup feta cheese, crumbled
3 eggs
a grating of nutmeg
freshly ground black pepper
½ pound fresh or thawed filo pastry
about 4 tablespoons extra virgin olive oil
4 tablespoons sesame seeds

Wash the spinach carefully and cook in a covered saucepan for 5 minutes or until tender. The water clinging to the leaves is sufficient to prevent scorching. Drain and chop coarsely.

Heat the olive oil in a large frying pan and cook the green onions over a moderate heat until they are softened. Add the spinach and cook gently for 2 or 3 minutes. Set aside to cool.

Mix the feta cheese and eggs together in a bowl. Add the spinach mixture and season with nutmeg and black pepper. There is no need to add any salt as the feta cheese is salty enough.

Brush a large baking dish with oil. Place a sheet of filo pastry over the top and brush lightly with oil. Repeat with two-thirds of the filo pastry. Spread the filling over the top and cover with a sheet of filo pastry. Brush lightly with oil. Repeat until all the filo pastry is used up. Sprinkle the sesame seeds over the top. Bake in a preheated 350°F oven for 35 to 40 minutes or until the top is golden. Serve hot or at room temperature. Serves 6 to 8.

Ligurian Swiss Chard and Potato Pie

Polpettone di Bietole

In other parts of Italy, a *polpettone* is a meat loaf, but in Liguria it is a kind of gratin or pie without pastry. It usually made with puréed vegetables, eggs, Parmesan cheese, and *quagliata* or *prescinsena*, a fresh cheese made from clabbered milk. If it is unavailable, ricotta may be used instead.

1 pound Swiss chard or spinach
3 tablespoons extra virgin olive oil
1 small onion, finely chopped
a handful of flat-leaf parsley, finely chopped
1 tablespoon fresh marjoram
1 pound potatoes
3 large eggs
¼ cup ricotta or *quagliata* cheese
¼ cup freshly grated Parmesan cheese
2 or 3 tablespoons butter
about ½ cup dry bread crumbs

Wash the Swiss chard and remove the stalks. Cook in a covered saucepan over a moderate heat for 5 minutes or until it is tender. Drain and chop finely. Heat the olive oil in a large frying pan and cook the onion over moderate heat until it is translucent. Add the herbs and cook for another 3 or 4 minutes.

Meanwhile, bring the potatoes to boil in lightly salted water for 20 minutes or until they are tender. When they are cool enough to handle, force through a sieve into a mixing bowl. Add the Swiss chard, onion mixture, eggs, ricotta, and Parmesan cheese and mix well. Season with salt and black pepper.

Grease the bottom and sides of a shallow baking dish with butter and dust with bread crumbs. Pour in the Swiss chard mixture and top with the remaining bread crumbs. Dot with the remaining butter. Bake in a preheated 350°F oven for 35 to 40 minutes or until it is nicely puffed and the top is golden. Serves 4 to 6.

VEGETABLE STUFFED PANCAKES
Palacinke Nadjevene Povrćem

The vegetables used for the filling vary according to the season. Tiny peas or green beans in spring, eggplant or zucchini in summer, or a little diced carrot, potato, or celeriac in winter.

PANCAKE BATTER:
1¾ cups flour
pinch of salt
3 eggs
about 1¾ cups milk (or half milk, half water)
2 tablespoons extra virgin olive oil

FILLING:
3 tablespoons extra virgin olive oil
3 garlic cloves, finely chopped
a handful of flat-leaf parsley, finely chopped
½ pound mushrooms, thinly sliced
2 cups fresh shelled peas or frozen *petit pois*

TOPPING:
2 cups béchamel sauce (see page 213)
2 tablespoons sour cream
¼ cup freshly grated Parmesan cheese
2 tablespoons butter

To make the pancakes, follow the directions for pancakes on page 207. To make the filling, heat the olive oil in a large frying pan and cook the garlic over moderate heat for 1 minute. Add the parsley and cook for 2 or 3 more minutes. Add the mushrooms and continue to cook for 8 to 10 minutes or until they are tender and any liquid is evaporated.

Meanwhile bring the peas to a boil in lightly salted water and cook until they are tender. Drain and add to the mushroom mixture. Simmer for 2 or 3 minutes to blend the flavors. Spoon a little filling into the center of each pancake and roll them up. Arrange the pancakes side by side in one layer in the bottom of a well-oiled shallow baking dish.

Prepare the béchamel sauce as directed on page 213, and stir in the sour cream. Pour the sauce over the pancakes and sprinkle over the grated cheese. Dot with butter. Bake in a preheated 400°F oven for 15 minutes or until the pancakes are heated through and the cheese is melted. Serves 4 to 5.

LIGURIAN VEGETABLE TORTA
Torta Di Verdura

Liguria is famous for its wide variety of vegetable *tortes* or pies. This one, which is made with spinach, potatoes, leek, and artichokes, is one of my favorites. The dough for torte is similar to that for filo pastry but it is not rolled out as thinly. If you like, you can use fresh or thawed filo pastry instead, which makes it very quick and easy to prepare.

PASTRY FOR TORTE:
2 cups unbleached white flour
½ teaspoon salt
2 tablespoons extra virgin olive oil
about ½ cup water or more

FILLING:
½ pound spinach
½ pound floury potatoes, peeled and quartered
2 eggs
⅓ cup freshly grated Parmesan cheese
salt
freshly ground black pepper
1 leek, white part only, thinly sliced
4 frozen artichoke hearts, thawed
3 tablespoons extra virgin olive oil

To make the pastry, follow the directions for pastry for *torte* on page 201. To make the filling, wash the spinach and cook in a covered saucepan over moderate heat for 5 minutes or until tender. The water clinging to the leaves is sufficient to prevent scorching. Drain, squeeze dry, and chop coarsely.

Bring the potatoes to a boil in lightly salted water and cook for 20 minutes or until they are tender. Drain and force through a sieve into a mixing bowl. Add the eggs and Parmesan cheese and mix well. Add the chopped spinach and season with salt and black pepper.

Heat 2 tablespoons olive oil in a heavy frying pan and cook the leek over moderate heat until it is softened. Add the artichokes and continue to cook for 8 to 10 minutes or until they start to turn golden.

Set aside to cool slightly, then add to the spinach mixture. Roll the dough out into two circles about one-sixteenth of an inch thick. Place the larger circle over the bottom of a well-oiled shallow baking dish about 12 inches in diameter. Spread the filling over the top and cover with the second sheet of dough. Press around the edges with your fingertips to seal in the filling. Brush the top lightly with the remaining olive oil.

Bake in a preheated 350°F oven for 40 minutes or until the top is golden. Serve hot. Serves 4 to 6.

ZUCCHINI STUFFED WITH SWISS CHARD

Callabacines Rellenos con Acelgas

There are dozens of recipes for stuffed zucchini in Spain. This one from Andalusia makes a very good light main course or you can serve it, as they do in Spain, as a separate course on its own. Manchego is a hard cheese made from ewe's milk that is widely used in Spanish cooking. If it is unavailable, Parmesan may be used instead

6 medium zucchini
½ pound Swiss chard
1 egg
½ cup grated Manchego or Parmesan cheese
a grating of nutmeg
salt
freshly ground black pepper
1 recipe béchamel sauce (see page 213)
2 tablespoons extra virgin olive oil

Trim the ends of the zucchini and cut them in half lengthwise. With an apple corer, scoop out the flesh to leave a shell about one eighth of an inch thick. (Reserve the flesh for a soup or stew). Steam the shells for 8 to 10 minutes or until they are just tender. Set aside.

Wash the Swiss chard and cut away the stalks. Cook in a covered saucepan for 5 minutes or until tender. The water clinging to the leaves is sufficient to prevent scorching. Drain, squeeze dry, and chop coarsely. Set aside to cool slightly. Transfer to a mixing bowl and add the egg and half of the cheese. Season with nutmeg, salt, and black pepper. Stuff the zucchini halves with the mixture.

Arrange in a single layer over the bottom of a well-oiled shallow baking dish. Pour over the béchamel sauce and sprinkle the remaining grated cheese over the top. Dribble over the olive oil. Bake in a preheated 350°F oven for 30 minutes or until the top is golden and the sauce is bubbling. Serves 3 to 4.

ZUCCHINI PIE

Kolokithopita

All kinds of vegetable pies are made in Greece—with spinach, wild greens, onions, leeks, potatoes, eggplant, pumpkin, and zucchini. They make delicious snacks as well as main courses and may be served hot or cold.

FILLING:
2 pounds zucchini
4 tablespoons extra virgin olive oil
1 medium onion, finely chopped
a handful of flat-leaf parsley, finely chopped
a handful of dill, finely chopped
3 eggs, lightly beaten
1 cup feta cheese, crumbled
⅓ cup freshly grated Kefalotyri or Parmesan cheese
freshly ground black pepper

½ pound fresh or thawed filo pastry
about 4 tablespoons extra virgin olive oil

Trim the ends of the zucchini and grate them coarsely.

Heat 4 tablespoons olive oil in a large frying pan and cook the onion over moderate heat until it starts to turn golden. Add the zucchini and continue to cook until they are tender and any liquid is evaporated. Add the parsley and dill and simmer for 2 or 3 more minutes.

Place the feta cheese in a mixing bowl and mash well with a fork. Add the egg and grated cheese and blend well. Stir in the cooked vegetables and season with black pepper. Mix well.

Place a sheet of filo pastry over the bottom of a well-oiled shallow baking dish and brush lightly with olive oil. Repeat until two-thirds of the pastry is used up. Spread the filling over the top. Place another sheet of pastry over the filling and brush lightly with oil. Repeat until all the pastry is used up. Brush the top lightly with oil. Bake in a preheated 350°F oven for 35 to 40 minutes or until the top is golden. Serve hot. Serves 6 to 8.

ZUCCHINI PASTICCIO
Pasticcio di Zucchine

A *pasticcio* is a layered pie, made with or without pastry, which usually contains béchamel sauce and eggs. This *pasticcio* from Trieste consists of layers of fried zucchini, a mixture of béchamel and tomato sauce, mozzarella and Parmesan cheese. It is also very good made with eggplant instead of zucchini.

2 pounds zucchini
flour
olive oil for frying
2 cups Béchamel Sauce (see page 213)
1 cup Tomato and Basil Sauce (see page 150)
½ pound mozzarella cheese
½ cup freshly grated Parmesan cheese

Trim the ends of the zucchini and cut them into slices lengthwise about one eighth of an inch thick. Dust them in flour and fry in hot oil until golden on both sides. Arrange a layer of fried zucchini over the bottom of a well-oiled shallow baking dish.

Combine the béchamel and tomato and basil sauce and mix well. Spoon a little sauce over the zucchini and top with slices of mozzarella. Sprinkle a little grated cheese over the top. Repeat the layers until all the ingredients are used up, finishing with mozzarella and grated cheese. Bake in a preheated 350°F oven for 30 minutes or until the top is golden and the sauce is bubbling. Serve hot. Serves 4.

TURKISH ZUCCHINI AND WHITE CHEESE FRITTERS

Kabak Múcveri

These delicious fritters make a very good light lunch or supper dish served with a salad on the side. If *beyaz peynir* is unavailable, feta cheese may be used instead.

1 pound zucchini
3 tablespoons extra virgin olive oil
2 green onions, thinly sliced
3 eggs
6 tablespoons flour
¾ cup feta cheese or *beyaz peynir*
2 tablespoons fresh mint leaves, finely chopped
2 tablespoons fresh dill, finely chopped
2 tablespoons flat-leaf parsley, finely chopped
salt
freshly ground black pepper
oil for frying

Trim the ends of the zucchini and grate them coarsely. Heat the olive oil in a large frying pan and cook the zucchini and green onions over moderate heat until they start to turn golden. Set aside to cool slightly.

Beat the eggs lightly in a mixing bowl and gradually add the flour to make a smooth batter. Add the cheese and herbs and season with salt and black pepper.

Heat a thin layer of oil in the bottom of a heavy frying pan. Drop heaping tablespoons of the mixture into the hot oil and fry until golden on both sides. Drain on paper towels and serve hot. Serves 4 to 6.

EGGS

On ne fait pas d'omelette, sans casser des oeufs.
You cannot make an omelette without breaking eggs.
—French proverb.

Eggs have been held in high esteem around the Mediterranean since the days of the pharaohs. The Egyptians and the Phoenicians loved ostrich eggs. The Romans preferred to eat the eggs of partridges, pheasants, and chickens, but peacock eggs were considered the greatest delicacy. The Romans cooked eggs in various ways: boiled, pickled, fried, and cooked over hot coals. They also liked *ova mellita*—a dish of eggs baked with honey that was the forerunner of the omelette. In the Middle Ages, eggs were widely eaten in France, Spain, and Italy, where they were often dubbed "the meat of the poor."

Today most countries around the Mediterranean have a vast repertoire of egg dishes, especially scrambled eggs and thick substantial omelettes filled with vegetables. These include the Spanish tortilla, the Italian frittata, the Arab *eggah,* and the North African *chakchouka.* These omelets are very good hot or served cold for a buffet or picnic.

SCRAMBLED EGGS WITH WILD MUSHROOMS

Brouillade aux Cèpes

This classic dish is very popular all over southern France. The secret of making good scrambled eggs is not to overcook them. Some French cooks are so fanatic about obtaining the desired soft, creamy consistency that they cook them in a *bain-marie*, but you can have very good success if you simply stir the eggs constantly with a wooden spoon over very low heat.

½ pound cèpes, or other good quality mushrooms
2 tablespoons butter
6 eggs
2 tablespoons crème fraiche or heavy cream
salt
freshly ground black pepper

Wash the cèpes carefully and wipe dry. Chop them fairly finely. Heat the butter in a heavy frying pan and add the cèpes. Cook over a gentle heat until they are tender. Beat the eggs with the crème fraîche in a bowl. Season with salt and black pepper.

Pour over the cepes and cook over gentle heat, stirring constantly with a wooden spoon until the eggs have a creamy consistency. Serve at once. Serves 3 to 4.

SCRAMBLED EGGS
WITH ARTICHOKES
Imbrogliata di Carciofi

Scrambled eggs with artichokes are also very popular in southern France and Spain. In this recipe from Liguria, the dish is delicately flavored with garlic, parsley, and Parmesan cheese. Frozen artichoke bottoms make it very quick and easy to prepare.

4 tablespoons extra virgin olive oil
5 frozen artichoke bottoms, thawed and thinly sliced
2 garlic cloves, finely chopped
2 tablespoons flat-leaf parsley, finely chopped
4 eggs
¼ cup freshly grated Parmesan cheese

Heat the olive oil in a heavy frying pan and cook the artichokes bottoms over moderate heat until they start to turn golden. Add the garlic and parsley and cook for a further 2 or 3 minutes.

Meanwhile beat the eggs in a bowl and add the Parmesan cheese. Mix well and season with salt and black pepper. Pour the egg mixture over the artichokes. Cook, stirring constantly with a wooden spoon, over gentle heat until the eggs have reached a creamy consistency. Serve at once. Serves 2 to 3.

Scrambled Eggs with Tomatoes

Strapasada

Variations of *strapasada* are made all over the Ionian Islands. This recipe comes from Corfu where it is usually flavored with basil or oregano and a little grated cheese. On the island of Zakynthos, they like to add garlic. Sometimes a little finely chopped fresh chili pepper is added, in which case the cheese is usually omitted.

2 tablespoons extra virgin olive oil
4 eggs
2 tablespoons torn basil leaves
¼ cup grated Kefalotyri or Parmesan cheese
½ pound ripe tomatoes, peeled, seeded, and chopped
salt
freshly ground black pepper

Heat the olive oil in a heavy frying pan and add the tomatoes. Cook over a moderate heat for 8 to 10 minutes or until the sauce is thickened. Beat the eggs in a bowl and add the basil and cheese. Mix well and season with salt and black pepper.

Pour the egg mixture over the tomatoes. Cook over gentle heat, stirring constantly with a wooden spoon until the eggs have a creamy consistency. Serve at once. Serves 2.

SCRAMBLED EGGS WITH SPINACH

Revuelto de Espinaka

Scrambled eggs with spinach are especially smooth and creamy. In Spain, they are usually served on top of slices of bread fried in olive oil.

2 pounds spinach
2 tablespoons extra virgin olive oil
3 tablespoons heavy cream
a grating of nutmeg
salt
freshly ground black pepper

Wash the spinach carefully and cook in a covered saucepan over moderate heat for 5 to 7 minutes or until it is tender. The water clinging to the leaves is sufficient to prevent scorching. Drain, squeeze dry, and chop finely. Set aside to cool.

Beat the eggs lightly in a bowl and add the cream. Season with nutmeg, salt, and black pepper. Stir in the chopped spinach. Heat the olive oil in a heavy frying pan and pour in the egg mixture. Cook over a gentle heat, stirring constantly with a wooden spoon until the eggs have reached a creamy consistency. Serve at once. Serves 4.

Scrambled Eggs with Peppers, Tomatoes, and White Cheese

Menemen

Menemen is prepared in most bus and train stations throughout Turkey. It is usually made with long green tapering peppers called *sivri biber* that can vary from mild to hot, but a combination of bell peppers and chili peppers is equally good.

2 tablespoons extra virgin olive oil
1 green bell pepper or 2 *sivri biber,* cored, seeded, and
finely sliced
1 green chili pepper, cored, seeded, and finely chopped
3 ripe tomatoes, peeled, seeded, and chopped
4 eggs
¼ cup feta cheese or *beyaz peynir,* crumbled
salt
freshly ground black pepper

Heat the olive oil in a heavy frying pan and cook the peppers over moderate heat until they are tender and about to turn golden. Add the tomatoes and continue to cook until the liquid is evaporated.

Beat the eggs lightly and add the cheese. Season with salt and black pepper. Pour over the pepper and tomato mixture and cook over a gentle heat, stirring constantly with a wooden spoon until the cheese is melted and the eggs have a creamy consistency. Serve at once. Serves 2.

POACHED EGGS WITH SPINACH AND YOGHURT

Ispanakli Çilbir

This dish makes a very good light lunch or supper dish. If you like, you can serve it with fried rather than poached eggs.

½ pound spinach
1 tablespoon butter or ghee
1 tablespoon extra virgin olive oil
1 small onion, finely chopped
4 poached eggs
4 tablespoons thick creamy yoghurt
3 garlic cloves, crushed
½ teaspoon paprika
a pinch of cayenne
salt

Wash the spinach and cook in a covered saucepan over moderate heat for 5 to 7 minutes or until tender. The water clinging to the leaves is sufficient to prevent scorching. Drain well and chop finely.

Heat the butter and olive oil in a large frying pan and cook the onion over moderate heat until it is softened. Stir in the spinach and cook for 2 or 3 minutes. Transfer to a serving dish and arrange the poached eggs over the top. Mix the yoghurt in a bowl with the garlic, paprika, cayenne, and salt. Pour over the eggs and serve at once. Serves 4.

Artichoke and Tomato Omelet

Omelette Niçarde

This omelette from Nice is usually made with baby artichokes that are so tender that they can be eaten raw. However, frozen artichoke bottoms (that are readily available in most Middle Eastern stores) make a quick and easy alternative.

4 tablespoons extra virgin olive oil
4 frozen artichoke bottoms, thawed and sliced fairly thickly
2 garlic cloves, finely chopped
1 tablespoon flat-leaf parsley, finely chopped
4 ripe plum tomatoes, peeled, seeded, and chopped
a pinch of thyme
4 eggs
salt
freshly ground black pepper

Heat half of the olive oil in a frying pan and cook the artichoke bottoms over a moderate heat until they are tender and starting to turn golden. Add the garlic and parsley and cook for 2 more minutes. Add the tomatoes and thyme and continue to cook for a further 10 minutes or until the sauce starts to thicken. Set aside to cool.

Beat the eggs in a bowl and add the artichoke mixture. Season with salt and black pepper. Heat the remaining olive oil in a heavy frying pan and pour in the egg mixture. Cook over gentle heat until the bottom is lightly browned, shaking the pan from time to time to prevent sticking. Place under a hot grill for 20 seconds to set the top and proceed as for *frittata con le melanzane* on page 238. Serve hot, cut in wedges like a pie. Serves 2 or 3.

EGGPLANT FRITTATA

Frittata con le Melanzane

This frittata is usually with *caciocavallo* cheese (a hard cheese with a sharp flavor that is widely used in Sicilian cooking). The name derives from the ancient custom of hanging the cheese in pairs *a cavallo* (on horseback) to ripen.

3 small eggplants, about 1½ pounds
salt
extra virgin olive oil for frying
4 eggs
¼ cup grated caciocavallo or pecorino cheese
a handful of flat-leaf parsley, finely chopped
2 tablespoons torn basil leaves
freshly ground black pepper

Trim the ends of the eggplants but do not peel. Dice into half-inch pieces. Sprinkle with salt and set in a colander for 1 hour to release the bitter juices. Wash off the salt, drain, and pat dry with a paper towel. Fry in hot olive oil until golden on both sides. Beat the eggs in a bowl and add the fried eggplant, grated cheese, and herbs. Mix well and season with salt and black pepper.

Heat 2 tablespoons olive oil in a heavy frying pan. When it is very hot, pour in the egg mixture. Cook over gentle heat until the bottom is lightly browned, shaking the pan from time to time to prevent sticking. Place the frying pan under a preheated grill for 20 seconds to set the top, then slide the frittata onto a saucepan lid or plate. Place the frying pan over the uncooked side of the frittata and hold it snugly against the saucepan lid.

Quickly flip the saucepan lid over so the uncooked side of the frittata is on the bottom of the frying pan. Continue cooking the frittata on the stove until the bottom is golden. Slide it onto a serving platter and serve hot or at room temperature, cut in wedges like a pie. Serves 3 to 4.

OMELETTE WITH BLACK OLIVES
Bayd bil Zitoun

This omelette is a good example of the mix of French and North African cultures. It is cooked in the traditional way of a French rolled omelette, but with the addition of two of North Africa's favorite ingredients—olives and cumin.

4 eggs
½ cup black olives, pitted and sliced
½ cup flat-leaf parsley, finely chopped
½ teaspoon ground cumin
salt
freshly ground black pepper
1 tablespoon butter

Beat the eggs in a bowl and add the olives, parsley, and cumin. Mix well and season with salt and black pepper.

Melt the butter in a heavy frying pan. When it starts to foam, pour in the eggs. Let the eggs cook for about 10 seconds to set the bottom, then tilt the pan away from you and gently push the eggs towards the center. Now tilt the pan towards you so the uncooked eggs cover the space you have made. Repeat a couple of times until the eggs are lightly set. Remove from the heat. Fold the omelette in half and slide onto a serving plate. Serve at once. Serves 2.

SEPHARDIC ZUCCHINI OMELETTES

Omleta de Kalavasa

This recipe is one of the many dairy dishes that were traditionally made in the Jewish communities of Greece for lunch, an evening meal, or as a snack.

½ pound zucchini
2 medium onions, peeled
3 eggs
a handful of flat-leaf parsley, finely chopped
salt
freshly ground black pepper
extra virgin olive oil

Trim the ends of the zucchini and grate them coarsely. Place in a mixing bowl. Grate the onions coarsely and add to the zucchinis together with the eggs and parsley. Mix well and season with salt and black pepper.

Heat a thin layer of olive oil in a heavy frying pan. When it is hot, drop heaping tablespoons of the mixture into the pan and spread out evenly with a fork to form little pancakes.

Cook a few at a time until they are golden on both sides. Remove from the pan and drain on a paper towel. Repeat until all of the mixture is used up. Serve hot. Serves 2 to 3.

GREEK COUNTRY OMELETTE

Omleta Horiatiki

The ingredients of this omelette can vary according to the season. This one is made with purple onions, red peppers, black olives, and feta cheese, but it is also very good made with eggplant, zucchini, tomatoes, new potatoes, or spinach instead of the peppers.

2 red bell peppers
4 tablespoons extra virgin olive oil
2 medium purple onions, thinly sliced
4 eggs
¼ cup black olives, pitted and sliced
2 ounces feta cheese, thinly sliced
2 tablespoons flat-leaf parsley, finely chopped
salt
freshly ground black pepper

Cut the peppers in half and remove the core, pith, and seeds. Cut into thin strips. Heat half of the olive oil in a heavy frying pan and cook the onions and peppers over a moderate heat until they are tender and starting to turn golden. Set aside to cool slightly. Beat the eggs in a bowl and add the onion mixture, black olives, feta cheese, and parsley. Mix well and season with salt and black pepper.

Heat the remaining olive oil in the same frying pan. When it is hot, pour in the egg mixture. Cook over gentle heat until the bottom is golden. Place under a preheated hot grill for 20 seconds to set the top and proceed as for *frittata con le melanzane* on page 238. Serve hot or at room temperature, cut in wedges like a pie. Serves 2 to 3.

EGYPTIAN LEEK OMELETTE
Eggah bil Korrat

This omelette is flavored with sumac, which gives it a tangy, lemony flavor that goes very well with the leeks. It is also very good made with a bunch of green onions instead of leeks.

2 leeks (including the green tops)
4 tablespoons extra virgin olive oil
1 tablespoon lemon juice
4 eggs
1 tablespoon flour
½ teaspoon sumac
¼ teaspoon paprika
a good pinch of cinnamon
a grating of nutmeg
salt
freshly ground black pepper

Trim the ends of the leeks and cut in half lengthwise. Wash away any dirt that collects between the leaves and cut into 1 inch slices. Heat half of the olive oil in a heavy frying and cook the leeks over moderate heat until they are tender and starting to turn golden. Remove from the heat and stir in the lemon juice. Set aside to cool.

Beat the eggs with the flour in a bowl. Add the leeks and spices and mix well. Season with salt and black pepper. Heat the remaining olive oil in the same frying pan and when it is hot, pour in the egg mixture. Cook over gentle heat until the bottom is golden. Place under a hot grill for 20 seconds and proceed as for *frittata con le melanzane* on page 240. Serve hot or at room temperature, cut in wedges like a pie. Serves 2 to 4.

SPANISH POTATO TORTILLA
Tortilla de Patata a la Espanola

The Spanish *tortilla* has been made in Spain for more than 400 years. Legend has it that it was originally created by a peasant for a hungry king—not, of course, with potatoes, which were not introduced into Spanish cooking until the eighteenth century. This version of the *tortilla* is made with separated eggs, which makes it very light and fluffy.

3 medium potatoes
5 tablespoons extra virgin olive oil
4 eggs, separated
salt
freshly ground black pepper

Peel the potatoes and slice them fairly thinly. Heat 3 tablespoons olive oil in a heavy frying pan until it is very hot. Add the potatoes and stir briefly so they are well coated in oil. Reduce the heat and cook gently until the potatoes are tender and starting to turn golden. Remove with a slotted spoonand set aside.

Beat the egg yolks until they are pale. Season with salt and black pepper. Beat the egg whites until they are stiff and fold into the egg yolks.

Lastly, fold in the potatoes. Heat the remaining olive oil in the same frying pan. When it is hot, pour in the egg mixture, spreading the potatoes evenly in the pan. Cook for a minute or two over fairly high heat to set the bottom. Reduce the heat and cook over gentle heat until the bottom is golden, shaking the pan from time to time, to prevent it sticking. Place the tortilla under a hot grill for 20 seconds and proceed as for *frittata con le melanzane* on page 240. Slice onto a serving plate and serve hot or at room temperature, cut in wedges like a pie. Serves 2 to 4.

LITTLE PARSLEY OMELETTES

Ejjet Ba'Doones

The Lebanese sometimes make their omelettes very small, like fritters or pancakes. They are usually served with a selection of salads or cooked vegetables dressed with olive oil and lemon juice.

1 bunch flat-leaf parsley, about 4 ounces
½ bunch fresh mint
4 eggs
2 spring onions, trimmed and finely sliced
¼ teaspoon cinnamon
¼ teaspoon allspice
salt
freshly ground black pepper
olive oil for frying

Remove the outer stalks from the parsley and mint and discard. Chop the herbs finely. Beat the eggs in a large mixing bowl and add the parsley, mint, and spring onions and mix well. Add the spices and season with salt and black pepper.

Pour in enough olive oil to cover the bottom of a large frying pan. When it is hot, drop 2 tablespoons of the mixture into the pan and spread out evenly with a spatula to form a thin circle about 3 inches in diameter.

Cook 3 or 4 omelettes at a time. Fry until golden on both sides. Remove and drain on paper towels. Repeat with the remaining egg mixture until it is used up. Serve hot, warm, or at room temperature. Serves 4.

CATALAN OMELETTE WITH SAMFAINA
Truita de Samfaina

This is one of the most popular omelettes in Catalonia. *Samfaina* is one of the five basic sauces of Catalan cooking. Reminiscent of the French ratatouille, it is made with a mixture of onion, sweet pepper, eggplant, tomatoes, garlic, and olive oil. When it is used as a sauce, a little water is added and the mixture is cooked down until it becomes the consistency of a jam or marmalade.

1 small eggplant, about ¼ pound
6 tablespoons extra virgin olive oil
1 medium onion
2 garlic cloves, finely chopped
1 small red pepper, roasted, cored, seeded, and cut into strips
3 ripe plum tomatoes, peeled, seeded, and chopped
4 eggs
salt
freshly ground black pepper

To make the *samfaina*, trim the ends of the eggplant and dice into half-inch pieces. Heat 4 tablespoons olive oil in a frying pan and cook the onion over moderate heat until it is softened. Add the garlic and cook for 2 more minutes. Add the eggplant and pepper and stir well so they are coated in oil. Cover and simmer for 10 to 15 minutes or until tender. Add the tomatoes and continue to cook uncovered until the sauce is very thick. Set aside to cool.

Beat the eggs in a bowl and stir in the *samfaina*. Season with salt and black pepper. Heat the remaining olive oil in a heavy frying pan. When it is hot, pour in the egg mixture. Cook over gentle heat until the bottom is golden. Place under a hot grill for 20 seconds and proceed as for *frittata son le melanzane* on page 240. Serve hot, cut in wedges like a pie. Serves 2 to 4.

NIÇOISE SWISS CHARD OMELETTE
Troucho à la Niçarda

This tasty omelette can be made with Swiss chard or spinach or a combination of both. In Nice, it is often served cold for a picnic.

1 bunch Swiss chard (about 1 pound)
4 tablespoons extra virgin olive oil
4 eggs
2 tablespoons flat-leaf parsley, finely chopped
1 tablespoon torn basil leaves
3 tablespoons freshly grated Parmesan cheese
a grating of nutmeg
salt
freshly ground black pepper

Cut away the stalks and thick ribs of the Swiss chard and reserve for a soup or stew. Wash carefully and pat dry. Shred it finely. Heat half of the olive oil in a frying pan and add the Swiss chard. Cover and cook over moderate heat for 5 minutes or until it is wilted. Set aside.

Beat the eggs in a bowl and add the Swiss chard, herbs, and grated cheese. Mix well and season with nutmeg, salt, and black pepper.

Heat the remaining olive oil in a heavy frying pan. When it is hot, pour in the egg mixture. Cook over gentle heat until the bottom is golden. Place under a hot grill for 20 seconds and proceed as for *frittata on le melanzane* on page 240. Serve hot or at room temperature, cut in wedges like a pie. Serves 4.

PROVENÇAL TOMATO OMELETTE

Omelette Provençale

In this recipe, the tomatoes are cooked down to make a kind of *jam* before they are added to the eggs. The omelette has a lovely orange color and a true Mediterranean flavor.

4 tablespoons extra virgin olive oil
1 garlic clove, finely chopped
1 tablespoon flat-leaf parsley, finely chopped
2 tablespoons torn basil leaves
5 ripe plum tomatoes, peeled, seeded, and chopped
4 eggs
salt
freshly ground black pepper

Heat the olive oil in a frying pan and cook the garlic and herbs over a moderate heat for 2 minutes. Add the tomatoes and cook for a further 10 to 15 minutes, stirring from time to time, until all the liquid is evaporated and the tomatoes are the consistency of jam. Set aside to cool slightly.

Beat the eggs in a bowl and add the tomato jam. Mix well and season with salt and black pepper. Heat the remaining olive oil in a heavy frying pan and when it is very hot, pour in the egg mixture. Cook over gentle heat until the bottom is golden, shaking the pan from time to time to prevent sticking. Place the frying pan under a hot grill and proceed as for *frittata con le melanzane* on page 240 Serve hot, cut in wedges like a pie. Serves 2 to 4.

PEASANT-STYLE ONION FRITTATA
Frittata Fredda Contadina

This frittata from Campania was traditionally eaten cold for lunch by peasants working in the fields. If *Scamorza* is unavailable, mozzarella may be used instead.

4 tablespoons extra virgin olive oil
2 large onions, thinly sliced
4 eggs, separated
2 tablespoons torn basil leaves
¼ cup *Scamorza* or mozzarella cheese, diced into small pieces
salt
freshly ground black pepper

Heat half of the olive oil in a heavy frying pan and cook the onions over gentle heat until they are very soft and starting to turn golden. Set aside to cool slightly. Beat the egg yolks in a bowl. Whisk the egg whites until stiff and fold into the egg yolks.

Carefully fold in the onions, basil, and cheese and season with salt and black pepper. Heat the remaining olive oil in the same frying pan. When it is very hot, pour in the egg mixture. Cook over gentle heat until the bottom is golden. Place under a hot grill for 20 seconds and proceed as for *frittata con le melanzane* on page 240. Serve at room temperature, cut in wedges like a pie. Serves 4.

SICILIAN EGG FRITTERS WITH BASIL

Piscirova cò basilico

A *piscirova* or *piscidova* literally means "fish made of eggs," probably because the eggs are mixed with bread crumbs and cooked, like fish, in hot oil. Be sure to leave plenty of room for these light fritters to puff out during cooking.

4 eggs
¼ cup freshly grated pecorino or Parmesan cheese
½ cup fresh basil leaves, coarsely chopped
¼ cup soft bread crumbs
salt
freshly ground black pepper
olive oil for frying

Beat the eggs lightly in a bowl and add the grated cheese, basil, and bread crumbs. Season with salt and black pepper. Fry tablespoons of the batter in hot oil until golden on both sides. Drain on a paper towel. Serve hot. Serves 2-4.

VEGETABLE CHAKCHOUKA
Chakchouka bil-Khodra

In Tunisia and Algeria, a *chakchouka* is a vegetable stew that is usually combined with eggs. In Morocco, it is made with meat rather than eggs. The vegetables vary according to the season—artichokes, broad beans, and potatoes in spring; eggplant, zucchini, peppers, and tomatoes in summer.

4 tablespoons extra virgin olive oil
2 medium onions, chopped
2 red or green peppers, cored, seeded, and chopped
1–2 red chili peppers, cored, seeded, and finely chopped
3 medium zucchinis, sliced into rounds
5 ripe plum tomatoes, peeled, seeded, and chopped
salt
freshly ground black pepper
4 eggs

Heat the olive oil in a frying pan and cook the onions over moderate heat until they are softened. Add the peppers, chilies, and zucchinis and stir well so they are coated in oil. Cover and cook over a gentle heat for 25 to 30 minutes or until the vegetables are tender and lightly browned, stirring from time to time so they cook evenly. Add the tomatoes and cook, uncovered, for a further 8 to 10 minutes or until the sauce starts to thicken.

Season with salt and black pepper. Make 4 depressions with the back of a spoon and break in the eggs. Cover and cook for 5 to 6 minutes or until the eggs are set. Serve at once. Serves 4.

LITTLE ROLLS STUFFED WITH SPINACH AND RICOTTA
Rollatine con Ricotta e Spinaci

These little omelettes from the Veneto are made with a little flour which gives them the consistency of very light pancakes. First they are stuffed with a mixture of spinach and ricotta, then they are topped with tomato sauce and grated cheese and gratinéed in the oven. If you like you can bake them in individual dishes—2 or 3 omelettes per person.

FOR THE OMELETTES:
3 tablespoons flour
3–4 tablespoons of water
6 eggs
salt
freshly ground black pepper
3–4 tablespoons extra virgin olive oil

FILLING:
¼ pound spinach
¾ cup ricotta
¼ cup freshly grated Parmesan cheese
a grating of nutmeg
salt
freshly ground black pepper

TOPPING:
1 recipe Tomato and Basil Sauce (see page 150)
½ cup freshly grated Parmesan cheese

To make the omelettes, place the flour in a bowl and gradually add the water until the mixture is free of lumps and the consistency of single cream. Beat the eggs in another bowl until they are light. Stir in the flour and water mixture and blend well. Season with salt and black pepper.

Heat a little olive oil in a heavy 6-inch frying pan. When it is hot, pour in about 3 tablespoons of the egg mixture. Quickly tilt the pan in all directions so the egg evenly covers the pan. Cook for about 1 minute on each side. Slide onto a plate and repeat until all of the egg mixture is used up.

To make the filling, wash the spinach carefully and cook in a covered saucepan over moderate heat for 5 minutes. The water clinging to the leaves is sufficient to prevent scorching. Drain, squeeze dry, and chop finely. Set aside to cool. Place the ricotta in a bowl and mash with a fork. Add the spinach and grated Parmesan cheese and blend well. Season with nutmeg, salt, and black pepper.

Spoon a little filling into the center of each omelette and roll them up. Place the omelettes side by side in the bottom of a well-oiled shallow baking dish and spoon over the sauce. Sprinkle grated cheese over the top. Bake in a preheated 400°F oven for 15 minutes or until the omelettes are heated through and the cheese is melted. Serve at once. Serves 4 to 6.

EGGPLANT PAPETON

Papeton de merinjano

Papeton, or *aubergines des papes* as it is sometimes called, is a kind of eggplant flan that was created in Avignon for one of the popes. Originally, it was cooked in the shape of a crown. It can be served hot or cold with a little tomato coulis on the side.

2 pounds eggplants
about ½ cup extra virgin olive oil
2 garlic cloves, finely chopped
2 tablespoons flat-leaf parsley, finely chopped
a pinch of thyme
4 eggs
salt
freshly ground black pepper
¼ cup freshly grated Parmesan cheese
1 cup Tomato Coulis (see page 156)

Peel the eggplants and dice into half-inch pieces. Heat the olive oil in a large frying pan and add the eggplant, garlic, and herbs. Stir well so they are evenly coated in oil. Cover and cook over a gentle heat for 15 to 20 minutes, stirring from time to time so they cook evenly, or until the eggplant is tender and starting to turn golden. Force through a sieve or purée in a food processor.

Beat the eggs lightly in a mixing bowl and add the eggplant purée. Mix well and season with salt and black pepper. Pour into a well-buttered soufflé dish and sprinkle the grated cheese over the top. Place in a pan of hot water and bake in the lower third of a 190°F oven for 40 minutes or until the top is golden and the center is done. Serve hot or cold with tomato coulis on the side. Serves 4.

Spinach and Ricotta Molded Soufflé

Sformato Verde

A *sformato* is a kind of molded soufflé or pudding that is usually made with puréed vegetables, béchamel sauce or ricotta cheese and eggs. It is much easier to prepare than a soufflé and makes a very good light lunch with a salad on the side.

1 pound spinach
1½ cups ricotta
3 eggs, separated
¼ cup freshly grated Parmesan cheese
a grating of nutmeg
salt
freshly ground black pepper
2 tablespoons butter
dry bread crumbs

Wash the spinach and cook in a covered saucepan over a moderate heat for 5 minutes, or until tender. The water clinging to the leaves is sufficient to prevent scorching. Drain, squeeze dry, and chop finely. Set aside to cool.

Sieve the ricotta into a mixing bowl and add the egg yolks. Blend well. Stir in the spinach and ¼ cup Parmesan cheese and mix well. Season with nutmeg, salt, and black pepper.

Beat the egg whites until stiff and fold into the mixture. Pour into a well-buttered soufflé dish that has been dusted with bread crumbs. Sprinkle the remaining Parmesan cheese over the top. Bake in a preheated 375°F oven for 30 minutes or until the *sformato* is well risen and the center is done. Serves 4.

POTATO MARKHOUDA
Markhouda bil-Batata

A *markhouda* is a cross between a French flan and a baked Italian frittata. In Tunisia, it is often called an *omelette juive* as it is a traditional dairy dish of Sephardic Jews.

1 pound potatoes
4 tablespoons extra virgin olive oil
2 medium onions, finely chopped
1 cup flat-leaf parsley, finely chopped
6 eggs, lightly beaten
½ teaspoon paprika
½ teaspoon turmeric
salt
freshly ground black pepper
2 tablespoons butter

Cook the potatoes in lightly salted water for 20 minutes or until they are tender. Drain and peel when they are cool enough to handle. Force through a sieve into a mixing bowl. Heat the olive oil in a large frying pan and cook the onions over moderate heat until the onions start to turn golden. Add to the potatoes together with the eggs, parsley, and spices. Mix well and season with salt and black pepper.

Pour into a well-oiled shallow baking dish and dot with butter. Bake in a preheated 375°F oven for 40 minutes or until the center is set and the top is nicely browned. Serve hot or at room temperature. Serves 4 to 6.

Zucchini Soufflé

Kolokythakia Soufflé

This soufflé is very light and easy to prepare.

2 pounds zucchini
about ⅓ cup extra virgin olive oil
3 large eggs
⅔ cup grated Kefalotyri or Parmesan cheese
a grating of nutmeg
salt
freshly ground black pepper

Trim the ends of the zucchini and slice them into rounds. Heat the olive oil in a large frying pan and cook the zucchini over moderate heat until tender and starting to turn golden, stirring from time to time so it cooks evenly. Force through a sieve or purée in a food processor. Add the egg yolks and ½ cup grated cheese and mix well.

Season with nutmeg, salt, and black pepper. Beat the egg whites stiff and fold into the mixture. Pour into a well-buttered soufflé dish and sprinkle the remaining cheese over the top. Bake in a preheated 400°F oven and reduce the heat immediately to 375°F. Bake for 25 to 30 minutes or until the soufflé is well risen and the center is done. Serve at once. Serves 4.

ARTICHOKE SOUFFLÉ
Soufflé di Carciofi

This savory soufflé from Liguria makes an elegant light lunch or supper dish with a salad on the side.

2 tablespoons extra virgin olive oil
8 or 9 frozen artichoke bottoms, thawed and sliced
2 tablespoons butter
3 tablespoons flour
¾ cup hot milk
a grating of nutmeg
salt
freshly ground black pepper
¼ cup freshly grated Parmesan cheese
3 egg yolks
3 egg whites

Heat the olive oil in a large frying pan and cook the artichoke bottoms over moderate heat until they are tender and starting to turn golden. Force through a sieve or purée in a food processor. Set aside.

Prepare a thick béchamel sauce with the butter, flour, and hot milk as directed on page 213. Remove from the heat and add the artichoke purée and grated cheese. Blend well and season with nutmeg, salt, and black pepper. Add the egg yolks one at a time and mix well. Beat the egg whites until stiff and fold into the mixture. Pour into a well-buttered soufflé dish and bake in a preheated 400°F oven and reduce the heat immediately to 375°F. Bake for 25 to 30 minutes or until the soufflé is well risen and the center is done, Serve at once. Serves 4.

VEGETABLES

*A table without vegetables is like an old man
devoid of wisdom.*
—Arab saying

Vegetables play an important role in the Mediterranean kitchen. They are often served as a separate course or even make up the entire meal. In Greece, Lebanon, and Turkey, vegetable dishes prepared without meat are so common they are given a special name—*ladera* in Greece, *zeytinyağli* in Turkey, and *bil-zeit* in Lebanon—all literally meaning "cooked in olive oil."

The mild Mediterranean climate gives most regions a growing season that is virtually all year round. Vegetables are always plentiful and eaten fresh and in season. So much so that the appearance of each new vegetable is awaited with great anticipation—wild asparagus, baby broad beans, and artichokes in spring, tiny peas in June, followed by green beans, eggplant, and zucchini in summer, an array of succulent mushrooms in early autumn and pumpkin and sweet corn in October and November. Flavorings vary from country to country. Dill, mint, and parsley are favored in Turkey. The Lebanese and Syrians prefer allspice and sumac, while North Africans like to spice their food with chili, ground caraway, coriander, ginger, and cumin. All around the Mediterranean, pine nuts, sesame seeds, almonds, olives, and capers are added for extra flavor and texture. Throughout the year, all kinds of cultivated dark green leafy vegetables are enjoyed as well as a variety of wild greens and herbs that are collected from the hillsides.

ASPARAGUS PARMA STYLE
Asparagi alla Parmigiana

This classic dish comes from Parma in Emilia–Romagna, the home of Parmesan cheese. Celery, leeks, and fennel can be prepared the same way. It is said that Parmesan cheese (Parmigiano Reggiano) has been made in the region around Parma for more than two thousand years. Today it is made in carefully designated areas between Parma, Bologna, and Mantua. When it is made elsewhere in Italy, it is called *grana*. Good Parmesan cheese is straw-colored with a pleasant, slightly salty taste. Always buy it whole, as it quickly loses its flavor once it is grated.

1 pound asparagus
½ cup freshly grated Parmesan cheese
4 tablespoons butter, melted
salt
freshly ground black pepper

Trim the ends of the asparagus and remove any fibrous inedible parts from the lower stalks with a sharp knife. Steam for 15 to 20 minutes or until tender. Place in a well-buttered shallow baking dish in a single layer.

Sprinkle the Parmesan cheese over the top and dribble over the melted butter. Place under a hot grill for 1 or 2 minutes or until the cheese is lightly browned. Season with salt and black pepper. Serve at once. Serves 3 to 4.

WHITE BEANS SIMMERED WITH TOMATOES AND CUMIN
Fassoulya bil-Banadoura

This dish is usually served as part of a *mezze*, but it is also very good served as a side dish or as a main course with a rice pilaf on the side. Cumin is usually added to pulse dishes in the Middle East not only for its fine flavor but also for its antiflatulent properties.

1½ cups dried cannelini beans
4 tablespoons extra virgin olive oil
2 medium onions, thinly sliced
2 garlic cloves, finely chopped
3 canned plum tomatoes, forced through a sieve or puréed
    in a food processor
2 tablespoons flat-leaf parsley, finely chopped
½ teaspoon cumin
salt
freshly ground black pepper

Soak the beans overnight and drain. Place in a saucepan and cover with water. Bring to a boil. Cover and simmer for 1 to 1½ hours or until the beans are tender. Drain and reserve about half a cup of the cooking liquid.

Heat the olive oil in a saucepan and cook the onions and garlic over moderate heat until they start to turn golden. Add the beans, tomato purée, parsley, cumin, and reserved cooking liquid and season with salt and black pepper. Bring to a boil. Cover and simmer for 15 to 20 minutes or until the liquid is reduced. Serve hot or at room temperature. Serves 4 to 6.

BRUSSEL SPROUTS WITH PARMESAN

Cavolini di Bruxelles al Forno

This recipe from Emilia-Romagnais a delicious way of preparing brussels sprouts—just take care that you do not overcook them.

1 pound brussels sprouts
salt
freshly ground black pepper
1/2 cup freshly grated Parmesan cheese
2 tablespoons butter, melted

Trim the root ends of the brussels sprouts and remove any yellowish leaves. Steam for 8 to 10 minutes or until they are just tender, taking care not to overcook them. Place in one layer in the bottom of a well-oiled shallow baking dish and season with salt and black pepper.

Sprinkle the grated cheese over the top and dribble over the melted butter. Bake in a preheated 400°F oven for 10 minutes or until the cheese is melted and the tops are golden. Serve at once. Serves 4.

BAKED SUMMER VEGETABLES
Horiatiki Briam

This delicious casserole is made all over Greece. Sometimes green beans or okra are added, or perhaps a little fennel. It is often served as a light lunch with some crusty bread and slices of feta cheese on the side.

1 pound waxy potatoes, peeled and cut into ¼-inch thick slices
3 medium zucchini, cut into rounds ¼ inch thick
2 long thin eggplants, cut into rounds ¼ inch thick
2 red or green peppers, cored, seeded, and cut into thin strips
2 medium, onions, sliced
1 pound ripe tomatoes, peeled, seeded, and chopped
¾ cup extra virgin olive oil
about ½ cup hot water
2 tablespoons fresh mint leaves, finely chopped
2 teaspoons dried oregano
salt
freshly ground black pepper

Arrange the vegetables in the bottom of a well-oiled shallow baking dish and top with the onions and tomatoes. Pour over the olive oil and water and sprinkle the herbs over the top. Season with salt and black pepper. Cover with foil and bake in a pre-heated 350°F oven for 1 hour. Stir once or twice during cooking. Remove the foil. Bake, uncovered, for a further 30 minutes or until the vegetables are tender and lightly browned and the sauce is syrupy. Serve hot or at room temperature. Serves 4 to 6.

CARROTS IN HOT SAUCE

Mzoura

This dish may be served as an appetizer or a side vegetable.

1 pound carrots, diced
3 tablespoons extra virgin olive oil
4 garlic cloves, crushed
½ teaspoon *harissa* (see page 124)
½ teaspoon paprika
¼ teaspoon ground caraway seeds
¼ teaspoon cumin
1-2 tablespoons white wine vinegar
salt
2 tablespoons finely chopped flat-leaf parsley

Steam the carrots 15 minutes or until they are tender. Heat the olive oil in a frying pan and add the carrots, garlic, *harissa,* and spices. Cook over a gentle heat for 2 or 3 minutes. Add the vinegar and salt to taste and simmer for 5 to 7 minutes or until the liquid is evaporated. Serve hot or at room temperature garnished with parsley. Serves 4.

SWEET AND SOUR CARROTS, JEWISH STYLE

Carote alla Giudea

This dish is a specialty of the *Levantini*—Levantine Jews from Turkey, Syria, and Egypt who once lived in one of Venice's three Jewish ghettos. (The others were for *Tedeschi* (German Jews) and Italian or Sicilian Jews). Some cooks like to soak the raisins in a little sweet wine before they are added to the carrots.

2 tablespoons extra virgin olive oil
1½ pounds baby carrots
¼ cup raisins
¼ cup pine nuts
1 or 2 tablespoons red wine vinegar

Heat the olive oil in a saucepan and add the carrots. Stir well so they are evenly coated in oil. Add ¼ cup water and bring to a boil.

Cover and simmer for 10 to 15 minutes or until the carrots are tender, adding a little more water if necessary. Add the raisins and pine nuts and cook for another 5 minutes. Pour in the vinegar and simmer for a further 5 minutes or until it is almost evaporated. Serve hot. Serves 4 to 6.

CABBAGE SIMMERED IN TOMATO SAUCE

Cromb Makmoor

This dish is a very simple but tasty way of preparing cabbage.

3 tablespoons extra virgin olive oil
2 medium onions
2 garlic cloves
1 small green cabbage, coarsely shredded
¼ cup flat-leaf parsley, finely chopped
¼ cup fresh dill, finely chopped
1 cup canned plum tomatoes, forced through a sieve
    or puréed in a food processor
1 teaspoon ground coriander
½ teaspoon cumin
salt
freshly ground black pepper
1 teaspoon red wine vinegar

Heat the olive oil in a saucepan and cook the onion and garlic over a moderate heat for 2 minutes. Add the cabbage and stir well.

Cover and simmer for 15 to 20 minutes or until the cabbage is tender. Add the parsley, dill, tomato purée, and spices, and season with salt and black pepper. Simmer for 15 minutes or until the sauce starts to thicken. Add the vinegar and simmer for 2 or 3 more minutes. Serve hot. Serves 4 to 6.

CHICKPEAS IN HOT SAUCE
H'missa bil-Dersa

Dersa, a garlicky hot sauce flavored with cumin or ground caraway seeds is widely used in Algerian cooking. Lentils, broad beans, or kidney beans may be prepared the same way.

3 tablespoons extra virgin olive oil
6 garlic cloves, finely chopped
3 ripe tomatoes, forced through a sieve or pureed in food processor
½ teaspoon paprika
½ teaspoon cumin
1–2 teaspoons *harissa*, see page 124, to taste
1 cup hot water
3 cups cooked and drained chickpeas

Heat the olive oil in a saucepan and cook the garlic over moderate heat for 1 or 2 minutes without browning. Add the tomato purée, spices, and *harissa,* and stir well. Simmer for 5 minutes. Add the hot water, chickpeas, and salt to taste.

Bring to a boil, cover, and simmer for 15 to 20 minutes or until the sauce is reduced. Serve hot. Serves 4 to 6.

CAULIFLOWER IN TOMATO SAUCE WITH OLIVES AND CAPERS

Cavolfiore Piccante

This recipe is usually made in Sicily with cauliflower with purple or pale green heads, but white cauliflower is equally good—just take care not to overcook it.

1 medium head cauliflower, about 2 pounds

2 tablespoons extra virgin olive oil

2 garlic cloves, finely chopped

½–1 small red chili pepper, cored, seeded, and finely chopped

2 teaspoons fresh oregano

1 pound ripe plum tomatoes, peeled, seeded, and chopped

¼ cup black olives, pitted and sliced

1 tablespoon capers

salt

Trim the ends of the cauliflower and break into florets. Steam for 7 to 8 minutes or until just tender.

Heat the olive oil in a large frying pan and cook the garlic, chili, and oregano for 1 or 2 minutes. Add the tomatoes and cook over moderate heat for 10 minutes or until the sauce starts to thicken. Add the cauliflower florets, olives, and capers and salt to taste and stir well. Simmer for 5 minutes to blend the flavors. Serve hot. Serves 4 to 6.

EGGPLANT WITH BÉCHAMEL SAUCE

Merinjano a la Béchamel

This delicious recipe from Provence also makes a very good light main course. If you like, you can sprinkle a little freshly grated Parmesan cheese on top instead of the bread crumbs.

2 pounds eggplant
salt
about ¾ cup extra virgin olive oil
1 cup Tomato Coulis, see page 156
1 recipe béchamel sauce, see page 213
¼ cup soft bread crumbs
2 tablespoons butter

Trim the ends of the eggplants and cut them into rounds a quarter inch thick. Sprinkle with salt and set in a colander for 1 hour to release the bitter juices. Wash off the salt and pat dry with a paper towel. Fry in hot olive oil until golden on both sides.

Arrange a layer of fried eggplant over the bottom of a well-oiled shallow baking dish. Spoon over a thin layer of tomato sauce and top with a layer of béchamel sauce. Repeat the layers until all the ingredients are used up. Sprinkle the bread crumbs over the top and dot with butter. Bake in a preheated 350°F oven for 20 minutes or until the top is golden and the sauce is bubbling. Serve hot. Serves 4.

EGGPLANT ROLLS

Melanzane a Beccaficio

This dish consists of slices of fried eggplant stuffed with a mixture of bread crumbs, parsley, pine nuts, sultanas, and grated cheese that are shaped into plump rolls that look like little birds or warblers. In Sicily, a *beccaficcio* is a warbler.

2 large eggplants, about 1¼ to 1½ pounds
salt
vegetable oil for frying
2 tablespoons extra virgin olive oil
1 small onion, finely chopped
2 garlic cloves, finely chopped
½ cup soft bread crumbs
½ cup flat-leaf parsley, finely chopped
¼ cup sultanas
¼ cup pine nuts
¼ cup freshly grated pecorino or Parmesan cheese
freshly ground black pepper

Trim the ends of the eggplants but do not peel. Cut them into rounds about a quarter-inch thick. Sprinkle with salt and set in a colander for 1 hour to release the bitter juices. Wash off the salt and pat dry with paper towels. Fry in hot oil until golden on both sides. Drain on paper towels.

Heat the olive oil in a frying pan and cook the onion over a moderate heat until it is softened. Add the garlic and cook for another 2 minutes. Stir in the bread crumbs, parsley, sultanas, and pine nuts and simmer for 5 minutes. Remove from the heat and add the grated cheese. Mix well and season with salt and black pepper. Spoon a little filling into the center of the eggplant slices and roll them up. Arrange side by side in the bottom of a well-oiled shallow baking dish. Bake in a preheated 350°F oven for 25 to 30 minutes. Serve hot. Serves 4.

LEBANESE MOUSSAKA

Moussaka'a

Unlike the famous Greek *moussakas,* the Lebanese *moussaka'a* is a vegetarian dish made with fried eggplants simmered in an onion and tomato sauce with chickpeas. It is usually served at room temperature, as its name implies. *Moussaka'a* means "cooled down" in Arabic.

1½ pounds small eggplants
olive oil for frying
2 medium onions, thinly sliced
3 garlic cloves, finely chopped
½ cup cooked and drained chickpeas
1½ pounds ripe tomatoes, peeled, seeded, and chopped
a good pinch of allspice
salt
freshly ground black pepper

Trim the ends of the eggplants. Peel off a strip of skin lengthwise about **half an** inch thick. Leave a portion of skin about the same size unpeeled and repeat so the eggplants appear striped. Cut into quarters lengthwise. Fry in hot oil until they are golden on both side. Drain on paper towels.

Heat 2 tablespoons olive oil in a large frying pan and cook the onions and garlic over moderate heat until they start to turn golden. Add the chickpeas and simmer for 2 minutes. Add the tomatoes and allspice and cook for 5 minutes. Season with salt and black pepper.

Arrange the fried eggplant over the top of the sauce. Cover and simmer for a further 15 to 20 minutes or until the sauce is thickened. Transfer to a serving dish and serve at room temperature. Serves 4.

EGGPLANT, POTATOES, AND TOMATOES
Plavi Palidžani, Krumpir i Rajčice

This simple stew from the island of Brač has a lovely Mediterranean flavor. Traditionally, it was prepared in the morning and eaten in the evening by peasants returning from the fields.

2 medium eggplants (about 1 pound eggplant)
6 tablespoons extra virgin olive oil
2 medium onions, thinly sliced
2 garlic cloves, finely chopped
1 pound ripe tomatoes, peeled, seeded, and chopped
1 pound potatoes, peeled and thinly sliced
parsley
salt
freshly ground black pepper

Trim the ends of the eggplants and peel. Slice into rounds an eighth of an inch thick.

Heat 4 tablespoons olive oil in a saucepan and cook the onion and garlic for 2 or 3 minutes. Cover with one third of the tomatoes and top with one third of the potatoes. Arrange one third of the sliced eggplant over the top. Sprinkle with parsley and season with salt and black pepper.

Repeat the layers until all of the ingredients are used up. Pour in enough hot water to just cover the vegetables and dribble over the remaining olive oil. Bring to a boil. Cover and simmer for 1 hour or until the vegetables are tender and the liquid is almost evaporated. Serve hot or at room temperature. Serves 4 to 6.

FENNEL IN BÉCHAMEL SAUCE

Finocchi in Besciamella

This lovely gratin from Emilia–Romagna also makes a very good light lunch or supper dish with a salad on the side.

4 large fennel bulbs
4 tablespoons butter
4 tablespoons flour
4 cups hot milk
¼ cup thin cream
a grating of nutmeg
salt
freshly ground black pepper
¼ cup freshly grated Parmesan cheese
2 tablespoons extra virgin olive oil

Remove the outer stalks and leaves from the fennel bulbs. Trim the bases and cut into wedges. Steam for 10 minutes or until they are tender. Prepare a béchamel sauce with the butter, flour, and hot milk as directed on page 213. When the sauce is very smooth, stir in the cream. Season with nutmeg, salt, and black pepper and simmer for another 3 or 4 minutes.

Spoon a little of the sauce into the bottom of a shallow baking dish. Arrange the fennel on top in one layer and pour over the remaining sauce. Sprinkle the Parmesan cheese over the top and dribble over the olive oil. Bake in a preheated 375°F oven for 20 to 25 minutes or until the top is golden. Serves 4.

GREEN BEANS BRAISED WITH POTATOES AND TOMATOES

Fassolakia me Patates Yiahni

This is one of the most popular Greek summer dishes. It is usually served at room temperature with some feta cheese and country bread on the side. The secret to making a good Greek *yiahni* (stove-top stew) is to use fresh, seasonal ingredients and plenty of extra virgin olive oil.

1 pound green beans
⅓ cup extra virgin olive oil
2 medium onions, thinly sliced
2 garlic cloves, finely chopped
½ pound new potatoes, scrubbed and diced
1 pound ripe plum tomatoes, peeled, seeded, and chopped
¼ cup flat-leaf parsley, finely chopped
1 cup hot water
salt
freshly ground black pepper

Trim the ends of the green beans and cut them in half. Heat the olive oil in a saucepan and cook the onions and garlic over moderate heat until the onions are softened. Add the green beans and potatoes and stir well. Simmer for 2 or 3 minutes. Add the tomatoes, parsley, and water and bring to a boil. Cover and simmer for 30 minutes, or until the vegetables are tender and most of the liquid is evaporated. Season with salt and black pepper. Serve hot or at room temperature. Serves 4 to 6.

BRAISED LEEKS COOKED IN OLIVE OIL
Zeytinyağli Eksili Pirasa

Zeytinyağli means a vegetable dish cooked in olive oil without meat that is usually served cold. It may be served as an appetizer, side dish, or as a separate course on its own. All kinds of vegetables are prepared this way in Turkey, especially artichokes, eggplant, celery root, zucchini, and all kinds of beans. Sometimes a tablespoon or two of rice is added to a *zeytinyağli* as a thickener.

1 pound leeks
¼ cup extra virgin olive oil
1 medium onion, thinly sliced
2 garlic cloves, finely chopped
a handful of fresh dill, finely chopped
a handful of flat-leaf parsley, finely chopped
1 small carrot, thinly sliced
1 tablespoon long-grain rice
1 tablespoon lemon juice
1 teaspoon sugar
a pinch of cinnamon
1 cup hot water
salt
freshly ground black pepper
1 lemon, cut into wedges

Trim the ends of the leeks and cut in half lengthwise. Wash carefully to remove any grit that collects between the leaves. Cut into 1½-inch lengths.

Heat the olive oil in a saucepan and cook the onions, garlic, and herbs over moderate heat for 3 minutes. Add the leeks and carrots and cook, covered, over a gentle heat for 15 minutes, stirring from time to time so the vegetables cook evenly. Add the rice, lemon juice, sugar, cinnamon, and water, and season with salt and black pepper. Bring to a boil.

Cover and simmer for 30 minutes or until the vegetables are tender and most of the liquid is evaporated. Serve at room temperature with lemon wedges on the side. Serves 4.

Egyptian Stewed Lentils

Ads Adsfar Matbookh

This spicy lentil stew is reminiscent of Indian *dhal*. It is made with tiny orange split lentils that that are widely used in Egypt.

2 cups split lentils
4 tablespoons extra virgin olive oil
1 medium onion, finely chopped
4 garlic cloves, finely chopped
½-1 small red chili pepper, cored, seeded, and finely chopped
5 cups hot water
½ teaspoon cumin
½ teaspoon ground coriander
salt
a handful of fresh coriander, finely chopped

Wash the lentils carefully and remove any stones or grit. Heat half of the olive oil in a saucepan and cook the onions, garlic, and chili over a moderate heat for 2 or 3 minutes. Add the lentils and stir well.

Pour in the hot water and bring to a boil. Cover and simmer for 45 minutes or until the lentils are tender. Add the spices and the remaining olive oil, and season with salt to taste. Simmer for a further 10 minutes to blend the flavors. Serve hot garnished with chopped fresh coriander. Serves 6.

MALLORCAN STUFFED MUSHROOMS
Bolets Farcit

Several million almond trees grow in Mallorca, so it is not surprising that almonds are widely used in Mallorcan cooking. In this recipe, they are combined with bread crumbs, garlic, and parsley to make a delicious stuffing for mushrooms.

8 large mushrooms
6 tablespoons extra virgin olive oil
4 garlic cloves, finely chopped
¼ cup flat-leaf parsley, finely chopped
1 cup bread crumbs
¼ cup unblanched almonds, finely ground in a blender or
     food processor
 salt
paprika

Wash the mushrooms and wipe them dry. Remove the stems and chop them coarsely. Place the caps in a well-oiled shallow baking dish and brush them lightly with olive oil. Bake in a preheated 350°F oven for 10 minutes or until they are semi-tender. Remove from the oven and set aside.

Heat 2 tablespoons olive oil in a frying pan and cook the garlic over moderate heat for 2 minutes. Add the mushroom stems and cook for a further 5 minutes or until they are tender. Remove from the heat and stir in the parsley, bread crumbs, and almonds. Mix well and season with salt and paprika. Stuff the mushroom caps with the mixture and dribble the remaining olive oil over the top. Return to the oven and bake at 350°F oven for a further 20 minutes or until the tops are golden and the mushrooms are tender. Serve hot. Serves 4.

MUSHROOM AND POTATO TORTA
Torta di Funghi e Patate

This *torta*, or pie, comes from the region around Trieste near the borders of Croatia. It is usually prepared with fresh porcini (cèpes) or *ovoli* (Amanita caersarea) mushrooms but, if they are unavailable, any quality mushroom may be used instead.

1 pound fresh *porcini*
1 pound waxy potatoes, peeled and sliced thinly
½ cup extra virgin olive oil
salt
freshly ground black pepper
6 garlic cloves, finely chopped
½ cup flat-leaf parsley, finely chopped

Wash the porcini carefully and wipe them dry. Slice them fairly thinly.

Arrange half of the potatoes in the bottom of a well-oiled baking dish. Dribble over a little olive oil and season with salt and black pepper. Cover with half of the porcini and sprinkle half of the garlic and parsley over the top. Repeat the layers and season with salt and black pepper. Dribble the remaining olive oil over the top. Cover tightly with tin foil. Bake in a preheated 350°F oven for 45 to 50 minutes or until the vegetables are tender. Serve hot. Serves 4.

WILD MUSHROOMS WITH GARLIC AND PARSLEY

Rovellons amb All i Julivert

Catalans love wild mushrooms, especially *rovellons* (*Lactarius sanguifluus*)—"bleeding milk caps." When the stems of these rust-colored mushrooms are cut, they exude a few drops of blood-like juice—hence their name. If you like, you can use a mixture of wild and cultivated mushrooms for this dish. Sometimes 2 tablespoons of fresh bread crumbs are added just before the end of cooking.

¾ pound wild mushrooms
4 tablespoons extra virgin olive oil
3 garlic cloves, finely chopped
3 tablespoons flat-leaf parsley, finely chopped
salt
freshly ground black pepper

Wash the mushrooms and wipe them dry. Slice them fairly thickly. Heat the olive oil in a large frying pan and cook the mushrooms over a moderate heat until they start to turn golden. Add the garlic and parsley and cook for a further 3 or 4 minutes. Season with salt and black pepper. Serves 4.

OKRA SIMMERED WITH TOMATOES
Bamya Ateh

Variations of this recipe are made all over the Middle East. In Syria and Lebanon, a little ground coriander and pomegranate syrup are included. This adds a subtle sweet and sour flavor that goes very well with the slightly sharp taste of the okra. Small okra are best for this recipe as large okra tend to be tough and stringy.

1 pound small young okra
vegetable oil for frying
3 tablespoons extra virgin olive oil
½ pound small white onions, peeled
4 garlic cloves, finely chopped
1 teaspoon ground coriander
1 pound ripe tomatoes, peeled, seeded, and chopped
2 tablespoons pomegranate syrup or lemon juice
salt
freshly ground black pepper
1 lemon, cut in wedges

Wash the okra and drain in a colander. Place them in a tea towel and gently pat dry. With a sharp knife, trim the ends without piercing the pods or they will disintegrate during cooking.

Heat the vegetable oil in a frying pan. When it is very hot, cook the okra in batches for 2 or 3 minutes or until the okra is crisp but not brown. This helps to seal in the mucilaginous juice inside the okra. Remove with a slotted spoon and drain on a paper towel.

Heat the olive oil in a saucepan and cook the onions over moderate heat for 10 minutes or until they are softened and starting to turn golden brown. Add the garlic and coriander and cool for 1 or 2 more minues. Add the tomatoes and okra and season with salt and black pepper. Cover and cook for 15 minutes or until the sauce is thickened. Stir in the pomegranate syrup and simmer for a few more minutes to blend the flavours. Serve hot or at room temperature with lemon wedges on the side. Serves 4

PEAS, VALENCIA STYLE

Guisantes Estilo Valencia

This dish from Valencia is usually served garnished with slices of roasted pepper and a little chopped hard-boiled egg.

2 pounds unshelled fresh peas
3 tablespoons extra virgin olive oil
1 medium onion, finely chopped
½ cup hot water
1 bay leaf
a pinch of thyme
2 tablespoons flat-leaf parsley, finely chopped
½ cup dry white wine
2 garlic cloves, peeled
¼ teaspoon saffron threads
salt
freshly ground black pepper

Shell the peas. Heat the olive oil in a saucepan and cook the onion over moderate heat until it starts to soften. Add the peas and herbs and cook for a further 2 minutes. Pour in the wine and hot water and bring to a boil. Cover and simmer for 15 minutes or until the peas are almost tender. Place the garlic and saffron in a mortar and crush with a pestle. Dissolve in a little hot water and add to the peas. Simmer for a further 10 minutes or until the peas are tender and most of the liquid is evaporated. Serve hot. Serves 4 to 6.

SWEET PEPPERS WITH RAISINS AND PINE NUTS

Peperoni all'Uvetta

This dish is prepared in the Veneto and across the border in Istria where it is still sometimes called by its Italian dialect name, *peveroni alla garbodolze.* It may be served as an appetizer or a side dish. It can also be made with zucchini or a mixture of peppers and zucchini.

3 tablespoons extra virgin olive oil
3 garlic cloves, finely chopped
4 red, green, or yellow bell peppers, cored, seeded, and cut into strips
3 tablespoons pine nuts
3 tablespoons raisins
1 tablespoon red wine vinegar
salt
freshly ground black pepper

Heat the olive oil in a frying pan and cook the garlic and peppers over gentle heat for 20 minutes or until they are tender and starting to turn golden. Add the pine nuts and raisins and cook for a further 5 minutes. Pour in the vinegar and season with salt and black pepper. Simmer for 2 or 3 more minutes to blend the flavors.

SICILIAN STUFFED PEPPERS

Peperoni Imbottite alla Siciliana

These delicious stuffed peppers may be served hot as a side vegetable or cold as an appetizer.

4 red or green sweet peppers
2 medium eggplants, about 1 pound
about ⅓ cup extra virgin olive oil
4 tablespoons Tomato and Basil Sauce (see page 148)
16 green olives, pitted and coarsely chopped
1 tablespoon capers
1 tablespoon fresh oregano
salt
freshly ground black pepper

Roast the peppers under a hot grill until they are blackened all over. Wash under cold water and remove the skins. Slice off the tops and reserve.

Meanwhile, trim the ends of the eggplant. Peel and cut into half-inch cubes. Heat ¼ cup olive oil in a heavy frying pan and add the eggplant. Stir well. Cover and cook over low heat until they are golden, stirring from time to time so they cook evenly. Add the tomato and basil sauce, olives, capers, and oregano and simmer for 3 minutes to blend the flavors. Season with salt and black pepper. Stuff the peppers with the mixture and place the reserved lids on top.

Place the peppers side by side in a well-oiled shallow baking dish and dribble the remaining olive oil over the top. Bake in reheated 350°F oven for 1 hour or until the peppers start to turn golden. Serve hot or cold. Serves 4.

POTATOES SIMMERED WITH ONION, TOMATOES, AND BLACK OLIVES

Fricot de Pommes de Terre aux Olives

There is no need to peel the potatoes. If they are very small, you can leave them whole, otherwise cut them in half or quarters.

3 tablespoons extra virgin olive oil
2 garlic cloves, finely chopped
2 medium onions, thinly sliced
2 pounds small new potatoes
2 cans plum tomatoes, forced through a sieve
    or puréed in a food processor
1 bay leaf
2 tablespoons flat-leaf parsley, finely chopped
a pinch of thyme
a pinch of powdered saffron
about 2 cups hot water
½ cup Niçoise black olives, pitted and sliced
salt
freshly ground black pepper

Heat the olive oil in a saucepan and cook the garlic and onions over moderate heat until they are tender and starting to turn golden. Add the potatoes and stir well so they are evenly coated in oil. Continue to cook for 3 minutes. Add the tomato purée, herbs, and saffron and simmer for another 3 minutes. Pour in the hot water and bring to a boil.

Cover and simmer for 15 to 20 minutes or until the potatoes are almost tender. Add the olives and cook for a further 5 minutes or until the potatoes are tender and the sauce is thickened. Season with salt and black pepper. Serve hot. Serves 4 to 6.

POTATO AND SPINACH PURÉE
Puré di Patate Verde

This dish comes from Emilia–Romagna, a region that is well-known for its love of butter and cream.

2 pounds floury potatoes
½ pound spinach
4 tablespoons butter
½ cup single cream (or half milk, half cream)
⅓ cup freshly grated Parmesan cheese
a grating of nutmeg
salt
freshly ground black pepper

Wash the spinach carefully and cook in a covered saucepan over moderate heat for 5 minutes or until tender. The water clinging to the leaves is sufficient to prevent scorching. Bring the potatoes to boil in plenty of lightly salted water.

Cover and cook over moderate heat for 20 minutes or until they are tender. Drain well and mash with a potato ricer. Add the spinach, butter, cream, and Parmesan cheese, and mix well. Season with nutmeg, salt, and black pepper and serve hot. Serves 4 to 6.

POTATO AND PINE NUT CROQUETTES
Cuculli di Patate

These delicious little croquettes are a specialty of Liguria. The name *cuculli* can also refer to a chickpea pancake similar to the Provençal *panisse*. *Cuculli* means "chubby little ones" in the Genoese dialect.

2 pounds floury potatoes
salt
3 eggs, separated
3 tablespoons pine nuts
3 tablespoons freshly grated Pecorino Sardo or Parmesan cheese
a grating of nutmeg
freshly ground black pepper
dry bread crumbs
vegetable oil for frying

Boil the potatoes in lightly salted water for 20 minutes or until they are tender. Drain and peel when they are cool enough to handle. Force through a sieve or mash with a potato ricer. Add the egg yolks and blend well. Add the pine nuts and grated cheese and season with nutmeg, salt, and black pepper.

Shape into small croquettes the size of a walnut and refrigerate for 30 minutes. Dip in lightly beaten egg white and roll in bread crumbs. Deep-fry in hot oil until golden on both sides. Drain on paper towels and serve hot. Serves 4 to 6.

SPINACH GRATIN

Epinards Cannoise

This delicious gratin from Cannes consists of spinach and sautéed mushrooms mixed with double cream, topped with grated cheese, and gratinéed in the oven. Sometimes the mushrooms are cooked in a little Madeira wine before they are added to the spinach.

2 pounds spinach
3 tablespoons extra virgin olive oil
1 garlic clove, finely chopped
½ pound mushrooms, thinly sliced
½ cup double cream
a grating of nutmeg
salt
freshly ground black pepper
¼ cup Gruyère cheese, grated

Wash the spinach carefully and cook in a covered saucepan over a moderate heat for 5 minutes or until tender. The water clinging to the leaves is sufficient to prevent scorching. Drain, squeeze dry, and chop finely.

Heat the olive oil in a large frying pan and cook the garlic over moderate heat for 1 minute. Add the mushrooms and continue to cook until they are tender. Add the spinach and stir well. Simmer for 3 minutes. Pour in the cream and season with nutmeg, salt, and black pepper.

Simmer for another 3 or 4 minutes or until the cream is heated through. Transfer to a well-oiled shallow baking dish and sprinkle the cheese over the top. Bake in a preheated 400°F oven for 15 minutes or until the top is golden. Serve at once. Serves 4.

SPINACH WITH RAISINS AND PINE NUTS

Espinacs a la Catalana

Variations of this dish from Catalonia are made all around the Mediterranean. It can also be made with Swiss chard instead of spinach.

2 pounds spinach
3 tablespoons extra virgin olive oil
¼ cup raisins, soaked in warm water for 30 minutes
and drained
¼ cup pine nuts
a grating of nutmeg
salt
freshly ground black pepper

Wash the spinach and discard any tough stalks. Cook in a covered saucepan for 5 minutes or until just tender. The water clinging to the leaves is sufficient to prevent scorching. Drain thoroughly.

Heat the olive oil in a large frying pan and cook the raisins and pine nuts over moderate heat until the nuts are golden. Add the spinach and stir well. Season with nutmeg, salt, and black pepper. Cook over a gentle heat for 3 or 4 minutes, stirring constantly. Serve hot. Serves 4 to 6.

SWISS CHARD AND POTATOES

Blitve Pirjana

This is one of the most popular side dishes in Dalmatia. Sometimes the Swiss chard and potatoes are simply boiled and chopped and then dressed with olive oil and garlic.

2 pounds Swiss chard
1 pound potatoes
5 tablespoons extra virgin olive oil
2 garlic cloves, finely chopped
salt
freshly ground black pepper

Remove the stalks of the Swiss chard and reserve for a soup or stew. Wash the leaves carefully and cook in a covered saucepan for 5 to 7 minutes, or until they are tender. The water clinging to the leaves is sufficient to prevent scorching. Drain and chop coarsely. Meanwhile cook the potatoes in plenty of slightly salted water for 20 minutes or until they are tender. Drain and peel when they are cool enough to handle. Dice into very small pieces.

Heat the olive oil in a large frying pan and cook the garlic over moderate heat for 1 or 2 minutes. Add the Swiss chard and potatoes and stir well so the vegetables are well coated in oil. Cook for 2 or 3 minutes without browning. Season with salt and black pepper. Serve hot. Serves 4.

Neapolitan Stuffed Tomatoes

Pomodori Gratinati

This classic dish comes from the Bay of Naples, which is famous for its fine tomatoes. The exact amount of the ingredients depends on the size of the tomatoes.

4 large ripe tomatoes
2 garlic cloves, finely chopped
½ cup flat-leaf parsley, finely chopped
1 tablespoon fresh oregano
1 teaspoon capers
½ cup soft bread crumbs
salt
freshly ground black pepper
2–3 tablespoons extra virgin olive oil

Cut the tomatoes in half horizontally and scoop out the seeds. Place the garlic, parsley, oregano, capers, and half of the bread crumbs in a bowl and mix well. Season with salt and black pepper. Spoon a little of the mixture into the tomato halves and sprinkle the remaining bread crumbs over the top. Dribble over the olive oil.

Arrange side by side in a well-oiled shallow baking dish and bake in a preheated 350°F oven for 30 minutes or until the tomatoes are tender and the tops are golden. Serve hot. Serves 4.

Zucchini Fritters with Yoghurt Sauce

Kunguj me Kos

This dish is made all over the Balkans. In Albania and Croatia, the yoghurt is sometimes replaced by sour cream.

FRITTER BATTER:
2 cups flour
about 1 cup water
salt
freshly ground black pepper

YOGHURT SAUCE:
1½ cups thick yoghurt
3 garlic cloves, finely chopped
2 teaspoon fresh mint leaves, finely chopped
salt
paprika

2 pounds zucchini
vegetable oil for frying

Place the flour in a bowl and season with salt and black pepper. Gradually stir in enough water to make a smooth batter the consistency of single cream. Mix the yoghurt in a bowl with the garlic and mint and season with salt and paprika. Trim the ends of the zucchini and cut them lengthwise into slices about half an inch thick. Dip the slices into the batter and deep-fry in hot oil until they are golden on both sides. Drain on paper towels and serve hot with the yoghurt and garlic sauce on the side. Serves 4 to 6.

ZUCCHINI WITH TOMATOES AND FETA

Kolokythakia me Feta me Domates

This dish also makes a very good light lunch or supper dish served with some whole-wheat country bread on the side.

1½ pounds zucchini
¼ cup extra virgin olive oil
3 garlic cloves, finely chopped
1 teaspoon dried oregano, crumbled
1½ pounds ripe plum tomatoes peeled, seeded, and chopped
6 ounces feta cheese, thinly sliced
freshly ground black pepper

Trim the ends of the zucchini and cut them into rounds a quarters-inch thick. Heat the olive oil in a large frying pan and cook the zucchini over moderate heat until they are lightly browned on both sides. Add the garlic and oregano and cook for 1 or 2 more minutes. Add the tomatoes and cook for a further 15 minutes or until the sauce starts to thicken. Add the feta cheese and season with black pepper. Simmer for 5 more minutes or until the cheese is melted. Serve at once. Serves 4 to 6.

ZUCCHINI PISTO WITH POTATOES

Pisto de Calabacin con Patatas

The Spanish *pisto* is a vegetable stew similar to the Provençal *ratatouille*. It has many variations. This one is made with zucchini, peppers, tomatoes, and potatoes. *Pisto* makes a very good light lunch served topped with fried eggs— one per person.

4 medium zucchini
1 green pepper
6 tablespoons extra virgin olive oil
1 Spanish onion, chopped
2 cups ripe plum tomatoes, peeled, seeded, and chopped
½ pound waxy potatoes, peeled and diced
salt
freshly ground black pepper

Trim the ends of the zucchini and cut into thin rounds. Roast the pepper in a hot oven until it is blackened all over. Wash under cold water and remove the skin and cut into thin strips.

Heat 4 tablespoons olive oil a large frying pan and add the onion and zucchini. Cook over moderate heat for 10 to 15 minutes or until they start to turn golden, stirring from time to time so the vegetables cook evenly. Add the pepper and tomatoes and cook for a further 15 minutes or until the sauce starts to thicken.

Meanwhile, heat the remaining olive oil in a heavy frying pan and add the potatoes. Stir briefly so they are well coated in oil. Cook over gentle heat until the potatoes are tender and staring to turn golden. Add to the *pisto* and stir well. Season with salt and black pepper. Serve hot. Serves 4.

ZUCCHINI FLOWER FRITTERS

Bignet de Fleur de Coucourdeto

This recipe comes from the region around Aix-en-Provence, which is well-known for its fine produce. If you are lucky enough to grow your own zucchini, pick the flowers just as they start to open.

FRITTER BATTER:
1 cup flour
½ teaspoon salt
1 tablespoon extra virgin olive oil
1 large egg, beaten
¼ cup dry white wine
about ½ cup water

10 to 12 zucchini flowers
vegetable oil for frying
lemon wedges

Place the flour and salt in a bowl. Gradually mix in the olive oil and egg. Add the wine and enough water to make a smooth thin batter. Let it sit for 30 minutes.Open the zucchini flowers carefully and remove the pistils.

Dip the flowers into the batter and deep-fry in hot oil until they are golden on both sides. Drain on paper towels and serve hot with lemon wedges on the side. Serve 3 to 4.

DESSERTS

Let us share a sweet dish. Let us indulge in sweet talk.
—Turkish saying

In most Mediterranean countries, meals usually end with fresh fruit, or, in winter, dried fruit and nuts. The variety of Mediterranean fruit is enormous: figs, apricots, peaches, nectarines, table grapes, plums, cherries, apples, pears, loquats, quinces, pomegranates, and all kinds of melons and citrus fruit, to name a few. Fruits are also made into compôtes, baked dishes, pastries and strudels, and jams and preserves. Cakes and pastries are seldom served for dessert. Instead they are usually bought at pastry shops and eaten with a cup of coffee or lemon tea. However, I have included a few traditional cakes and pastries in this chapter that can easily be made at home.

All kinds of custards, creams, and ice creams—made with eggs, milk, cream, crème fraîche, yoghurt, ricotta, or mascarpone—are made throughout the Mediterranean. They are much enjoyed by children and adults alike and make very good light endings to both family meals and dinner parties.

SEPHARDIC ALMOND SPONGE CAKE
Pallébé aux Amandes

This cake is often served in Moroccan Jewish households to break the fast of Yom Kippur. An amazingly elaborate version called a *paille* is often served for weddings and special occasions. It consists of layers of almond sponge cake filled with chocolate mousse and a mixture of strawberry preserves, ground almonds, and egg yolks, topped with royal icing, and decorated with sugared almonds and marzipan flowers.

butter
2 tablespoons flour
4 eggs, separated
½ cup + 2 tablespoons sugar
grated rind of 1 organic lemon
1 cup unblanched almonds, finely ground
     in a blender or food processor

Butter an eight-inch spring-form pan and dust it with flour. Preheat the oven to 350°F degrees. Beat the egg yolks and sugar until they are pale and creamy. Stir in the lemon rind. Beat the egg whites until stiff and fold into the mixture.

Lastly fold in the ground almonds and flour. Pour into the prepared pan and bake for 40 to 45 minutes or until a knife comes out clean from the center of the cake. Remove from the oven. Unclip the pan and allow the cake to cool for 5 minutes. Turn out onto a wire wrack and set aside to cool completely. Serves 6 to 8.

ISTRIAN APPLE CAKE

Torta od Jabuka

This delicious apple cake is also very good served hot as a pudding. It is very light and moist as it contains just enough batter to hold the cake together.

3 pounds cooking apples
3 tablespoons butter
¼ cup sunflower seed oil or melted butter
⅓ cup sugar
1 egg
grated rind of ½ organic lemon
¾ cup flour
⅓ cup milk
½ teaspoon cinnamon

Preheat the oven to 325°F. Butter an 8-inch spring form pan and dust it with flour. Peel and slice the apples fairly thickly. Melt the butter in a large frying pan and cook the apples over moderate heat for 5 minutes or until they are half cooked and still retain their shape. Set aside.

Place the oil, sugar, and egg in a bowl and mix well. Stir in the lemon rind and flour. Add the milk and mix well. The batter should be fairly thin. Pour half of the batter into the bottom of the prepared pan. Cover with the apple slices. Pour the remaining batter over the top.

Bake in a preheated 325°F oven for 45 to 50 minutes. Halfway through cooking, place a sheet of tin foil over the cake. This will prevent the cake from browning too much. Serve hot or cold. Serves 6.

CARROT FILBERT CAKE WITH MASCARPONE CREAM

Torta di Carote alla Crema di Mascarpone

This light carrot cake makes a very good teatime snack, as well as the ending of a meal. *Mascarpone* is a delicious creamy cheese made from cow's milk that is widely used in Italian desserts (especially in the Veneto, Lombardy, and Emilia–Romagna), the most famous of which is *tiramisù*.

3 eggs, separated
½ cup sugar
1 cup carrots, finely grated.
 grated rind of 1 organic lemon
⅔ cup unblanched filberts, finely ground
       in a blender or food processor
2 tablespoons flour
1 teaspoon baking powder

TOPPING:
1 cup mascarpone
1 egg yolk
1/3 cup sugar
1 or 2 teaspoons brandy or rum

Preheat the oven to 350°F oven. Butter a 7-inch spring form pan and dust it with flour.

Beat the egg yolks with the sugar until they are pale and creamy. Add the carrots and lemon rind and mix well. Beat the egg whites until stiff and fold into the mixture. Lastly, fold in the hazelnuts and flour. Pour into the prepared pan and bake for 30 to 35 minutes or until a knife comes out clean from the center of the cake. Remove from the oven. Unclip the pan and allow to cool for 5 minutes. Turn out onto a wire rack and set aside to cool completely. To prepare the topping, place the mascarpone, egg yolk, sugar, and brandy in a bowl and blend well. Spread over the cake. Serves 6.

Corsican Cheesecake
Fiadone

All kinds of cheesecakes are made in Corsica. Some are baked on chestnut leaves. Others are cooked with or without a pastry shell. *Fiadone* is the lightest and most popular. It originated in Corte in central Corsica, but today it is made throughout the island. Corsican cheesecake is always made with *brocciu*, a fresh cheese made with ewe's or goat's milk. If it is unavailable, ricotta may be used instead.

1 pound fresh *brocciu* or ricotta cheese
4 eggs, separated
¾ cup sugar
grated rind of 2 organic lemons
2 tablespoons flour

Butter a 9-inch spring form pan and dust it with flour. Preheat the oven to 350°F oven. Force the cheese through a sieve into a mixing bowl. Add the egg yolks and sugar and blend well. Stir in the lemon rind and flour. Beat the egg whites until stiff and fold into the mixture. Pour into the prepared pan and bake for 35 to 40 minutes or until a knife comes out clean from the center of the cake. Remove from the oven. Unclip the pan and allow to cool for 5 minutes. Turn out onto a wire rack and set aside to cool completely. Serves 6 to 8.

CHERRY STRUDEL

Savijača od Trešnanja

All kinds of strudels are made in Croatia—with apples, pears, apricots, plums, dried fruit and nuts, and *pujine* (a fresh white cheese similar to ricotta). Cherry strudel is usually made with sour cherries, but if they are unavailable, sweet black cherries may be used instead. Commercial filo pastry makes strudel very quick and easy to prepare.

1 pound sweet or sour black cherries
2 or 3 sheets fresh or thawed filo pastry, approximately 12 x 16 inches
3–4 tablespoons butter, melted
½ cup dry bread crumbs
½ cup shelled walnuts, finely ground in a blender or food processor
¼ cup sugar, or to taste
1 teaspoon cinnamon
grated rind of 1 organic lemon
powdered sugar for dusting

Cut the cherries in half and remove the pits. Set aside.

Cover the table or work surface with a clean cloth. Lay a sheet of filo pastry on the cloth and brush lightly with melted butter. Place another sheet over the top and brush lightly with melted butter. Sprinkle the bread crumbs along the side of the pastry nearest to you in a strip about 3 inches wide. Sprinkle the walnuts over the top. Arrange the cherries over the top and sprinkle with sugar, cinnamon, and lemon rind.

Carefully lift the corners of the cloth nearest to you to allow the strudel to roll over on itself. Lift up the cloth again to then allow the strudel to roll over completely. Brush the top lightly with melted butter.

Pick up the cloth with the strudel and very carefully flip it over onto its buttered side on a greased baking sheet. Brush lightly with melted butter. Bake in a preheated 350°F oven for 30 minutes or until the cherries are tender and the pastry is crisp and golden. Remove from the oven and sprinkle lightly with powdered sugar. Allow to cool before serving. Serves 4 to 6.

SEPHARDIC FRUIT- AND NUT-FILLED PASTRIES

Sansantikos

These delicious triangular filo pastries are a Jewish specialty from Salonika, where they were traditionally made for *Sukkot*, the Feast of the Tabernacles. They can be served dredged in sugar syrup, but I prefer them lightly dusted with powdered sugar.

FILLING:
2 apples, peeled, cored, and chopped
1 cup raisins
½ cup currants
½ cup unblanched almonds, finely chopped
1 teaspoon cinnamon
¼ teaspoon cloves
2 tablespoons butter, melted
2 tablespoons honey
2 teaspoons sugar

12 sheets filo pastry, 12 x 8 inches
2–3 tablespoons olive oil
powdered sugar for dusting

To prepare the filling, place the chopped apple, raisins, currants, almonds, cinnamon, and cloves in a bowl. Add the melted butter, honey, and sugar and mix well. Set aside. Cut the filo pastry in half lengthwise to make rectangles approximately 12 x 4 inches. Place them in a pile and cover with a cloth to prevent them from drying out. Take one sheet of filo pastry and brush lightly with melted butter. Place a heaping tablespoon of the filling over the bottom end of the pastry strip.

Carefully lift up the right-hand corner and fold over to make a triangle. Fold over and over again until you have reached the top. Repeat with the remaining filo pastry and filling. Place the filled pastry triangles side by side on a greased baking sheet and brush the tops lightly with melted butter. Bake in a preheated 350°F oven for 20 to 25 minutes or until the pastries are crisp and golden. Makes 24 pastries.

CROATIAN PEPPER BISCUITS
Paprenjaci

Variations of these spicy biscuits are made all over Croatia. Some recipes include a little chocolate; others use walnuts instead of almonds. Sometimes they are decorated with white icing. Although they are called pepper biscuits, often they include no more than 1 ground peppercorn. *Paprenjaci* are usually served with a glass of *prošek*—a sweet red wine made from grapes that are left to shrivel on the vine to increase their sweetness.

2 cups flour
¼ teaspoon baking soda
½ cup liquid honey
¼ cup sweet marsala or *prošek*
¼ cup sunflower-seed or extra virgin olive oil
½ cup sugar
½ teaspoon vanilla
1 teaspoon cinnamon
½ teaspoon ground cloves
freshly grated nutmeg
freshly ground black pepper
¼ cup unblanched almonds, finely ground
      on a blender or food processor

Preheat the oven to 350°F oven.

Sift the flour with the soda and set aside. Place the honey, marsala, oil, sugar, vanilla, and spices in a mixing bowl and blend well. Stir in the almonds and enough flour to make a soft dough. Roll out on a floured board or work surface into a rectangle about an eighth of an inch thick. Cut into diamond shapes. Bake on a well-oiled baking sheet for 10 to 15 minutes or until the biscuits are golden. Remove from the oven and allow to cool. Makes about 24 biscuits.

CATALAN BREAD FRITTERS
Torrades de Santa Teresa

This dish is traditionally made in October for the Feast Day of Santa Teresa. Sometimes it is flavored with anise and topped with a dusting of powdered sugar instead of pine nuts and honey.

about 1¼ cups milk
1 tablespoon orange flower water
4 slices bread, about a half an inch thick
3 eggs, beaten
about ¼ cup extra virgin olive oil for frying

TOPPING:
2–3 tablespoons honey
¼ cup pine nuts, lightly toasted in a 300°F oven

Mix the milk and orange-flower water in a bowl. Soak the bread slices in the mixture for a few minutes. Dip each slice briefly in the beaten egg and fry in hot oil until golden on both sides. Transfer to a serving dish. Dribble over the honey and sprinkle the pine nuts over the top. Serve at once. Serves 4.

RICOTTA FRITTERS

Fritelle di Ricotta

These delicious fritters from Calabria make a very good teatime snack as well as dessert.

2 cups ricotta cheese
2 eggs
4 pairs of *amaretti*, crushed
3 tablespoons sugar
grated rind of 1 organic lemon
3–4 tablespoons flour
flour
vegetable oil for deep frying
powdered sugar for dusting

Place the ricotta, eggs, *amaretti*, and sugar in a mixing bowl and blend well. Add the lemon rind and just enough flour to form a solid mixture. Form into small balls the size of a walnut. Dip in flour and fry in hot oil until golden on both sides. Drain on paper towels. Dust with powdered sugar and serve at once. Serves 4.

PANETTONE PUDDING
Budino di Pannetone

This lovely pudding may be made with *panettone, pan dolce,* or any other kind of sweet brioche. It is always served at room temperature. Legend has it that *panettone* was named after a fifteenth-century aristocrat named Toni, who fell in love with the beautiful daughter of a poor baker. In order to be close to his beloved, Toni became an apprentice of the baker. Soon after, he created a rich bread with more butter, eggs, and candied peel that became so popular it was nicknamed "Tony's bread" or *pan di toni,* whichwas later shortened to *panettone.*

2 cups milk
3 tablespoons marsala
grated rind of 1 organic lemon rind
2 eggs, separated
3 tablespoons sugar
1 tablespoon candied citron or organic orange rind
4 ounces *panettone* or sweet brioche

Bring the milk to a boil and remove from the heat. Stir in the marsala and lemon rind and set aside to cool.

Beat the egg yolks with the sugar and add to the warm milk together with the candied citron. Cut the *panettone* into slices and pour over the milk mixture. Beat the egg whites until stiff and gently fold into the mixture, taking care not to break up the bread too much.

Bake in a preheated 375°F oven for 1 hour. Reduce the heat to 300°F and bake for 15 more minutes or until the pudding is firm. Serve at room temperature. Serves 4 to 6.

PEACHES IN SWEET RED WINE

Préssec amb Vi Dolç

This recipe comes from Catalonia where it is usually made with *pressec de vinya* (peaches ripened on the vine), which are highly prized for their fine flavor.

8 small peaches, peeled
2 cups sweet red wine
3–4 tablespoons sugar, or to taste
½ cinnamon stick
2 cloves
¼ teaspoon mace
2 strips lemon rind (no white part)

Place the peaches in a saucepan with the wine, sugar, spices, and lemon rind. Bring to a boil. Cover and simmer for 45 to 50 minutes. Slow simmering removes any bitterness from the wine. Remove the peaches with a slotted spoon and place in a glass serving bowl. Boil the cooking liquid down to a syrupy consistency.

Remove the cinnamon stick, cloves, and lemon rind and pour the syrup over the peaches. Chill thoroughly before serving. Serves 4.

BAKED APPLES WITH WALNUTS
Mila Psita me Karyda

Baked apples are especially good the Greek way, stuffed with a mixture of chopped walnuts, raisins, Greek honey (Hymettus if possible), cinnamon, and brandy.

4 large cooking apples
¼ cup shelled walnuts, coarsely chopped
¼ cup raisins
1 teaspoon cinnamon
4 tablespoons Greek honey, or to taste
⅓ cup brandy
2 tablespoons butter, melted
⅔ cup hot water

Wash and core the apples, but do not peel. Arrange them side by side in a shallow baking dish. Place the walnuts, raisins, cinnamon, honey, and brandy in a bowl and mix well. Stuff the apples with the mixture. Dribble over the melted butter.

Pour in the hot water and bake in a preheated 350°F oven for 45 minutes to 1 hour, or until the apples are tender. Baste once or twice during cooking. Serve hot. Serves 4.

BAKED BANANAS FLAMBÉED WITH RUM

Greixera de Bananas amb Rom

This recipe comes from the Roussillon in French Catalonia. The bananas are usually flambéed with white rum, but brandy or Curaçao may be used instead. *Greixera* is the Catalan name for the shallow earthenware dish in which it is baked.

4 bananas
2 tablespoons butter
2 tablespoons liquid honey, preferably orange blossom
½ teaspoon freshly grated ginger
½ teaspoon cinnamon
grated rind of 1 organic lemon
juice of 1 orange
¼ cup white rum, Curaçao or brandy

Peel the bananas and slice them in half lengthwise. Arrange side by side in a shallow baking dish. Dot with butter and dribble over the honey. Sprinkle with the ginger, cinnamon, and lemon rind. Pour in the orange juice.

Bake in a preheated 375°F oven for 15 to 20 minutes, or until the bananas are tender. Remove from the oven. Heat the rum and pour over the bananas. Set alight and serve at once. Serves 4.

DRIED APRICOTS WITH CLOTTED CREAM

Kaymakli Kayisi Tatlisi

Kaymak is a kind of thick clotted cream that is made in Turkey from cow's or buffalo's milk. It is usually sold rolled up and cut into slices. If it is unavailable, clotted cream or thick strained yoghurt may be used instead.

½ pound dried apricots
3 tablespoons sugar or honey, or to taste
1 teaspoon lemon juice
1 tablespoon orange-flower water
1½ cups hot water
¼ cup blanched almonds or pistachios, finely chopped
1 cup clotted cream or *kaymak*

Place the apricots, sugar, and hot water in a saucepan and bring to a boil. Cover and simmer for 30 to 35 minutes or until the apricots are tender and the cooking liquid is reduced by half. Remove from the heat and stir in the lemon juice and orange-flower water. Set aside to cool.

Spoon into 4 individual glass serving dishes and top with clotted cream. Sprinkle the chopped nuts over the top. Chill thoroughly before serving. Serves 4.

STRAWBERRIES WITH MARSALA
Fragole al Marsala

This is a very simple but delicious way of serving strawberries. If you like, you can serve them topped with a dollop of whipped cream. Marsala is an amber-colored fortified wine from Sicily that is widely used in Italian desserts. It can be sweet or dry, but the best is *Marsala Vergine*, which is very dry.

1 pint strawberries
2 to 3 tablespoons sugar, or to taste
about ½ cup sweet or dry marsala

Wash and hull the strawberries and place in individual glass serving dishes. Sprinkle with sugar and pour over the marsala. Chill thoroughly before serving. Serves 4.

DRIED FRUIT AND NUT COMPÔTE
Khoshaf

This classic dessert is made all over the Middle East. Traditionally, it is made in Syria and Lebanon with raisins and dried apricots, but today prunes or dried figs are often included. The compôte is always macerated, not stewed, which not only increases the nutritional value, but also makes the nuts much easier to digest.

1 cup seedless raisins
1 cup dried apricots
1 cup pitted prunes
¼ cup blanched almonds
¼ cup blanched pistachios
¼ cup pine nuts or blanched walnuts
4 cups cold water
2 tablespoons rose water
2 tablespoons orange-flower water

Place the dried fruit and nuts in a bowl and cover with cold water. Stir in the rose water and orange-flower water. Cover with a plate and leave to soak for 24 hours, or until the fruits are tender and the juice is syrupy. Serves 6 to 8.

DRUNKEN FIGS

Pijane Smokve

This Dalmatian dish is usually served at the end of a meal with a cup of Turkish coffee. Traditionally, the figs are dried in the sun for 15 days, then cut open, stuffed with an almond, and soaked for 8 hours in grappa (a fiery spirit made from grapes after the juice has been extracted for wine-making). If grappa is unavailable, brandy makes a good substitute.

12 dried figs
12 blanched almonds
about ¾ cup brandy or grappa

Make a small incision in the stalk end of each dried fig and insert an almond. Place the stuffed figs in a small bowl and pour over the brandy. Leave to marinate for 6 to 8 hours or until the figs are softened and most of the brandy has been absorbed. Serves 3 to 4.

FRESH DATES STUFFED WITH ALMOND PASTE
Degla bi-H'risset Ellouz

These delicious stuffed dates make an elegant ending to a meal—served with a glass of mint tea or a cup of Turkish coffee. In Algeria, *degla nours* or large *mejdoul* dates are generally used for stuffing.

16 medjoul dates
½ cup blanched almonds, finely ground in a blender or food processor
3 tablespoons sugar
1 tablespoon butter, melted
1–2 tablespoons orange-flower water

Make an incision in the side of the dates and remove the pits. Place the ground almonds and sugar in a bowl and mix well. Add the melted butter and enough orange-flower water to make a smooth paste. Stuff the dates with the almond paste and close up. Arrange on a serving dish and serve. Serves 4 to 5.

VENETIAN CHOCOLATE AND RICOTTA PUDDING

Budino di Ricotta alla Veneta

This traditional Venetian recipe is probably the forerunner of *tiramisu*. It consists of layers of *savoiardi* (ladies' fingers) soaked in marsala, topped with a chocolate–flavored ricotta cream, and a layer of ricotta mixed with ground almonds, egg yolks, brandy, and candied fruit. If you like, you can soak the *savoiardi* in strong black coffee mixed with 3 or 4 tablespoons of rum instead of the marsala.

3 cups ricotta
⅓ cup sugar
4 tablespoons brandy
2 eggs, separated
2 ounces baking chocolate, broken into squares
12–16 *savoiardi*
about ⅔ cup sweet marsala
¼ cup blanched almonds, finely ground in a
    blender or food processor
2 tablespoons chopped candied cherries or citron

Place half of the ricotta, 3 tablespoons sugar, and half of the brandy in a bowl and blend well until smooth and creamy. Beat the egg whites until they are stiff and fold into the mixture. Melt the chocolate in a small bowl over hot, not boiling, water and stir into the ricotta mixture.

Dip half of the *savoiardi* in the marsala and arrange in the bottom of a glass serving dish. Place the remaining ricotta in a bowl with the egg yolks and the remaining sugar and brandy. Blend well.

Stir in the ground almonds and candied fruit. Dip the remaining *savoiardi* in the remaining marsala and arrange over the chocolate and ricotta cream. Cover with the ricotta and almond mixture. Chill for at least 2 hours before serving. Serves 6.

STRAWBERRY TIRAMISÙ
Semifreddo allo Fragola

A *semifreddo*, which literally means "half cold," can refer to various Italian desserts such as ice cream, baked custard, all kinds of creamy desserts made with ricotta, as well as trifle or *tiramisu*. For a variation, you can use raspberries, blueberries, or sliced peaches, instead of the strawberries.

8 *savoiardi* or sponge fingers
½ cup sweet marsala
1 egg yolk
2 egg whites
1½ cups mascarpone
3 tablespoons sugar
1–2 tablespoons brandy
½ pound strawberries, hulled

Dip the *savoiardi* in marsala and place in the bottom of a glass serving dish. Beat the egg yolk and sugar until pale and creamy. Gradually add the mascarpone and blend well. Stir in the brandy. Beat the egg whites until stiff and fold into the mixture. Spoon over the *savoiardi* and arrange the strawberries over the top. Chill for at least 2 hours before serving. Serves 4.

Chocolate Mousse with Almonds
Molsa Xocolata amb Ametlles

This delicious chocolate mousse from the Roussillon (French Catalonia) is delicately flavored with brandy and topped with lightly toasted chopped almonds. It is also very good made with amaretto instead of brandy.

6 ounces baking chocolate
4 tablespoons hot water
2 tablespoons brandy or amaretto
2 eggs, separated
½ cup whipping cream
2 tablespoons powdered sugar
¼ cup blanched almonds, lightly toasted in a 325°F oven
    for 5 to 10 minutes

Melt the chocolate with the water over a pan of hot (not boiling) water. Remove from the heat and allow to cool slightly. Stir in the brandy and the egg yolks, one at a time. Whip the cream until it is stiff and fold into the mixture. Lastly fold in the stiffly beaten egg whites. Spoon into individual glass dishes. Chop the almonds finely and sprinkle over the top. Chill for at least 4 hours before serving. Serves 4.

COFFEE ZABAGLIONE
Zabaione al Caffè

Zabaglione or *zabaione* is one of Italy's most famous desserts. It was invented in Turin in the seventeenth-century by one of the King of Savoy's chefs, who accidentally poured some dessert wine into a bowl of egg custard. The dish was named after San Giovanni Babylon, the patron saint of pasty makers. Zabaglione is usually made with egg yolks, sugar, and Marsala wine. This version is made with a mixture of strong black coffee and brandy instead of wine.

4 egg yolks
4 tablespoons sugar
¼ cup cold, very strong black coffee
1–2 tablespoons brandy, to taste

Whisk the egg yolks and sugar together in the top of a double saucepan over hot, not boiling, water. Mix the coffee with the brandy. Gradually add to the egg yolk mixture, beating constantly, until the mixture starts to thicken. Spoon into individual glass serving bowls and chill thoroughly before serving. Serves 4.

DALMATIAN CREAM CARAMEL
Rožada

Rožada or *rožata* (a kind of cream caramel) is one of the most popular desserts in Dalmatia. It is named after the drops of rose oil that was originally used to flavor it. Today it is usually flavored with *Maraska*, a liqueur made from black Maraska cherries, but if it is unavailable, maraschino or rum may be used instead.

FOR THE CARAMEL:
½ cup sugar
3 tablespoons water

FOR THE CUSTARD:
2½ cups milk
3 eggs
3 egg yolks
¼ sugar
1–2 tablespoons maraschino or Maraska liqueur

To make the caramelized mold, place the sugar in a small heavy saucepan with the water. Cook over moderate heat for 4 to 5 minutes or until the sugar starts to caramelize. Pour at once into a 1-quart mold or soufflé dish. Tilt the dish in all directions until the caramel evenly lines the bottom and sides of the mold. Set aside.

Preheat the oven to 350°F. Scald the milk. Do not let it boil or the custard will curdle. Remove from the heat and leave to cool slightly. Beat the eggs and egg yolks with remaining sugar until light. Gradually add the hot milk and blend well. Stir in the maraschino. Pour through a sieve into the prepared mold. Set the mold in a pan of hot, not boiling, water, and place in the oven.

Lower the heat to 325°F and bake for 40 to 45 minutes or until a knife comes out clean from the center. Remove from the oven and chill thoroughly before serving. Serves 4.

YOGHURT MILK PUDDING

Yoğurtlu Muhallebi

A Turkish *muhallebi* is a chilled milk pudding thickened with rice flour or corn flour. This recipe may look like a *muhallebi* but it just consists of sweetened yoghurt flavored with orange-flower water and topped with chopped nuts. It may be simple, but it is very delicious.

3 cups thick creamy yoghurt
3 tablespoons sugar or honey, to taste
grated rind of 1 organic lemon
3 tablespoons orange-flower water
⅓ cup finely chopped unblanched almonds or pistachios

Combine the yoghurt, sugar, lemon rind, and orange-flower water in a bowl. Spoon into 4 individual glass dishes and sprinkle with chopped nuts. Chill thoroughly before serving. Serves 3 to 4.

NEAPOLITAN COFFEE ICE CREAM

Gelati al Caffè

Neapolitans like to add a touch of dark cocoa to coffee ice cream, which they say brings out the flavor of the coffee.

2 cups milk
2 tablespoons instant coffee granules
2 teaspoons dark cocoa
4 egg yolks
⅔ cup sugar
2 cups whipping cream

Heat the milk in a saucepan until it is very hot. Place the coffee granules and cocoa in a mixing bowl. Pour over the hot milk and mix well until they are dissolved. Beat the egg yolks with the sugar until they are pale and creamy. Gradually add the hot milk and blend well. Pour into a heavy-based saucepan and cook over gentle heat until the mixture is thick enough to coat the back of a spoon. Make sure that it does not boil or the eggs will curdle. Remove from the heat and leave to cool.

Whip the cream until it forms soft peaks and fold into the coffee mixture. Pour into a mold and cover with a lid or foil. Freeze for about 2 hours or until the ice cream is half frozen. Remove from the freezer and whisk thoroughly to break up the ice crystals that have formed. The more air that is incorporated into the ice cream, the smoother the texture. Pour back into the mold. Cover and freeze for a further 2 hours or until firm. Serves 4.

STRAWBERRY ICE CREAM

Helado de Fresa

This ice cream is very light and has a superb flavor.

1 pint strawberries
¾ cup sugar
¼ cup sweet sherry
2 cups whipping cream
2 egg whites

Purée the strawberries with the sugar in a food processor. Transfer to a mixing bowl and stir in the sherry. Mix well. Whip the cream until it forms soft peaks and fold into the mixture. Lastly, fold in stiffly beaten egg whites. Pour into a mold and cover with a lid or foil. Freeze for 2 or 3 hours or until the ice cream is half frozen.

Remove from the freezer and whisk thoroughly to break up the ice crystals that have formed. The more air that is incorporated into the ice cream, the smoother the texture. Pour back into the mold. Cover and freeze for a further 2 hours or until firm. Serves 4.

BANANA CRÊME FRAÏCHE ICE CREAM

Booza ala Moz

Similar ice cream is also made in Algeria. For a variation, you can use mangoes, peaches, or fresh figs instead of the bananas. Crême fraïche is a thick pasteurized cream that is widely used in French cooking. It has a very high butterfat content (up to 60%) and contains lactic acid and other ferments that give it its characteristic slightly sour taste.

1 cup milk
½ cup sugar
4 to 5 bananas, peeled
1 cup Crême fraïche
1 tablespoon rose water

Scald the milk. Stir in the sugar and set aside to cool. Purée the bananas in a blender or food processor. Strain the milk and add the banana purée. Process until very smooth and creamy. Transfer to a mixing bowl. Add the crème fraiche and rose water and blend well. Pour into a mold and cover with a lid or foil. Freeze for 2 hours or until the ice cream is half frozen.

Remove from the freezer and whisk thoroughly to remove any ice crystals that have formed. The more air incorporated into the ice cream, the smoother the texture. Pour back into the mold and freeze for further 2 hours or until the ice cream is firm. Serves 4 .

RUM-RAISIN RICOTTA ICE CREAM
Gelati di Ricotta con Ruma e l'Uvetta

Ricotta ice cream has a lovely texture and is very easy to prepare. The addition of rum and Marsala give it a very special flavor.

⅓ cup seedless raisins
¼ cup rum
2 cups ricotta
3 egg yolks
½ cup sugar
2 tablespoons Marsala
1 cup whipping cream

Soak the raisins in the rum for 30 minutes. Force the ricotta through a sieve into a mixing bowl. Add the egg yolks, sugar, and Marsala and blend well. Stir in the raisins and the rum. Whip the cream until it forms soft peaks and fold into the mixture. Pour into a mold and cover with a lid or foil. Freeze for 3 to 4 hours or until firm. Serves 4 .

APRICOT FROZEN YOGHURT

Vericoco Pagoto Yaiourti

This frozen yoghurt is light and refreshing and has a fantastic flavor.

10 ounces ripe apricots, peeled and pitted
⅓ cup sugar
1¾ cups Greek-style yoghurt
1 tablespoon orange-flower water
2 egg whites

Process all the ingredients except for the egg whites in a food processor until the mixture is smooth and creamy. Transfer to a mixing bowl. Beat the egg whites until stiff and fold into the mixture. Pour into a mold and cover with a lid or foil.

Freeze for 2 to 3 hours or until half frozen. Remove from the freezer and whisk thoroughly to break up the ice crystals that have formed. The more air incorporated into the frozen yoghurt, the smoother the texture. Pour back into the mold and freeze for a further 2 hours or until firm. Serves 4.

STUFFED PEARS

Pere Ripiene

This dish is delicous and very easy to prepare. The pears are stuffed with a mixture of ground almonds, sugar, egg yolk, and grated lemon rind and baked with Marsala in the oven until golden. Barlett pears are best for this recipe.

4 ripe but firm pears
⅓ cup unpeeled almonds, finely ground
       in a blender or food processor
3 tablespoons sugar
grated rind of ½ small organic lemon
1 egg yolk
4 tablespoons Marsala

Peel, halve, and core the pears. Arrange them, cut side up, in a lightly buttered baking dish.

Combine the almonds, sugar, and lemon rind in a bowl. Add the egg yolk and 1 or 2 teaspoons of Marsala and mix well. Fill the pear halves with the mixture. Pour the remaining Marsala into the baking dish and bake in a 350°F oven for 20-25 minutes or until golden. Serve hot, warm, or cold. Serves 4.

Notes

NOTES

INDEX

CPSIA information can be obtained at www.ICGtesting.com
Printed in the USA
BVOW061905190212

283228BV00001B/7/P